1617~1967~2000

ROYAL BURGH
of
STRANRAER

To Jim and Margaret Kelly, with best wishes.

Donnie Nelson.

Christine Wilson

HISTORY AND
DEVELOPMENT

The Trust is grateful to Mrs Anna Boyd for granting permission to reprint the Royal and Ancient Burgh of Stranraer 1617-1967, written by her husband, J.S. Boyd, to celebrate the 350th anniversary of the Royal Burgh.

ISBN 0 9535776 4 3

Edited by JACK HUNTER

Thanks are expressed by the trust for generous grants from
THE HERITAGE LOTTERY FUND - AWARDS FOR ALL
THE MILLENNIUM FUND - DUMFRIES AND GALLOWAY COUNCIL

Published by

Stranraer and District Local History Trust
Tall Trees
London Road
Stranraer DG9 8BZ

JOHN SHEARER BROWN BOYD

1911 - 1978

JOHNNY BOYD was born in Newark, New Jersey, the son of Scottish parents, who had emigrated, but who returned to Glasgow within a few years. His schooldays were spent at Bellahouston Academy and his first connection with newspapers came as a copy boy with the Glasgow Evening Citizen. Reporting jobs with the Daily Mail, the Irish Times, the Sunday Post and the Sunday Dispatch followed and he came to Stranraer in the early 1930s "to get some experience of a weekly" with Fleet Street as his ultimate aim.

But he quickly discovered that Stranraer had its own particular attractions, especially golf, and apart from a war-time spell in bomb disposal with the Army he was to spend the rest of his life in the town serving the Free Press for almost fifty years.

He played for Stranraer Football Club, and was secretary of that group for some years, but it was in the local golf scene that he really made his mark. He held the posts of secretary, chairman and ultimately president and life member of Stranraer Golf Club; was secretary of the Wigtownshire Golf Association and president of Dumfries and Galloway Golfers' Association. Though he rarely mentioned it he was very proud of the fact that he had won his club's championship and also the Wigtownshire title.

Through his journalistic offerings and his intimate knowledge of local government he was not without influence in Stranraer and Wigtownshire affairs. He attended all town and county council meetings, on which he reported with some style, and was not averse to using the leader column to express his views trenchantly on council matters.

He was editor of the Free Press for eighteen years and during his time in charge took the firm from its original works in Castle Street to a new printing plant in St. Andrew Street and a whole new way of life for the staff with the change-over from letterpress to litho printing; from hot metal to computerised setting.

He also produced the original part of this History of Stranraer, regarding it as the Free Press contribution to mark the 350th anniversary of the foundation of the Royal Burgh.

CONTENTS

PREFACE

FROM TWO SMALL CLACHANS, The Chapel and Strand-rawr, Stranraer has risen to its present eminent position as the principal town in Galloway. It owes the distinction to its geographical location and the persistence of an Irish family. Sheltering behind a raised beach, on level ground, above the high spring tide mark of Lochryan, it was but one among several early settlements. Nomadic tribes seeking permanence sought first of all for pure water supplies, shelter from the elements and an encampment easily defended from marauding foes, human and otherwise. Habitations were not selected at the whim of the Chief; these essentials had to be on hand. And around the shores of Lochryan, an area generally known to the Romans as Rerigonium, several sites presented themselves. They are mentioned in the campaigns of Agricola in A.D. 82.

From later history, it would appear that the most important of the permanent abodes of the native Gallovidian, in the Rhins at any rate, was Innermessan. Indeed, up until the end of the sixteenth century Innermessan, and not Stranraer, might well have been the centre. There is an opinion that Stranraer might be the site of an early Roman settlement.

Around the Chief's dwelling were built rude houses of stakes and branches, later turf and earth were added. To the habitations on Lochryan came Irish crofter-fishermen, many of whom were welcome and settled amicably. Later, in successive centuries, there arrived not so welcome and not so peaceful invaders, among them Celts and Saxons and still later, bent upon pillage and plunder — though there must have been little in the way of booty, came Danes and Norsemen. Gipsies first appeared from Ireland in 1452. Of all the overseas visitors, the Celts had the greatest impact and influence. The Irish had an engaging habit of burning their long, black, curved boats on landing, showing they had reached the point of no return.

Marshes abounded, roads were almost unknown, the Romans had not thought it worth their while to colonise, General Wade did not pass this way and Macadam was many centuries off. Whilst there were whins and broom in profusion, the district was almost treeless; there were no great forests, but there was flat and fairly easily cultivable land, and moreover the loch provided safe fishing grounds.

Around the town burn which, generally speaking, still flows through what is the centre of the burgh, the small clachan grew almost imperceptibly. The rivulet provided the first necessity of life and the district was settled. Later, considerable use was made of a well, to become known as St. John's Well, to the east of the original settlement. This part was subsequently known as Chapel and for a considerable time Chapel and Stranraer vied with each other in importance, both however being overshadowed by Innermessan. However, the existence of a spring, which ran from a bank on which Agnew Crescent now stands and which flowed down to the beach to the west of the foot of Backrampart, led to the formation of a village, Clayhole. A fourth source of water was found near what is now High Street and around this grew Hillhead. Drainage was simple and the town spread westwards in a reasonably straight line running parallel to the loch and becoming, in course of time, Charlotte Street and George Street with offshoots of Castle Street and Strand Streets.

As drainage improved a fifth area was settled, to become known as Tradeston for the simple reason that most of the inhabitants were tradesmen, and also to the south in much later days, Little Ireland became the nomenclature, for obvious reasons, of still another district.

Spreading out from what became Castle Street, the inhabitants moved into St. John Street, Rose Street and Thistle Street as the town increased in size. This district, the old Stranraer, became the burgh for it was not until last century that Hillhead and Clayhole were regarded as part and parcel of the town; they were referred to as villages adjoining Stranraer.

Possibly because of the ease of water-borne transport as compared to the difficulties of movement over land, Stranraer may have been influenced more by St. Columba, even though the remainder of the Province regards St. Ninian as their apostle. There is no record of St. Patrick. Not until 1124, at the time of David I, was there mention made of the Church of Rome. It was St John the Evangelist who became the patron saint of the burgh. In 1148 Fergus, Lord of Galloway, brought the district into the medieval comity. Founder of Soulseat Abbey, he dedicated it to St. John, and a well on the east shore as well as one nearer the town centre, became known as St. John's Well.

The shore well which remained in operation until the second world war, 1939-45, had a free flow of water, pure and fresh, even though at high tide it was completely immersed. It was reputed once to flow in the garden of the manor of the Knights of St. John of Jerusalem who held the lands on the east side of the town burn. The Well, the Croft and the Fey all constituted a manor of the Knights Hospitallers. St. John Street retains the association; Chapel Fey, however, later became Thistle Street. The Templars owned, too, the lands of Spittal Croft of Creachmore, now the town's golf course on the western side of Lochryan.

No doubt because of its inaccessibility by land, Galloway was in the early centuries an independent Province of which it was said she "ance had Kings of her ain." She owned allegiance neither to Scotland nor to England; her closest ties were with Carrick and her affinities were with Ulster and it was to natives of these parts that she owes her rise.

In 1300, troops of Edward I invaded Galloway and garrisoned Lochnaw. Most of the older families, though few were native to the district, the McDoualls, Mc-Cullochs, Dunbars, Hannays, Kennedies, and Adairs, supported the English King and showed their allegiance to him when, in 1306, Thomas and Alexander Bruce landed at Lochryan from Ireland with some 700 men to take part in their brother's struggle against the English. The McDoualls were the oldest family in Wigtownshire and claimed to have come over as a tribe from Ireland after the departure of the Romans. In King John's reign Alan McDouall was one of the Barons who forced the signing of the Magna Carta. He fled from England to avoid reprisals and transferred his allegiance to King Alexander of Scotland. Sir Dougal Mc-Douall, described as a Sergeant of Galloway, who favoured Baliol, was later restored to favour with the English kings and raised an army of Gallovidians which met the invaders and routed them, taking the two brothers captive and delivering them to the English king at Carlisle.

It may be added that, later, Robert the Bruce marched into Galloway and avenged the deaths of his brothers, and in 1317 Edward Bruce, who had been acclaimed King of Ireland, sailed from Lochryan to Carrickfergus on his fatal foray to claim the throne.

Fergus de Mandeville, in the reign of Robert the Bruce, was granted a charter of "half of the lands of Stranrawer." This gift was probably the lands which had fallen to the Crown through the downfall of the Knights Templars or part taken from those of the resident chiefs for their temerity in opposing the cause of Scottish independence. It is the first mention of a charter in Stranraer. A family which rose to some eminence as a result of the victories of Bruce were the Douglases. Archibald the Grim was created Lord of Galloway in 1369 and three years later was appointed Sheriff of Wigtownshire. Patrick Agnew of Lochnaw, who had been appointed in 1320, was superseded by the Douglases for a time but later returned. The influence of the Douglas family was felt more in the Stewartry than in the Shire. But in any event the Douglases were not so influential, so far as Stranraer was concerned, as the families of Kennedy and Adair, both of which provided early Provosts of the burgh.

The Kennedies were probably indigenous to South Ayrshire. They were numerous and prosperous. One of them established himself near the site of St. John's Chapel and became known as Kennedy of Chappell. The family for a time were in possession of the castle. They also owned the lands of Ochtrelure. John, the second Lord Kennedy, added to the family's patrimony particularly obtaining ownership of Lochinch and ground in Leswalt Parish. So much did they hold sway in the Shire that it was said:

> 'Twixt Wigton and the town of Air,
>
> Portpatrick and the Cruives of Cree,
>
> Nae man needs think to bide there
>
> Unless he court a Kennedie.

In a deed of March, 1596, there was disponed to the burgh St. John's Croft, extending to six acres from the burn which comes from the Loch of Chappell to the Loch of Lochryan, and the lands of Aird, on the East; the tower fortalice, manor-place and yards of Chappell on the west; the water-gang, which runs to the Mill of Chappell, on the south; and the Loch of Lochryan on the north, reserving to Elizabeth Kennedy, heretrix of the said croft, the tower, the fortalice, manor-place, yards and orchards of Chappell.

During the century after Flodden, however, the influence of the Kennedies waned, so far as Stranraer and Wigtownshire were concerned and though the family had played a noble part in the making of Stranraer, it was not in evidence when the royal accolade was bestowed.

Similarly with the other family which had such a profound influence on the town in its earlier history.

Adare of Kilhilt came from Ireland, a son of the Earl of Desmond, and a supporter of Bruce. He fled to Galloway, no doubt with excellent reasons, and seized the main chance when it presented itself. He retrieved his fortunes by the simple expedient of capturing Dunskey Castle and putting the owner to death.

By so doing he earned royal patronage, for the owner of Dunskey had been, like the majority of the Wigtownshire lairds, not entirely sympathetic to the cause of Bruce. The family, whose home in Ireland was Adere, obtained lands at Portree, took the name Adair, built a castle and called it Kilhilt.

A saintly scion was known as Bishop Adair. He had three maiden sisters each of whom erected a chapel, the second of which was built in Stranraer in 1484, replacing an earlier chapel. It is presumed to have been built on the south side of what is now known as George Street or on the south side of Charlotte Street, at any rate, it was in the neighbourhood of the Old Castle built by Bishop Adair in 1510 and, some historians thought, erected near the site of the chapel. Adair dedicated the castle to St John, though it was also known as the Castle of Chapel, and later, as has been seen, as Kennedy Castle.

In the very heart of old Stranraer, the keep is referred to nowadays, simply as the Old Castle. It is a good example of a sixteenth century L-shaped keep, and was constructed of stone from a quarry four miles away, beyond the present village of Lochans. The stone was manhandled, being carried from one labourer to another spaced out at intervals.

7

The walls are of great thickness and contain a wheel stair which has been described as of great architectural beauty. At the South-East and South-West angles are the remains of two circular turrets, and the continuous corbelling which supports what was, at one time, the parapet walk, is practically complete.

There are indications that the building was heightened during the seventeenth century. Various alterations were carried out to make it a town jail. The two upper floors were used for that purpose and the strong iron gates in the passages can still be seen. The building had the small windows, pepper-box turrets at the corners, and crow-stepped gables, peculiar to Scottish architecture of the time. In later years, a pend was constructed and to accommodate other buildings, some 10ft. of the structure was carved away.

Ninian Adair, of the same Kilhilt family, on 12th November, 1595, had conferred on him by King James VI, the Barony of Kilhilt. The same charter raised the clachan of Stranraer into a burgh of barony and gave Adair the right to have a tolbooth, dispone the burgh lands, hold burgh courts three times a week and indulge in the usual privileges attached to a burgh. This included the holding of a market, imposing tiends or tithes and levying payment from farmers and others bringing produce into the town.

The charter went far beyond any normal charters but a third charter dated 30th March, 1596, went even further. King James considered that as "Stranraer was situated some 24 miles from the nearest Royal Burgh, was populous, and likely to be most convenient for trade," he forbade the erection of any other burgh or port, or any market within four miles. His Majesty was well aware of the situation of Stranraer for he had landed at Lochryan and had stayed at Castle Kennedy. Then, having left an indelible mark on the town and obtained for it, its first charter as a burgh of barony, the main branch of the Adair family, in 1608, went back to Ireland from whence they had originated. They disposed of their lands amicably, quite unlike the normal custom and in direct contrast to the manner in which they had obtained them. The Kennedies came in for a share, including the Castle.

The Agnews had not the same authority in the town as they had in the country. They were an old French family. They came to England during the reign of William the Conqueror and they took part in the conquest of Ulster under Henry II. They settled in Lochnaw and in 1451 became Hereditary Sheriffs of Galloway, undergoing in the succeeding years some vicissitudes. The family did not make an impression on Stranraer, however, until the Royal Burgh was created.

Towards the end of the sixteenth century, after the Kennedies had built what was then a mansion near the castle, and others had followed with more modest establishments, the area of the burgh extended until it covered some 59 acres. The population was in the region of 500. There were houses on both sides of Charlotte Street and George Street of fairly respectable dimensions and smaller, more modest dwellings, in the two Strand Streets and St John Street locality.

The Convention of Royal Burghs were not at all impressed by the charters granted in 1595 and 1596 and, in fact, in 1599 declined to recognise the claims. The Convention expressed their dissatisfaction with the growing practice of lairds having burghs of barony erected on their lands with the privileges thereto. It forbade trading at these "unfrey touns upoun the sey coist" and refused to accept them until "they had been inrollet be the conventioun".

Though the Convention disapproved, the effect of the barony charters on Innermessan was such as to end any hopes the people of that village or burgh as it had become entitled to be called might have had.

Innermessan, on the South-Eastern shore of Lochryan, had as early a history as that of Stranraer. Under the Agnews there arose a town or village according to Andrew Symson, writing in 1684, which was "of old the most considerable place in the Rinds of Galloway, and the greatest town thereabouts, till Stranrauer was built". A deed dated October, 1426, confirmed by a Great Seal Charter of February, 1430, conveyed to Andrew Agnew, the right to the mill at Innermessan, with its toft and croft, and the seals appended were those of Alexander Cambel, laird of Corswall and provost of the burgh. But even though it survived into the seventeenth century, its fate had been sealed by the emergence of Stranraer thanks to the Kennedies of Carrick and the Adairs of Ulster and despite the Agnews of Lochnaw. The Agnew family, however, did provide the first two Provosts and were active in the west end of the town subsequently. Two Agnews were Bailies in 1601.

Stranraer's status troubles were by no means over. The granting of the Royal Charter by King James VI of Scotland and I of England, on 24th July, 1617, though it created the town a Royal Burgh, did not, ipso facto, so enrol it.

...Birth of a Burgh

WHEN WITH COMMENDABLE ENTERPRISE, the Magistrates seized the opportunity to take advantage of the visit of His Majesty, who had been crowned King James I 14 years earlier, to Scotland in 1617, they took with them gifts as well as expressions of loyalty when they hurried to Dumfries to renew their acquaintance with the King and to repeat their obeisance.

They were accompanied by a body of influential men and their mien and expressions of deep-seated loyalties made a firm impression, emphasised, no doubt, by the gifts they bore. So much so that His Majesty graciously agreed to grant a Royal Charter creating the Royalty into a Burgh.

The Charter was presented at Paisley on Saturday, 24th July, 1617.

Thus armed, and as successors to Ninian Adair, the original charter holder, Provost William Agnew of Crooch, Bailie Andrew McCronnald and Bailie Gilbert Agnew saw the birth of a burgh. It was not without travail for the Convention of Royal Burghs looked askance at this signal of Royal favours from one termed the "wisest fool in Christendom".

Even though Charles I renewed the Charter in 1633, the stern opposition of Wigtown postponed acknowledgment from the Convention until 1683 when at long last Stranraer was "enrollit."

John Kennedy was in possession of Chappell, and Patrick Agnew, successor to Ninian Adair of Kilhilt, who later became Provost, owned most of the other land round about. Wide and varied were the duties of the new Council.

They were granted "superiorities" of certain lands, but William Adair of Kilhilt drew the annual rent for most of it; they were given authority over St John's Croft and the "harbourie"; in return they were to sustain ane kirk, hold ane market, admit burgesses and hold "court with pitt and gallows" for keeping the peace.

The "pitt" was for the simple purpose of drowning women by immersion if and when they were convicted of capital crimes. There is no record of it ever being required. They were to collect customs from those charged with making "thankful payment" and they were ordered to detain "malefactors, hurtfull persons, fighters and other sicklyke."

To accomplish these things, and many more, they had to "make, constitute, choose and create yearlie, Provost, Bailies, Treasurer, Dean of Gild, Councillors, Burgesses and other Officers."

How these were accomplished during the succeeding 350 years is detailed in the following pages.

... For the better government

FOR THE BETTER GOVERNMENT of the burgh, present and to come, in the words of the Charter, Stranraer had "to constitute, choose and create yearlie, Provost, Bailies, Treasurer, Dean of Gild, Councillors, Burgesses and other Officers." And also "to remove the said Officers and Governors for reasonable causes as they shall think expedient."

A list of the earliest Council and officials obtainable is that of 1684 and comprised Patrick Patersone, Provost (re-elected); Andro Hervy and James Hutchissone, Bailies (both re-elected); James McMaister, Treasurer; William Kennedy, Dean of Gild; Gilbert Craford, John Vance, Andrew Baillie, Alexander McCredy, Robert Hervy, Archibald Cowand, Thomas Hervy, James Lavor, William Knibloe, William Torbrane and Johne Torbrane, Hew Beard, Thomas McCrakin, Johne Beard, Councillors; Thomas Hervy, Water Bailie; Thomas Hervy, Procurator Fiscal (re-elected). James Hutchissone and Andro Hervy were also elected Barony Bailies within the five merkland of Stranraer and Markslavy and Thomas Hervy was Procurator Fiscal thereof. Hew Beard, John McCroune, Robert Hervy and Alexander McCredy, prysers; William Torbrane and Johne Torbrane, Burgh Officers.

These appointments were made at what was termed a meeting of the Michaelmas Head Court of the Royal Burgh of Stranraer, held in the Tolbooth on 6th October, 1684.

In 1688 local Council elections were suspended during His Majesty's pleasure when Stranraer had one, John Row, as Provost. Lists of the Civic Chiefs are given elsewhere.

An unusual duty in 1699 was the appointment of the council as the guardians of a female minor.

The extra Councillor is explained by the fact that the Dean of Gild was an office apart in the early days. By 1711 the sett of the Council was Provost, two Bailies and 15 Councillors. Patrick Patersone was the representative chosen to go to Dundee for the Convention of Royal Burghs in 1692.

There was a Town Clerk in 1692 but not until 1795 is there a record of a Town Chamberlain who was then termed Collector of Revenue for the Burgh. James McComb was offered the job. There was a Treasurer in 1768.

For some reason or other the Council, in 1724, ordered a page to be cut out of the minute book and this was done. Possibly the reason was that in 1725 the public were admitted to the council meeting. No meeting was to be held without one day's notice.

Despite the terms of the Charter, the Council decided in 1730 that three new Councillors should be elected annually, two from the west side of the burn and one from the other side. The number could be changed or increased if thought necessary. The arrangement held good until 1775 when the Council decided thereafter to choose the new Councillors from whichever side of the burn they pleased. Provost, Bailies and other Officers continued in office for only two years. The Magistrates and Councillors and sundry inhabitants, in 1723, met and opened the Burgh's "Charter Chist" and "found secure their Towne Charter"; they also found two bonds payable to the town. All were perused and returned to the "chist", each Bailie taking one of the keys, a copy of the town's accounts, and an English copy of the Charter. The Charter chest was shifted from Provost McCredie's house to the house of Robert Ker, the Town Clerk, and the two Bailies were made masters of the keys.

So well were the town's taxes coming in, in 1773, that the Council decided to increase the yearly salary of the Treasurer from 5/- to 25/-, retrospectively for five years. The town's mortcloth "on an unlucky occasion" was rendered useless and the Magistrates appointed a proper person who could apply for velvet to make a new one. The mortcloth was hired for one year to one person by the Council.

Under the Reform Act, the new Council was elected in 1833 by vote of the Burgesses and Heritors and the election month was changed from October to November. One-third of the Council were to retire each year. The Council decided to hold fortnightly meetings, on every second Thursday evening. The following year one of the meetings was adjourned until the Saturday as the clerk had other pressing business.

Provost Morland, who was the dominating figure in municipal affairs around this time, was one of the retiring councillors in 1839. The town clerk declared the result of the election: Charles Morland, Thomas Taylor, Wingate Robertson, William Galbraith, John Ritchie and David Guthrie. There was a protest that as a retiring councillor, Provost Morland should not be presiding officer and William Sprott, another member, declared that it was his duty to act and he intimated the following had been elected: Charles Morland, William Black, snr., John Adair, Alexander McFarlane, George Todd and Alexander Louis Guilmette.

All except Provost Morland took the oath, the Provost declining on the reasonable ground that he had done so two days earlier. All signed the minutes, so that for a day, Stranraer had 23 councillors. The matter was simply resolved by the town clerk, who omitted to send the odd five a notice of meeting. Mr Sprott's nominees disappeared from the municipal scene.

Andrew Irving, however, did not let the council settle. He claimed that, as one elected in 1837, he should not have had to retire. William Black, merchant, held the view that Mr Guthrie should not have been a retiring member and consequently was still a councillor, and by this process of thought, reasoned that he, as the one who was highest up among those unsuccessful, had been elected. George Todd and Alexander Louis Guilmette attended and claimed Provost Morland was incompetent. Mr McNeel-Caird protested that Archibald McMeikan should not be on the Council.

Matters reached such a pass that the town clerk read out the Act against bribery and the original 18 took the oath as did Messrs Black, Todd, Guilmette and Irving. Stranraer had now 22 councillors. None of the extra four, however, attended any subsequent meeting and Mr Morland's re-election as Provost was unanimous. William Black, who later became town clerk, was later co-opted on the death of John Kerr.

On an earlier occasion the three men who topped the poll each had 35 votes and in 1840 there was another three-way tie when Thomas King, innkeeper, Thomas Dalrymple, tanner, and William Bruce, blacksmith, recorded 71; James Buyers had 66, Archibald McMeikan 65 and William McGowan 64.

Samuel Black was the only member to turn up for a meeting in April, 1841, and after waiting half an hour he and the town clerk adjourned. After deciding that the meetings would be monthly and on the last Thursday of each month, with the Provost being given authority to vary the day if necessary, the council agreed in 1844 to have evening meetings. Provost Morland and Alexander McDowall, who had earlier been involved in a three-way tie, each recorded 58 votes in 1845 with another member. Each member of council signed the minutes.

There must have been a measure of public apathy in 1851 for the top three gained 35 votes each.

In 1854 six new councillors were returned and five of them had each 145 votes with the odd man out having only one fewer.

11

A dispute occurred among the councillors in 1856 over the numerous adjournments which had taken place at meetings. Some members had received an interdict from the Lord Ordinary to suspend council business. Other members endeavoured to carry on but the majority refused to attend meetings. Counsel's opinion was taken and on 27th December a meeting was held at which neither the Provost nor the Bailies were present. A letter from the First Division of the Court was read recalling the interdict and those present agreed that the minutes of meetings held subsequent to 17th November should be expunged.

Sixteen members were present in 1857, including the Provost, when members accused others of creating salaried posts for friends for work which previously had been done for nothing. The past treasurer was ordered to hand over the books to the new treasurer but this he refused to do. The Provost, it was noticed, did not attend any adjourned meetings thereafter, retiring at the end of his term. It is noteworthy that the six members returned as a result of the following election did not include any of the retiring members. The new council decided to take legal action against the former treasurer for £21 which they said he had retained from Burgh funds.

The salary of the town clerk in 1865 was fixed at £12, but he also held in addition the position of clerk to the harbour trust, £8 8s; clerk to the commissioners of police, £5; and clerk to the magistrates' and police court, £10. The registrar was paid £21 and the valuator, £20. The council, however, considered the services of the valuator should be gratuitous. Police, it was considered, were adequately remunerated though perhaps overworked, and an additional constable was appointed for night duty.

Two important steps forward in the more efficient conduct of public business were taken in 1870 when the council agreed that no motion be brought before it unless it was urgent, or had been notified at the previous meeting or to the town clerk at least three days before the meeting at which it was to be discussed. The council also agreed that members address the chair.

Conveners were required, in 1872, to give at least 24 hours' notice of a meeting, or at all events, to give notice at least on the morning of the day on which the meeting was to be held.

In 1874 there were 13 candidates for six seats and among the newcomers was John Mackie Adair, solicitor, who topped the poll as had a fellow lawyer, John M. Rankin, in the previous election.

Monthly meetings were agreed in 1877, with special meetings in between, if necessary. There were 13 candidates for seven seats in 1878 and Robert Hannay, Sheuchan Mill, a newcomer, topped the poll.

George Garrick was appointed treasurer without salary, at his own offer, in 1883, and the duties of assessor and collector of revenue were joined in 1883 when James McMaster was made chamberlain. This was an unfortunate appointment as coming events showed.

As a shareholder in the Gas Company, Mr Garrick's re-election was opposed as being illegal but the council paid so little notice to the objection that he was elected Provost. This was a period of intense interest in the elections. There were ten candidates for six seats in 1883 and four newcomers were returned to the council, including James McHarrie, ironmonger, who had led the opposition to the extensive works at Dindinnie some years earlier. Two years later three former members were again defeated and to fill a vacancy Peter Barr was co-opted on petition from 108 ratepayers in Sheuchan Street. The electorate remained fickle and in 1887 three former members were again defeated when there were nine candidates for six seats so that within four years a majority of the council were new

12

members. When beaten in the vote for the Provostship, George Dickson Baillie, a magistrate, resigned. Despite a petition by ratepayers, John Lithgow, highest up among those unsuccessful, was co-opted. Two months later another vacancy had to be filled and this time the council showed its independence by co-opting Archibald Hunter who had not even been a candidate. In 1888, the following year, there were eleven candidates for seven seats and again three former members lost their seats.

Objections were taken by a councillor, Thomas Wheatley to John Lithgow, and to William Hay, grocer, who topped the poll but the allegations proved unfounded and these two remained in office as did the objector who was a railway manager.

Parish Council elections caused some stir and it was commonplace for councillors to stand in all three of the parishes with more than a modicum of success, naturally, as they were in the public eye. Provost W. McGibbon, Councillors Wm. Dyer and David Logan became members of the County Council in 1890 following the setting up of that body.

Trouble with the auditor led to a serious situation between the chamberlain and the council which lasted from 1896 to 1902. The council found the chamberlain's system of book-keeping was "imperfect, incorrect and misleading; it threw the whole system into confusion." In 1900 the chamberlain, for reasons best known to himself, refused to sign the books, intimating he was not bound by statute so to do and he told the town council bluntly they had nothing to do with it. The auditor was of the opinion that "the town council do not exercise a sufficiently strict supervision over the chamberlain." The council drew up rules but these were ignored and in 1902 because the chamberlain "for a considerable period had, and is still performing his official duties in an unsatisfactory manner notwithstanding repeated remonstrances and admonitions" the council dispensed with his services. The matter did not end there, it ended in a court action and a Sheriff Court decree before the books were taken over by his successor, John Bradford, who held office until 1944.

There was only one item of business at a meeting in 1890—the purchase of blinds for the Old Town Hall.

One who was to play a most prominent part in the life of Stranraer for more than half a century took public office in 1896, Robert Broomfield Dyer, who joined William Dyer on the council. Ex-Bailie William Dyer, who had had 26 years' service, died two years later.

Robert Broomfield Dyer, born in 1862, started public service at the comparatively early age of 23 years when he joined the Parochial Board, later to become the Parish Council, and still later the Public Assistance Committee of which he was chairman. In 1916 he was elected interim Provost on the death of Provost Wm. Fox, the second Civic Head to die while in office. Wm. Fox had taken over in 1914 on the death of Robert Young, who occupied the position of Chief Magistrate for five years and who had, in all, service of 36 years, extending back to 1876 with one short break. He held the office of Provost for 12 years.

Provost Dyer was a member of the County Council of which he was vice-convener and chairman of the Education Committee as well as chairman of the Wigtownshire Education Trust. He was still a member of the council when he died in 1938, having been a member for 42 years.

The family association did not end there. William Dyer, the third generation of the family, entered the council on the death of his father and subsequently became Provost and like his father was honoured with the Order of the British Empire. He completed 24 years' service, making in all a total of 92 years' family service with the civic authority of Stranraer.

Petitioners in 1898 were no more successful than had been their predecessors when it came to filling a casual vacancy; the council simply ignored the 304 ratepayers.

Under the Act, the council in 1900 confirmed their burgh officers were: Wm. Black, clerk; David McMaster, town chamberlain; William Bradford, surveyor; Thomas Harper, medical officer; Augustus Smith Carnochan, burgh prosecutor; Captain John Walls, harbour master; Alexander Carrick, superintendent of slaughterhouse; John Douglas, water inspector; Robert Kerr, keeper of the weigh house; and James Davidson, public analyst. They also obtained robes for the Chief Magistrate and found that only ten ratepayers paid their rates on a Saturday night even though the chamberlain kept open until 8 p.m.

Resignations were intimated from the two Bailies and the Treasurer in 1900 but no reason was given though one of the Bailies was ill.

As there was no contest in 1902 the council fixed the order of retiral of the seven new members. For some reason or other the Provost refused to sign the minutes in 1906 and Dr A. Duke Munro appended his signature. Four members did not seek re-election that year, but there were still eight candidates with the Hon John Hew North Gustave Henry Dalrymple, later Lord Stair, topping the poll. The four who had resigned had all taken a prominent part in the formation of the water scheme at Dindinnie. There was, however, another reason for protest, for the council in 1905 had decreed that admission to the ratepayers' meeting was by ticket only.

Councillor Hay, in 1902, persuaded the council to take steps "to make Stranraer in place of Wigtown the County Town, as in all respects it is the principal town in the county," but Stranraer had to remain content with the fact, not the fiction.

There were no polls in the years from 1911 to 1918; elections were suspended during war-time. Vacancies were filled by co-option.

In 1913 the council petitioned the House of Lords against a Bill which would have meant burghs of under 2000 ratepayers becoming part of the county. This was apparently one of the earliest steps in local government reorganisation. On the resignation of Wm. Black, town clerk, W. G. Belford, who had been treasurer, resigned to act as interim clerk. He held the post until 1916 when John Bennoch, who had been a co-opted member, resigned to fill the office. This followed a precedent of 1692 when S. Paterson was a Bailie and later clerk. Among the candidates for the clerkship in 1918 were Alexander Aitken, who became County Clerk, and John D. Ker, who was later a Bailie of the Burgh.

William Black, who was the third generation of his family to serve the council in a period of over a century, left a bequest for a new town clock.

History was made in 1920 when Miss Elizabeth Wallace McGibbon became the first woman member. Miss Annie McDowall Fox was unsuccessful. Later, in 1932, two women were returned. They were Miss Grace McMath, who served until 1941, and Miss Janet McG. McConnell, who became a Bailie and whose tenure of office extended to 1946 and which coincided with the service of her brother, James McConnell, a Dean of Guild, whose main interest appeared to be the reclamation work of Clayhole Bay. The election of the women resulted in the defeat of two Bailies. There were 11 candidates for seven seats. In 1956 another of the female sex was returned, Mrs Mary Murray, who became Treasurer in 1967 and was the first woman to hold the post. Mrs Elizabeth Brown served on the council from 1957 to 1964.

In order to keep the members more informed, minutes of meetings were copied and circulated in 1922 and to encourage public interest the Provost was instructed

14

to call a ratepayers' meeting four days before the election. This system lasted for over 30 years before being abandoned. A special meeting to consider the unemployment situation was called in 1922 when various schemes were put forward, some of these came to fruition in the years that followed and ultimately resulted in an approach to the Secretary of State for Scotland in 1945 to make Stranraer an area for industrial development, paving the way for the Industry and Transport Committee which was to do such good work in the 20 years or so which followed.

Maintaining their desire to continue their ancient prerogatives, the council vigorously opposed the 1929 Local Government (Scotland) Act which transferred some of their rights and duties to the County Council.

Housing of the people was the main concern through the 1920s and 1930s and indeed since, even although in 1937 one councillor created a record by proposing five motions at one meeting. In 1938 a councillor was suspended. From 1939 to 1945, however, war emergency proposals kept the council fully employed, though it did not keep them from taking an active opposition to the Town and Country Planning Measures which ultimately became law. There was considerable concern, too, with flooding which took place mainly because of the terrific additional load being imposed on the Town and Laundry Burns.

When more normal times returned in 1945, there were 12 seats vacant on the council when election time came round and despite the fact that five of the sitting members did not seek re-election, there were 19 candidates. Alfred A. Walker, who topped the poll, had a record number of votes. One of the new members insisted on the minutes of the previous meeting being read and not taken for granted and this led to some discussion before the matter was cleared up. He was more successful in a subsequent motion that the minutes be made available in the public library.

The system of having all members of council on all committees, constituted in 1923, has remained and under an Act of 1960, committee meetings are held in public.

Since its erection, Stranraer Town Council has held its public meetings in the New Town Hall, and on the death of Mr John Bennoch, purchased 25 Lewis Street as offices for his successor. The offices were sold in 1947 when the council purchased their present official office for the town clerk and his staff, including the town chamberlain and burgh surveyor.

Therein all committee meetings are held and since 1960 by the Admission of the Press Act these are attended by newspaper representatives and occasionally, though rarely, by members of the public.

As such the premises have proved unsuitable and plans are afoot for changes in this connection.

Before the new Act was passed, there was a motion in 1949 to admit Press representatives to committee meetings. It failed by only one vote.

Apathy in the country generally led to the changing from November to May for elections in 1949. This apathy had not been a disease in Stranraer as the number of candidates indicate—19 for 12 seats in 1945, 10 for seven the following year, 11 for six in 1947, 14 for eight in 1950. In the first May election, among three newcomers, for the voters liked changes, was a minister of religion.

Electing councillors as burgesses, ipso facto, ceased in 1948. One hopeful councillor, in 1949, brought forward three motions at the one meeting, two of them ended with the charming query, "If not, why not?" All were defeated without the majority deigning to answer the questions.

In 1955 a motion consisted of 211 words in one sentence. It was approved.

Four new members made their appearance in 1950 and the new council drew up Standing Orders which have since remained unchanged. A by-election, an unusual decision, was held in 1951 to fill a vacancy.

Politics had never played any significant part in the council but in 1951 for the first time four candidates stood as official Socialists. All subsequently became members of the council but only one pursued a party line, in fact, the innovation was felt to be a curb though for a few years following there was an official Labour Municipal Group which considered the minutes prior to the council meeting. They made little impact and the procedure was soon dropped.

Attempts were made to end the ratepayers' meeting in 1950 and though these were unsuccessful they were a forerunner of things to come for not since 1955 has there been a "hecklers" meeting held. The last one was memorable. It had been agreed in 1954 to discontinue the ratepayers' meeting but it was overturned and one councillor, who had successfully persuaded the council to have the order of speakers drawn by lot, objected to the time limit, and amid general disorder when he refused to obey the chair, the meeting was closed abruptly by the Provost before all parties had been heard. There were 12 candidates for seven seats and three more vociferous councillors were not amongst those re-elected; there were five newcomers.

Twice during the 1950s the election of a Provost was held up, in 1951 and 1957. In the latter year Stranraer had only one Magistrate for a month.

At one meeting in 1954 there were 13 motions and amendments and at another three members left during a housing debate.

In 1954 there was again trouble between the elected treasurer and the chamberlain which culminated in the treasurer objecting to the audited accounts. After considerable discussion and reports to the Secretary of State the accounts were ultimately approved.

There was another storm in 1966 when the chamberlain's rate notices were described as "curt," "discourteous" and "brusque." Notices had been issued in accordance with the strict letter of the law and many recipients made strong objections. The upshot was a change in approach and a decision that the town clerk's position as chief official emphasised.

At the second meeting after the election in 1966 the Provost made a public appeal for less bickering among councillors and asked for more co-operation in view of the serious affairs which faced the burgh. For the most part their time was taken up with consideration of the need to encourage industry, to aid unemployed and to improve the appearance of the burgh. There was a slight breeze over council appointments but the trouble soon passed in 1966.

Stranraer, with 350 years of burghal history behind it, is actively opposing reorganisation proposals which would result in loss of status and the withdrawal of many more of the rights, duties and responsibilities granted to it in 1617.

...Not only for building

ONE OF THE OFFICES created by the Charter was Dean of Gild. It was and is entirely separate and is unique in that the Dean is all powerful, for although appointed by the Council he acts completely independently of that body. Recent legislation merely emphasised the importance of the position, even though in a small burgh like Stranraer the authority of the Planning Committee overlaps and at times over-rides his authority. The office is by no means an anachronism today.

No building in the town is permitted to be erected without his sanction. At times his authority spread to other matters; he was called in to settle disputes other than those related to building.

In 1769 he was asked to ascertain the marches of the Castle Yard, formerly excused from taxation, with a view to bringing the eastern part, extending to the Land of Aird, into taxation. He gave permission to Archibald Naismith, merchant, to erect a tan works, and he took stern measures in 1770 when it was found that the plans submitted to him had been deviated from. He found the gable of Hugh McKeag's house had overlapped on to Hugh Aitken's ground by two and a half inches, so he ordered it to be removed. Aitken received compensation and reasonable expenses. The exact boundary was later agreed by parties. Andrew Campbell was ordered to rebuild his house three feet nearer the street to make a more regular line. After Robert McCulloch had been granted a lining to build on the east side of the Burn of Chapel, adjacent to the bridge, it was found the bridge was too narrow, therefore, McCulloch had to build so as to leave 20ft. clear from the inside of the south ledge and to build a ledge of equal thickness on the north side.

The Dean gave permission for the opening up of a new street in 1771 when Adam Hanna, mason, asked authority to build in the Chapel Fey of Stranraer. The width of a street was measured by the Dean personally and after an inspection he found that Charles Baird and Alexander McWhinnie "hath a building which encroached on to the King's public road by two feet." He ordered the house to be pulled down.

Despite protestations that he had built on the foundation of a house "that had been there since the memory of man," John McWilliam, who had erected a dwelling upon the west side of the road to Stephenkirk in 1772 was ordered to have it pulled down. McWilliam considered that 21ft. was wide enough for any road. On the other side of the town, on the Glenluce Road, Alexander Gibson, in Chapel, had to knock down a wall and rebuild in a straight line between the houses of Robert Handcock and Alexander Adair.

At times his authority was questioned by the Magistrates. He had given permission in 1775 to one, Thomas Martin, to build a new house opposite the church, but the Magistrates ruled the gable windows of the church would have their light impeded, from outwith presumably.

James McKie had earlier been warned not to set up "tann pitts" near the Cross and the church, close by Mrs McHarrie's door. A subsequent application for "tann pitts" was turned down on the ground that the council intended to use the site for a slaughterhouse themselves.

One of the earliest town improvements was in 1803 when James McDowall, cooper, proposed pulling down the range of old houses at the foot of the East Vennel (Princes Street) to form an easy access to the shore. The court, having considered the proposal, agreed and paid Mr McDowall £12 10s for his trouble.

Authority was given, for a financial consideration, to John Agnew who had bought a house belonging to Mrs McCrea on the east side of the burn formerly called Wauck Mill Stead, to arch over the burn, and in 1817, two years later, Thomas Lindsay was granted authority to build on waste ground on the north-west side and arch the building over the burn to join with a house being built by Alexander McDowall.

A further improvement followed in 1825 when permission was given for old houses on the north side of the High Street to be pulled down and replaced by new buildings. This part of High Street became George Street.

Peter Gibson, ship master, petitioned the court concerning his new stone house on property to the south side of the High Street (George Street) and bounded on the east by the Chapel Burn (McHarrie's Corner at George Street-South Strand Street). He wished to leave a passage for his own, but not for the public convenience. The court refused after an inspection and decreed a public passage must be left along the side of the burn. He could, if he wished, arch over this passage but the arch must be at least 11ft. high.

The attention of the Dean was not always concerned with building, as has been indicated, for in 1840 he was authorised to investigate complaints about weights and measures.

His court decided in 1845 to construct an archway over the town burn from George Street to Bridge Street, and in 1869, after inspecting a site for a new house in Hanover Square, to which conterminous proprietors had objected, the Dean upheld the objections.

He himself raised objections on the ground of amenity to a new shed proposed for the bottom of King Street and the west end of Market Street, in 1872, and in 1879 he authorised work at the Old Castle.

In later years, the authority of the court was shown in several instances. A lining by N. Bonugli to create a new cafe on a site at the corner of George Street and Queen Street led to record sittings, the British Linen Bank objecting to a window which would look into their property over an alleyway, no doubt fearing a possible threat to the safety of the vaults. The hearing lasted several months in 1934 and after an agent, accompanied by his dog, had attended the court, which was until then rather informally held in the jury room of the New Town Hall, the Dean moved into the court house proper. The Dean is no respecter of persons: when there was no agent present to move for approval of a lining for a new police station in the town in 1950, he refused to consider the plans, and in 1960 he drew the attention of the county council to his powers. His wishes are a different matter for in 1966 he had to pass plans for erections near the sea front against his inclination. In the last decade or so one proprietor at least has been ordered to demolish work started without authority and another has received public warning as to the consequences that could follow the erection of any building without prior sanction of the Dean of Guild Court.

... To have ane Kirk

ONE OF THE CONDITIONS of the Charter was that the new burgh should provide "ane kirk."

So far as ecclesiastical buildings in the town are concerned, the Old Parish had the most changes. Built in 1649, in pursuance of the obligation placed upon the Royal Burgh, it was replaced in 1694 but not very successfully and it was rebuilt in 1784. Four years earlier the Magistrates appointed a special meeting of all interested to view the ruinous state of the kirk and to buy land if necessary contiguous to the kirkyard, on which to build a new one. The Earl of Stair offered to build a new church. In 1784, considering the kirk was still ruinous, nothing having been done in the interval, the council decided to purchase houses and yards belonging to John Cowand and the heirs of the late John Agnew, smith, adjacent to the kirkyard. Estimates were limited to £400 for the building. Archibald Paterson, who was Dean of Guild, was the builder and a door was included in the east gable built against the Kirk Vennel (now Church Street). Lord Stair met the bill and also the account for the purchase of the ground.

In the old church in 1725, Patrick McDowall of Freugh and Robert Agnew of Sheuchan, burgesses of the burgh who intended to live in the town, were granted permission to build a loft in the church for themselves, their families and their servants. The loft was to be so high as to allow those seated below to see the minister when they stood.

In 1809 the council considered the building too small and additions were made. In 1818 they opposed the building of a manse for the simple reason they had no tiends.

The new building did not meet with acceptance and in 1833 the Presbytery ordered the burgh and heritors to rebuild once more. In 1841 they did rebuild "a plain structure, crowded between other buildings in Church Street."

An offer from the Relief Church to give shelter was accepted, but a suggestion of a tax on all inhabitants for the Parish Church was turned down as the council thought it "would be disagreeable to those who were Dissenters and might ultimately deprive the burgh of its principal revenue." The principal revenue was that derived from seat lets but it was illusory. However, the council feared the Presbytery would insist upon them providing a church capable of holding two-thirds of the examinable population of the burgh and they decided to issue shares of £25. Each shareholder was to receive five per cent interest from the revenue from the seat rents.

The council were allowing the new church to be built upon the site of the old but not if it encroached on the burial ground. Rev. David Wilson, minister of the church, who was also a councillor, was informed he had no church for his congregation. The Presbytery intervened and laid down a time limit when the new church was to be completed. They demanded a building to accommodate 1048 persons. Plans prepared by James Adair were approved by Presbytery. Mr A. Taylor offered ground on the north side of Greenvale Street of the exact size less one foot, but the council, on the casting vote of Provost Morland, turned down the offer.

Contractors for the new building were Hugh McDowall and Andrew McCrea, masons, James Adair, carpenter, glazier and plasterer, and the cost was to be £2035. A stent master was appointed to raise the amount from the heritors and inhabitants. Considerable difficulty was experienced by the stent master, Abram Campbell, who was later harbour master. He resigned and his successor, Wingate

Robertson, had to execute letters of Horning. Heritors and council joined in a petition to Presbytery asking for a smaller church and the minister wrote for his arrears of stipend.

In 1838 matters eased a little and the council, in return for their good offices, requested three pews, one for the minister, one for the magistrates, and one for the elders. They also ordered seats to be retained for the poor.

The minister was by this time suing for his stipend and his claim was upheld by the Magistrates against the council. Ground was sold by the council to the Gas Company to pay off the arrears.

There was a slight deficit on the fund for the church but the council decided to pay this off from the income derived from seat rents after the minister's stipend, the school master's salary and repairs had been paid.

On 16th May, 1841, the new church was accepted from the builders and consecrated by Rev David Wilson.

A "forced entry" into the church by two councillors led to a protest by a member of the public but the council decided to enforce their civil rights of entering the church at any time.

By 1846 the debt on the church building had been paid off, but that was by no means the end of the strife.

As far back as 1734 there had been difficulty in collecting seat rents and various methods had been tried. One ratepayer, William McCracken, attended the council and objected to being wrongly stented on the roll for trade, house and seat in the church. He succeeded and in the next stent roll he was put in only for trade and house. Seat letting continued to be a bone of contention until ultimately in 1864 the council left the matter in the hands of the Kirk Session. This was by no means a bargain for the Kirk Session who, in 1882, collected £206 but spent £426 on repairs. A claim by the minister in 1884 for payment was refused by the council who, after examining the books for the previous 40 years, found they had paid his income tax and that, therefore, they did not owe him anything.

In 1867 H.M. The Queen was pleased to present Rev. Thomas Little, A.B., B.D., to the church and parish of Stranraer as a result of a memorial by the members to the Home Secretary.

The condition of the fabric was causing concern up until 1928 when the General Trustees called on the Council to make certain repairs prior to the building passing from the council to the Church Trustees, but the local authority considered that as there had been an agreement with the Kirk Session in 1875 whereby the Session, in exchange for the seat rents, assumed responsibility for the fabric, they had the right to refuse to accept any responsibility in the matter of repairs. Approval was sought of the council in 1953 for a new vestry.

Under the plan of Union of the Churches, commissioners making up the General Assembly were from 1930 elected by Presbyteries, and Stranraer Council's prerogative of appointing a representative elder ceased.

... To the honour and service of God

RELATIONSHIPS BETWEEN THE CHURCH and state, as represented by the council, were often less than amicable.

Before the Reformation there was a Chapel of St John and in March, 1600, the General Assembly sanctioned the founding of a parish for the Stranraer district. The disjunction from Leswalt and Inch took some time during which the duty of administering the parish was the responsibility of "the reidars," Cuthbert Adair, Adam Thomsone and Thomas Makalexander, from Leswalt and Inch around 1570. Their stipends were twenty merkis.

When Jenney Geddes threw her "cutty stoole" in St Giles in 1625 her action had a far-reaching effect on Stranraer and Galloway. King James had tried to enforce bishops on Presbyterians and Charles imposed the revised prayer book. There were uprisings by the Presbyterians. During the covenanting troubles Colonel John Graham of Claverhouse is believed to have had his headquarters in the Old Castle. In March, 1682, he wrote a letter from Stranraer in which he said "I am just beginning to send out many parties, finding the rebels become secure, and the country so quiet in all appearance. I sent out a party with my brother Dave three nights ago. The first night he took Drumbui and one McLellan, and the great villain McClurg, the smith at Moniegafe, that made all the clikys, and after whom the forces have trotte so often. It cost me both pains and money to know how to find him; I am resolved to hang him; for it is necessary I make an example of severity lest rebellion be thought cheap here. There cannot be alive a more wicked fellow!" There is evidence, however, that McClurg escaped; his name occurs in a list of fugitive outlaws proclaimed by the Government in 1684.

Sir John Dalrymple of Stair the following year was deprived of his bailiery of Glenluce and fined £500 Scots and ordered to be confined in Edinburgh Castle until his fine was paid. He was held responsible for his tenants attending Conventicles. Grierson of Lag was an able henchman of Claverhouse.

In 1652, Parliament passed the Act legally establishing the Presbyterian form of church government. Presbyteries and Synods had been set up as early as 1581, the Presbytery of Wigtown, with which Stranraer is now joined, being one of the earliest. With the Presbytery of Kirkcudbright it formed the Synod of Galloway. Stranraer, with the eight other parishes in the West, became the Presbytery of Stranraer, in 1633, and in 1699, these were joined by Colmonell and Ballantrae. Church patronage remained with the Bishop of Galloway until 1689. Though King James VI had established the Reformed Church, he superimposed the Bishops whom the General Assembly had deposed fifty years earlier.

Mr Robert Aird, M.A., was ordained by the Bishop of Galloway to Stranraer Parish in 1633 but demitted his charge in 1638 "as he could not withdraw his affection for Episcopacy."

Stranraer's next minister, Mr John Livingston, was not ordained by the Bishop. His diary is in the County Museum, Stranraer. He was appointed on the invitation of Sir Robert Gordon of Lochinvar and he was probably the most outstanding personality in the annals of the historic parish church of Stranraer. A son of the manse, he was inducted in the year of the National Covenant. Earlier he had come to Galloway but had not accepted the call and eventually went to Killinchie. He was compelled to remove from Northern Ireland because of the hostility of the Bishop of Down.

Rev. John Livingston, describing his ministry, said the Stranraer people met in the local church for psalms, a prayer, a scripture reading and an explanation thereof, "only so long as an half-hour glass ran."

"The people," he wrote, "were very tractable and respectable." He mentions, too, that the whole parish is "within the bounds of a small town."

He journeyed to London as one of the ministers who took copies of the Covenant, and he was an attender at the General Assembly of 1638 when the Marquis of Hamilton ordered it to disperse as he was displeased with the proceedings. His Lordship, however, felt friendly enough to warn Livingston to decamp from London as he had heard the King threaten to "put a pair of fetters about his feet." The Assembly was obdurate. Also present on that occasion which restored the church to the state it was in when King James had made his first attempts to subdue the Presbyterian form of ecclesiastical Government, was James Glover, clerk to Stranraer Presbytery.

The Stranraer minister was chaplain to the Scottish Army at the Battle of Newburn in 1639.

When Charles II was proclaimed King of Scotland in 1649, Mr Livingston was among the commissioners who went to The Hague. He was at Breda when His Majesty agreed to the Solemn League and Covenant and presided and delivered the sermon. In the storm of protest against the Repeal of the Act of Classes, condemned by the General Assembly, he took a strenuous and active part, and in 1654 he again visited London, this time to make a personal appeal to Cromwell for the relief of fines imposed on Galloway men, though at that time he was not, in fact, a Galloway minister. Among those fined for upholding the Solemn League and Covenant were James Johnston and Adam Martin, Stranraer, each fined £600, Patrick Agnew of Sheuchan, fined £1200, and John Gordon, described as a merchant, Stranraer, fined £240.

Mr John Park, M.A., succeeded Mr Livingston in 1649, and, as Moderator of Synod, he protested against the dissolution of that court by James, Earl of Galloway in 1661. He was also concerned in a Court of Session action anent his stipend. As a Nonconformist, Mr Park was banished in 1661 but, however, was restored to grace and favour in 1669 when the King empowered the Lords of Privy Council to reinstate deposed ministers.

Wodrow described Mr John Park as "a worthy person, a man of great solidity, very sufficient learning, and is the author of a treatise on Patronage, so well-known in this church." The book was later enlarged by his son, Mr Robert Park, who was clerk to the General Assembly.

Thus, in its earliest days, the Parish Church of Stranraer, had as ministers, two men of national, even international repute.

Another minister, gratefully remembered in the annals of the church, was Mr Walter Laurey, who, on his death in 1742, bequeathed to the Parish Church a house and garden, a seat in the church, a tomb and about 40 acres of land in the parish of Leswalt "to be enjoyed by and to encourage my successors in office in all time coming, on condition of keeping my tomb in repair."

Notwithstanding this munificent legacy, Mr David Wilson, who became minister in 1807, on the passing of an Act by George III, claimed £20 in lieu of a glebe. He raised an action in the Court of Session in 1821.

Rev. David Wilson appeared to have a more justifiable complaint. Among the obligations on the council were "to pay yearly to their minister 400 marks and four bolls of meall for which their inhabitants are taxed." There was no reneging on this from 1682 until 1705 when the Magistrates considered the bolls of meall were awkward currency but Mr Wilson found, no doubt to his pecuniary embarrassment, that for four years the Magistrates had not contributed to his maintenance. On their part the Magistrates met an increasing reluctance by the people to be taxed; they resisted the assessment. Mr Wilson's comment was wry, "I believe that

22

Stranraer is the only instance in Scotland of a royal burgh, the seat of a Presbytery, having only one minister, and that minister on the small stipend list."

Libelled on various charges, Rev David Wilson was deposed but the following year, despite the shattering events of the time, 1843, the superior court of the Church had time to deal with more mundane matters and on his appeal found the sentence "illegal and unconstitutional". He was readmitted.

Another of the perquisites of the charge was that there was a tiend of herring from Lochryan. This was paid, spasmodically, as the minister claimed it but as he had to uplift the claim personally at Clayhole Bay where the fishing vessels landed their catches he probably did not think it worth the trouble. In 1907, however, Rev Dr H. P. Charlton attempted to revive the payment simply to establish the right but the Church was disinterested.

Schisms in the Church toward the end of the seventeenth century also had their effect on Stranraer. Branches of the Cameronians in 1690 were followed by the McMillanites and the Smeatonites. These soon disappeared without trace. Not so the Anti-Burghers, formed in 1759. This church signed the Bond and Covenant as required by the Act of the Associate Presbytery, passed in 1743.

After meeting, for several years, in a house in Stoneykirk Road, the Associate Congregation of Anti-Burghers, in 1773, built a church in Ivy Place. Records of the Session showed, among other things, members were tried for smuggling and listening to other communions. It was not made clear which offence was considered the more heinous; but, at any rate, one member was expelled in 1830 for an offence committed twenty years earlier.

The congregation became the First United Secessionist Congregation, Stranraer, with, it was said, about 300 communicants. Subsequently it changed to the United Presbyterian Congregation of Ivy Place, and, under the leadership of Rev Robert Hogarth, a new church was built on the same site in 1840. When the United Presbyterian and Free Churches came together the name changed to Ivy Place United Free Church. In 1893, three years after the induction of Rev J. Somerville Smith, despite opposition from the Kirk Session, a mission hall was built in Glen Street and plans for a new building for the congregation were approved, and a new church opened in 1898. Union followed with St Mark's U.F., a church of the Disruption, in 1926, and the united charge was known as St Andrew's U.F. Church. Three years later the congregation joined the Church of Scotland retaining the name of Scotland's Patron Saint.

In 1797, another branch of the United Presbyterian Church was founded in Bellevilla Road. In 1850 the congregation moved to Bridge Street, to the building now used by the Parish Church for Sunday School and other purposes which was then known as the West U.P. Church. Still a United Presbyterian congregation, a new church was erected in Lewis Street in 1894, "the handsomest ecclesiastical structure in the town". At the union of the United Presbyterian and Free Churches it became St Ninian's United Free Church which it remained until 1929. At the union it, too, retained the name of the Saint.

Another strong minority of Presbyterians, before the Disruption, was the Original Seceders, who had two churches in the town. In 1839 one of these had built in Sun Street a regular meeting place and the congregation attracted an eminent divine in Rev John Smellie. The Original Seceders joined with the disaffected Anti-Burghers, the strongest of the original breakaway branches of the Church and subsequently the majority of them joined with the congregation at Ivy Place.

Their building was acquired in 1922 by the Stranraer Freemasons Lodge Kilwinning No. 208. The building vacated by the congregation of St Ninian's became, for a time, a Good Templars' hall before being later sold to the Army as a drill hall in 1900.

At the Disruption when 450 ministers came out, the greatest impact was felt by a new congregation, that of Sheuchan Parish Church. This parish had been created out of part of Leswalt and part of Portpatrick and the church was formed because "there is no church between Stranraer and Leswalt though there is a population of about 1800." It was officially recognised as a parish in 1867.

Services had been held by the congregation in various places around Sheuchan Street from 1830 and in 1839 many influential people in the west end of the town decided to erect a church. They included Sir Andrew Agnew of Lochnaw, whose forebears had been Hereditary Sheriffs of Galloway, Colonel Patrick Vans Agnew of Sheuchan, whose progenitors were the Vaus's of the Machars, and Major Robert McDowall, who was a sept of the Agnew family, and who occupied the dower house of Park. They made gifts of lands and of money. The new church had just been completed when came the Disruption.

Following the Union of Parliaments in 1707, an Act was passed restoring the patron's rights to appoint pastors. It was a disastrous Act, particularly so far as Sheuchan was concerned. The church had been built by heritors and the congregation left, almost to a man. After meeting in a loft in Sheuchan Street, a permanent church was built in Park Lane, the building latterly passed into the hands of the Salvation Army who made excellent use of it until this year when it was purchased by Stranraer Town Council for demolition to make way for new houses.

The building was not large enough and in 1884 the congregation of Sheuchan U.F. Church built a fine new church in King Street. The fact that the site was not within the bounds of Sheuchan Parish caused some discord and disaffection. However, it prospered and remained until 1929, the United Free Church of Sheuchan. In 1929 it became St Margaret's and continued under that name until 1956 when, following a vacancy, the congregation was united with Sheuchan Parish, thus returning to the home of their forefathers. The name of the united congregation is the High Kirk of Stranraer.

In 1743, the Presbytery of the Reformed Presbyterian Church was constituted and on 7th August, 1796, a congregation was formed in Stranraer which called Rev Robert Douglas. When Rev Wm. Symington took over the ministry in 1819 it was said there was a congregation of between 400 and 500 which seems inordinately large even though it had been joined by the second of the Original Seceders. At any rate, the building was too small and in 1824 it was taken down and the following year the present church in Dalrymple Street was built in its place.

There followed a period of great unrest and in 1863 many of the congregation left to join the Free Church. Those remaining suffered a period of difficulty not resolved until 1896 when Rev Wesley Rodger was called. It still remains a Presbyterian congregation separate from the Church of Scotland.

Though without a regular place of worship, through the immigrations from Ireland, there had arisen by 1843, a fairly responsible section of the Roman Catholic faith in Stranraer. For the most part they had settled down in one area in the town, termed obviously, "Little Ireland" and like other small denominations they had their place of worship in various houses. Around 1840 Rev John Moore was appointed first parish priest and the congregation held regular services in a room next to the Assembly Rooms in Castle Court.

In 1852 they built St Joseph's Church in Lewis Street.

In 1924 the tower containing the present sanctuary was added to the east end and the donor also gave a set of chimes. The most imposing feature of the sanctuary is the circular antique glass window above the altar, depicting the Crucifixion, the work of Stalens of Antwerp. The original choir loft was demolished in 1961 and the small porch beneath it was incorporated into the main part of the church, a new porch being built on to the front of the church. The convent of the Sisters of St Joseph of Cluny was the gift of a parishioner in the 1890s.

That they were a congregation earlier is on record for at the time of the Disruption they were acknowledged as having 161 adherents, together with the established church, with 1729 communicants, a Reformed Presbyterian Church and two United Secession Churches, whose congregations totalled 1053. There were 151 adults not known to belong to any religious organisation.

In 1892, the Episcopalian Church was built in London Road and one writer in the following year commented that "there are ten churches in the town, a supply far in excess of the population." The number is the same today. There are Stranraer Old Parish, the High Kirk of Stranraer, St Andrew's and St Ninian's of the Church of Scotland, Reformed Presbyterian, St Joseph's R.C., St John's Episcopalian, the Salvation Army, Christian Brethren and Jehovah's Witnesses.

In September, 1929, the Synod of Galloway met for the last time, as did the United Free Church Presbytery though for many years there was a congregation of the United Free Church (continuing) in Lewis Street, which, after suffering many vicissitudes, disappeared in 1966. The building, which had been in use as a dance hall, at an interval when the congregation was disbanded, is now being restored, if not to the Presbyterian Church, at any rate to divine worship.

Stranraer Presbytery also had its final meeting in 1929 but was reconstituted and operated as a separate entity until in 1963, after three years' negotiation, it joined with the Presbytery of Wigtown taking with it in all 17 congregations including three in Ayrshire, Ballantrae, Colmonell and Arnsheen-Barrhill and assuming the name of the former United Free Presbytery, that of the Presbytery of Wigtown and Stranraer, with the Synod of Ayr as the immediate supreme court.

...Of certain knowledge

THOUGH FORMAL EDUCATION was introduced in 1616, by decree of the Privy Council, scant attention was paid to the decree in Stranraer for already by that time there were many private establishments as well as the ecclesiastical schools.

Even when the Act was repeated in 1646 and 1696, Stranraer paid no heed, holding that it did not apply to the town for they already had had a parish school prior to the Parliamentary decrees.

In 1684, the council continued Alexander Bruce in office of school master from "Witsonday nix to cum, 1685, to Witsonday nixt thereftir at a salary of £60 Scots." The masters were engaged annually but in 1688 Archibald Griersone obtained a regular appointment to "teach and instruct all the weins and others that shall be put to the publick skooll." In 1712, James Johnstoune, the master, received 50 merks "and if he extravaig or faile in his dewty and in punchuall attendance, he shall lose his sallery."

School masters doubled as session clerks.

In 1787 the Magistrates and Councillors "were of opinion that the manner of conducting education in the burgh was defective," and two years later they "built a very convenient school and schoolhouse." The same site was used and the architect was Archibald Paterson with Edward Wallace the builder and the cost was £80.

Fees ranged from 2s 6d for English and Writing to 3s 6d for Greek or French. The building was in North Strand Street on premises now occupied by Inch Motors Ltd., having passed through stages of a brewery and a bakery. And at the time of erection the site was described as "quite in the country."

There was a private establishment in Fisher Street and in addition several church schools. The burgh school was convenient enough to take in boarders, there were 33 pupils although at that time, 1791, there were 260 children under the age of eight and 1276 over that age, practically adult.

By 1814 there were eight recognised schools in the town. The teachers, two in the burgh establishment, taught six subjects: English, practical maths, French, Latin, Greek and writing, for £50 per annum. Many prominent citizens guaranteed an Endowment Fund and a two-day bazaar which coincided with Lochryan Regatta raised £200.

Four years later, however, it was the opinion of many responsible citizens that the schools were by no means adequate owing to the rising population. More power was wanted by the Magistrates for providing schools and employing school masters. Another school was erected on a site later taken over by Stranraer Academy in 1843. The original burgh school and ground at the east corner of Fisher Street and Market Street were sold in 1823.

Church schools tended towards the classical side of education and the burgh leaders became concerned for the less fortunate of the population. Ragged schools and a penny-a-week school were started; the former met in a building provided at Bishopburn by the Earl of Stair. The pupils cultivated land at Clenoch, one and a half miles away. The name was later changed to the Industrial School and was accommodated in the Old Castle in 1850 replacing a girls' school there.

For almost 50 years James Carnochan was head master of the burgh school. He was joined in 1789 by Stephen Addison who brought with him the pupils he had been teaching in a private establishment. A third school to accommodate 60 scholars had been built on the present site of the gas holders in 1791. In 1839 the council agreed to meet four years' arrears of salary, amounting to £80, owed to William Main, school master.

Various premises were rented for use as a burgh school; rooms in King Street belonging to Mr William Morland, a brother of the Provost, and a bale-room in Castle Close belonging to Mrs Gifford, were used for this purpose at a cost of £6 per annum.

In 1842 Dr. Robert Cunningham conducted an open examination in the Mechanics Institute, Stranraer, then in the Old Castle, of all scholars in all Church schools; many scholars subsequently became eminent lawyers, honoured ministers or attained high office in Government service, banking and commerce.

The council claimed by this time that "there were few who could not either read or write." In direct opposition to the classical schools of the Church, and indeed of their own, Stranraer Academy was planned in 1841, the foundation stone was laid in 1842 and the building occupied a year later when the Society for the Advancement of Education was formed. The penny-a-week school, established in 1771, was accommodated in the basement of the new school; the boys repaired nets and did gardening, and girls, who were admitted later, did sewing.

In 1822, Lord Stair gave Glenwell Park as the site for a school and schoolhouse, and other buildings, necessary for the education of youth, including a playground, for a feuduty of one penny.

There were enrolled in burgh schools in 1847, 536 pupils in addition to those attending the many private schools in the town. The council were warned out of Castle Close in 1843 and in 1845, following the success of the Academy, gave up the burgh school. The burgh had pride in claiming in 1850 that "there was not one child under ten years of age in prisons." The attendance at the penny-a-week school varied from 100 in 1853 to 250 in 1861 and in 1862 a bazaar was held which raised £400 for a school in Glenwell Park. The project never materialised.

In 1868 the council was relieved of its obligations towards the Academy building by paying £5 for the rector's house elsewhere and making good a liability of £300.

Life for the schoolboy was tough, discipline was hard. The yew and oak rod were the forerunners of the tawse. Despite the number of private schools, the public schools were taxed to their utmost. With the opening of Sheuchan (Madras) School in 1862 the crowded situation was somewhat eased. A grant for this establishment came from Dr. Bell's Madras Trust.

A former Free Church school in Lewis Street was taken over in 1873 as the elementary school and became familiarly known as "Tully's School" after the head teacher. Son of a head master at Lewis Street School, Professor Mavor became head of the University of Toronto. He died in 1927. Part of the Academy had also been occupied from 1849 to 1858 by McNeil's School, a private affair.

The first lady teacher, Miss Cormack, was appointed in 1866 to the Academy, under Dr. Macgregor. Critics were soon answered for in 1868 the dux was Elizabeth M. Lyall, later the founder of the Wm. R. Lyall Memorial Prize for Essays.

The Acts of 1872 secularised the schools. In 1888 there was a serious dispute amongst those responsible for the Academy. When the representatives of the board arrived they found the gates locked, the key removed and the bell missing. They were greeted with hisses and groans from the pupils. An intriguing aspect was a procession of 600 children marching in protest led by four itinerant German musicians.

In the following year free education was offered to all, up to and including the fifth standard.

In 1893 the county committee on secondary education was offered a grant of £240 provided a secondary school was established in Stranraer to cover the Rhins. The school board was asked to join in with the other parishes but the members were divided on the question, the chief opponent being Rev. William Johnston on the ground that it would be a rival school to the Academy and the work of the two would overlap.

The majority decided in favour of the scheme and the top flat of the Academy was given over in 1894 to the governors of what is now called the High School.

In 1894 Mr John Machrey was appointed head master. Elementary number two was transferred to Lewis Street School, fees in the Academy having been done away with. A long period of overcrowding in the Academy ensued. Many parents objected to paying fees at the High School and refused to accept one of the free places provided so the school board arranged to have an advanced class in the Academy from which pupils were presented in single subjects, English, mathematics, Latin, etc., at the Leaving Certificate Examination. These pupils were taught along with the pupil teachers of the school.

In December, 1894, fire broke out in the upper flat and completely gutted the whole interior of the Academy. Classes for the next year were held in the Parish Church Hall and the Old Town Hall.

During 1897, Sisters of St Joseph of Cluny came to Stranraer at the request of the Bishop to take charge of St Joseph's Primary School, also in Lewis Street, which is for children of the Roman Catholic faith. Until this date the school had been staffed by secular teachers. From 1897 to 1918 the school was governed by the Parish Priest but since the Education Act of 1918 it has been the property of the Education Committee.

27

The Academy was reopened in 1895. Accommodation was still a problem but the school board would do nothing and the High School governors had no money to build a new school. Mr Joseph Hood took over on Mr Machrey's resignation. The problem was aggravated in 1903 by the raising of the school leaving age. In 1904 a temporary building was erected in the playground to accommodate the senior class. Since that time the building has been used as a dental clinic, a maternity welfare clinic, a classroom for Glasgow evacuees and before its closure was used as a metalwork and woodwork classroom.

In 1906 the attendances were: Academy 336, Sheuchan 255, Lewis Street 255 and St Joseph's 106. In 1967 the attendances are: Academy 513, Sheuchan 301, Rephad 263, Park 500, Dalrymple 107, St Joseph's 126, Stranraer High School 500, and at a junior occupational centre there are 18 pupils.

The fact that in 1909 fees were abolished may have helped to aggravate the difficulties. The High School at that time was made responsible for all grades of education, the only entry qualifications being the passing of an examination. Just two years later, in 1911, Stranraer High School became a separate entity, with its own building across the road from the Academy. When this happened the Academy was gutted and redesigned.

From 1937 to 1939 preparations were being made to raise the school leaving age to 15. Extra accommodation was required at the Academy and thus for practical work one of the classrooms was converted into a laundry room and new equipment provided in both domestic science and woodwork departments.

To obviate overcrowding in the advanced division classes and also to cope with the raising of the school leaving age, an annexe of six rooms was opened in August, 1939.

In September, 1939, the school was closed to allow for its being used as a distribution centre for evacuees from Glasgow owing to the impending threat of war. On the day after war was declared the school was used to billet troops proceeding to Northern Ireland. At one point at the beginning of the war, the total number of evacuees housed in the Academy was 850. In 1940 the Academy and annexe were occupied by servicemen and was not vacated by them until October, 1941. Not until March, 1942, were classes resumed and it was October before the annexe was ready for occupation.

A new school was born in 1938. Park Primary School was, and still is, the only double-stream school in the county. It is also the largest primary. Built to replace the aging Sheuchan and Lewis Street primaries, the Park, as it is known, cost £24,000 and had accommodation for 650 pupils. One rather strange feature is that upstairs there is a large room with two smaller adjacent rooms, which were designed to be used as an operating theatre during the war.

Sheuchan School itself had, in fact, been built to replace two schools—Sheuchan Free Church Female School and Agnew Crescent School. The total cost was £1058. Despite that it had only three rooms, the school had a roll of 200 pupils. When the roll rose to 300, one room was divided into two. Although criticised severely by H.M. Inspectors from 1926 onwards it was not closed until 1933 when the pupils joined to Lewis Street School. When it was realised in 1947 that the Academy could not cope with the increase in pupils, Sheuchan was reopened. Extensive alterations and modernisation were carried out in 1958 to make a 13-classroom school. The alterations cost £115,000.

Opened in 1958, Rephad Primary School, erected on the site of a former golf course at Ladies' Walk and London Road, cost in the region of £360,000 and has accommodation for 340 pupils. Most of the staff came from the Academy. Thus began a new era in the history of education in Stranraer. Zoning of children into the schools nearest at hand took place.

The 1929 Act brought into being the Wigtownshire Education Authority which was responsible for schools, appointments, and curriculum. The Education Act of 1936 raised the leaving age from 14 years to 15 in spite of widespread opposition, only before equalled in intensity when the age had been raised from 13 years. Stranraer Town Council were amongst the objectors and the change was not enforced until 1946. At present there is a third agitation on the same subject for the proposal is that the leaving age be raised to 16 years in 1970.

Following a centralisation scheme all post-primary children in the Rhins, apart from Sandhead, were brought to Stranraer for secondary education, being split into two streams in accordance with their age, aptitude and ability. Sandhead Junior Secondary Department is to be absorbed this year.

The influx taxed the already overburdened secondary schools. Primary pupils were fairly well off with three, one of them the two-stream, but secondary pupils were so cribbed, cabined and confined, that according to a High School magazine of the day "branches had to be opened everywhere."

This state of affairs led in 1963 to work starting on two new secondary schools which were erected in London Road and completed in 1965, being officially opened by the Secretary of State for Scotland, Mr William Ross, who had been a school teacher.

There is every possibility that the two schools will be joined under one rector for the former method of selection is to be ended and streaming of pupils will take place no longer at 12 years of age; a comprehensive school instead of a senior and junior secondary is imminent.

With the provision of modern schools for secondary education the problem moved over to the primary once again and the former Academy had to be reopened and renamed Dalrymple School. St Joseph's, which had been under severe strain for many years, even though improved in 1941, was to be this year moved lock, stock and barrel to an annexe of the Academy, which had been built in the grounds of the High School in Lewis Street.

This will enable the Roman Catholic pupils to have fair facilities which they had never enjoyed before; playing fields were naturally included in the plans for the new schools, both secondary and primary. Stranraer High School had had a gymnasium from 1928 and now, with the Academy, shares a swimming pool. Park School is still without adequate playing fields.

Of the private schools of the former centuries, Ruddicot in London Road remained in being longest as a school for girls. It was described as a seminary. For a time there was a preparatory private school in the Ritz Restaurant premises in Dalrymple Street, latterly occupied as a Youth Club, and now a private club. There was also a private kindergarten in Lewis Street which ceased in the thirties. The Youth Club has been accommodated for the last two years in the former High School building which in 1967 was converted for the purpose.

Following the 1918 Act, Mr William McClelland, a native of Wigtown, was appointed Education Executive Officer. He was succeeded in 1921 by Lt.-Colonel J. Johnstone, O.B.E., by H. Stewart Mackintosh in 1931 and by Hugh K. C. Mair in 1937 who became the first Director of Education in 1945.

... Safely defending of all ships, barks and other vesseles

LOCHRYAN WAS USED FAIRLY EXTENSIVELY by ships of all types and it was the port for the paddle steamers *Maid of Galloway* and *Lochryan* regularly plying between Glasgow and Belfast. These were, in 1843, under the command of Captain John D. Haswell, and when he retired he was succeeded by Captain Douglas. The *Albion* was also for a time on the route but was transferred to the short sea crossing and other ships on the Stranraer-Ayr-Campbeltown service in the middle of last century were *Mary Queen of Scots, The Oswald, Robert Burns, Lady Kelburne, Scotia, Briton, Caledonian* and *Ayrshire Lass.*

The steam packet ferried the mails to Portpatrick and Ayr. In 1850, Captain Haswell of the *Albion,* on a passage to Belfast from Stranraer, fell in with the *Hercules of St John,* laden with coal, and dismasted. "Her captain and crew were in a pitiable state," he reported. The distressed vessel was towed to Belfast. Captain John Donaldson Haswell was later appointed Harbourmaster.

A pleasure steamer, *Lochryan,* was permitted to use the pier free of charge but if on duty as a cargo vessel, the cost was 15s 8d a trip into harbour. The local shareholders were considering another ship in 1835. Stranraer was the headquarters for the revenue cutters, in 1848.

There was considerable excitement in 1852 when several smacks and small ships brought stones and earth for the new battery at the Clayhole. An area reclaimed at Portrodie was granted to the burgh by the Admiralty in 1857. Other reclamation work took place this century at the West End at what was to become Agnew Park.

Yachting was a popular pastime. All the local lairds and landowners held two- and three-day regattas in the latter years of last century and older residents were wont to talk nostalgically of the fine sights they had seen. In more modern times there were smaller yachts, many of these built in the town by amateurs, which also gave and do give considerable pleasure in Lochryan.

The steamer *Pirate,* later sunk in a collision with the *Princess Maud,* plied between Stranraer and Campbeltown in 1906 and the *Neptune* and *Juno* landed excursionists in the summer months.

Eight torpedo boats anchored in the loch in 1907 and in 1908 a destroyer flotilla visited Lochryan, and, as there were also berthed 42 fishing boats, the loch presented an animated picture. A picture of another kind was observed two years later when the harbour was frozen over!

Around this time there was a proposal to run train-carrying boats from Stranraer but the idea never materialised.

War-time developments transformed the loch. A shipyard was constructed at Innermessan in 1918 planned for the building of concrete vessels, and at Cairnryan in 1940 a large military port was constructed. It was closed in 1959. The battleship *Ramillies* was broken up there in 1948.

In addition to normal craft, Lochryan was the base for seaplanes from 1926 and during the war years. These huge craft were rendered obsolete and withdrawn in 1957. One of the R.A.F. mooring craft, *Foam,* was blown up in 1947 and sank by the stern, incidentally damaging the West Pier.

Salmon fishing on a commercial basis has been carried on for many years from the Kirkcolm side and there is still a fishing boat in Cairnryan but very little commercial fishing has taken place in Lochryan this century. Sea anglers, however, continue to enjoy much sport in the loch.

In 1840, the Council made arrangements to light the quay and to place a buoy on the Scar.

Stranraer's claim to the whole loch led them, in 1840, into litigation with General Sir Alexander Wallace who complained of the Burgh Tacksman uplifting anchorage dues at Cairnryan. The committee perused the copy of the Town's Charter and requested a copy of General Wallace's Charter, which, after inspection, they considered was not so specific as their own. So they asked the General what rights he thought had been infringed. The General's Agent denied that from time immemorial the Council had uplifted dues at Cairnryan but having taken counsels' opinion the Magistrates confirmed their rights. They held the General liable for interference.

Objections were taken in 1893 to John Alexander Wallace of Lochryan extending his right to oyster fishing to the Scar and foreshores. The council claimed free access on behalf of the inhabitants to the foreshore and Mr Wallace withdrew his claim.

The Council was not the only body to insist on immemorial rights, for in 1907 Rev. Dr. Charlton, parish minister of Stranraer, claimed £3 out of every £100 worth of herring landed. The Campbeltown fishermen who were getting the lion's share of what were termed enormous hauls of herring naturally enough resisted.

...Convenient for subjects

GROWTH OF TRADE AND TRAFFIC led to considerable improvements through the years in the two main arteries to Stranraer, from Ayrshire in the north, and Dumfriesshire in the east. The main Dumfries-Portpatrick Road had always run through the town. Around 1760 a military road between Dumfries and Portpatrick was formed through the representations of Lord Hillsborough who had been stormbound in Galloway and "could not proceed owing to the badness of the existing road" and had to remain in his carriage all night. Later, in 1800, the line of the road was changed in many places and the surface improved. The new road was finally opened in September, 1807, and tolls established for its maintenance.

So far as the immediate environs were concerned there was little difficulty in widening it to cope with the load it was called upon to carry following the invention of the internal combustion engine.

Similarly the road to the north presented no obstacle that could not be overcome although on many occasions the Cairnryan Road, as it is now termed, was washed away by high tides. Stranraer took an active part in having it widened farther north of Cairnryan and in this respect was aided by the necessities of war.

Mail coaches from Dumfries to Portpatrick had their route through Stranraer in 1805 and from Portpatrick to Glasgow and by 1820 there was a regular service; in 1835 there was what was termed the Machars coach running daily from Stranraer. Several small local bus concerns were amalgamated into one which radiated from the town but which, with changing fashions, is not now so lucrative as it once was.

Though admirably placed, geographically, for an air service there has been little activity in this mode of travel. There was an aerodrome established at Cults, outside the town, in 1956, but it lasted only a few years. Aeroplanes had landed at Cults as early as 1913 and ever since there were efforts by the council to get operators interested. Sir Alan Cobham visited Stranraer in 1929 and made a survey and the area was again examined in 1935.

...Ane sure port

THOUGH STRANRAER RECEIVED ITS CHARTER for "the burgh and harbourie of Stranraer" there was no harbour as such in existence. Ships merely anchored in the Roadsteads or came as close inshore as possible and the goods were unloaded into small skiffs and boats.

The burgh was given the extensive rights of harbourage by the Charter within all the creeks and landing places of Lochryan. The council was claiming in 1692 that they had "a sufficient harbour of their own, if they had any trade." They had been permitted by the terms of the Charter to impose customs and duties on all who "shall happen to come within the bounds of the Loch with their vessells and goods to come to the Burgh and there disloaden."

The latter part of the sentence was to lead to a considerable dispute with those using the safe harbour of Lochryan, particularly with the railway companies two hundred years later.

There were jetties of a sort at Cladyhouse and at Clayhole. There are indications that the Clayhole Bay was a favourite place in 1720 but in 1731 the council issued an injunction on the inhabitants "forbidding them to buy or handle goods which have come from vessels unloading within Lochryan but away from the town, such as at Cladichhouse". And in 1793 the council were appointing overseers as measurers for vessels carrying coals into the harbour. In 1799 they were tightening up on the collection of customs and anchorage fees because of the state of the town's finances. All foreign vessels unloading at the port had to pay 2d per ton as well as anchorage. The council thought of placing buoys in the loch but decided against it.

It was becoming increasingly obvious that a proper pier was necessary and in 1802 the Magistrates and Councillors called a meeting of the inhabitants to decide the best method of erecting a harbour. Estimates for the quay were taken. The Exchequer agreed to contribute £2000 in 1817 on condition that the Magistrates assigned the harbour dues for payment of the legal interest. A similar sum was borrowed from the Paisley Banking Company and the Convention granted £500. The council had no funds but hoped for dues from all vessels entering Lochryan. The work was completed in 1820 and the cost was £3800.

Shipmasters and owners were not anxious to pay the dues and repayment of the loan to the Exchequer became a matter of concern — to the Exchequer. The Magistrates were shocked at the result of the legal action raised against the traders and shippers. The rates were found to be invalid, the decision was that "the Burgh had enjoyed no possession whatever of the dues now claimed." In fact the defenders were granted the expenses of the action. The council considered shutting off all access to the harbour to prevent unloading. Another snag was the Court of Session action raised by the builder who claimed payment for extra work; the burgh settled out of court with an offer of £450, which, if not accepted "would lead to a sequestration owing to the state of the burgh funds." Five of the councillors guaranteed repayment and were given a bond over the lands of Greenfield, the shop below the town court room and property lying on the shore immediately east of the burn and north of the public street, at Portrodie. The council had later to sell Greenfield, the Markslavie of the Charter, to liquidate the debt; it was bought by Mr Gifford for £460. In 1830 the council carried out their threat and ordered a chain to be fixed across the end of the quay so that those who refused to pay were denied the benefit of the harbour.

The custom of the harbour was still let by public roup but the council did not guarantee that dues would be paid; It was up to the successful tenderer to gather in the money. Andrew Shillan took a chance at £71. In 1866, John Kerr, innkeeper, Fisher Street, presented a petition to the council, purporting to be signed by many ratepayers complaining about the harbour master. The council considered all the names had been written in one hand and dismissed the petition. They bore no grudge, for a few years later John Kerr was given the right to the dues.

The Commissioners became awkward in 1831, giving the council eight days in which to pay the balance of the £2000 loan. The burgh had no funds.

Troubles multiplied. Despite repairs in 1831 Mr McDouall reported that the harbour would not stand winter storms. He proposed driving about 120 piles along the 180 feet of the back of the head of the pier, six to nine feet into the foundations. The Earl of Stair was asked to provide the piles gratis.

In their official return under the Burgh Reform Act, the council showed a debt of £2128 18s 9d in 1833, mainly attributable to the building and maintenance of the quay. Yet the council agreed that the harbour was now a source of revenue!

The Exchequer Loans Commission were pressing hard for a return of their money. The Magistrates enlisted the aid of Members of Parliament to ask for a moratorium.

The committee of the council responsible for the harbour had other worries. They laid down two anchors and chains which were purchased for warping vessels, also a "dead man" within the basin to hold vessels in an easterly gale and they carried out further repairs in 1836. They agreed to ask for an Act of Parliament so that they might exact dues and the Exchequer Commissioners, no doubt by this time having given up all hope of a return of their money, agreed not to interfere so long as the revenue was applied for harbour purposes; the Magistrates asked the Exchequer to depart from their claim which amounted to £2373 7s 7d. A compromise was reached but it was not until 1929 that the Government departed from its claim and permitted a harbour debt, then standing at £5000, to be wiped off.

In 1843, however, shippers were beaching their boats at Clayhole in order to avoid harbour dues. Work on the quay continued, deepening it and lengthening it. Farmers were up in arms at the charges being made and suggested a harbour at Soleburn or Innermessan to avoid the iniquitous taxes and customs payable.

In 1909, the Kirkcolm farmers used a small jetty at Marian Port, Wig Bay, opposite Clendrie, but when they proposed to build a pier there, the Council immediately took umbrage and called to mind the terms of the Charter. The harbour at that time, 1909, was £14,000 in debt and the Council did not relish any opposition.

Under the new Burghs Harbours (Scotland) Act, 1853, the council fixed rates to be levied at the harbour. Objections by General Wallace and others were repelled. It was felt the objections were not so much to the rates as to the Council's right to levy them. They dispensed with the letting of the customs as formerly and exposed the dues to public set for one year, receiving £1065 from William Galbraith. Petty customs ceased in 1912.

Still, the trade improved and in 1855 an extension costing £11,500, or a new harbour at a cost of £28,000, was under consideration. It must be borne in mind the council still had no money for such grandiose schemes, relying on faith.

Into the scene came the Railway Company in 1861 when the whole country was suffering from railway mania. They advanced a loan of £20,000 for the erection of a second pier.

The agreement gave the Railway Company berthage priority at the East Pier which the council would build, own and maintain. The Company was to pay £1000 annually in lieu of harbour dues, petty customs, etc., and the money was to be spent on pier repairs and interest repayments. The dues from the old pier by this time had reached between £800 and £900 yearly.

The new pier was badly built, it consisted of a long, wooden trellis framework from the shore, widened into a stone-built termination for the berths. The council, despite their earlier experiences, borrowed a further £2600 to complete the work. Between 1865-70 the council found the railway payment was not enough; it was all swallowed up in repairs and in addition all the dues had to go to meet bills for maintenance. There was a big threat, too, facing the council for with the unsatisfactory condition of the piers there was a strong possibility of the Portpatrick-Donaghadee route being reopened; fortunately for Stranraer, nature intervened and in 1869 a storm almost completely wrecked the harbour at Portpatrick and tore down the lighthouse.

In 1874 an engineer reported to the council that the pier had so deteriorated it was unsafe and the wooden portion was too weak for trains. The repair bill was estimated at £1200. Some of the councillors wished to erect a new pier even though little or nothing had been paid back on the capital of the loans. Dredging became expensive, £600 was spent in 1874. The railway company kept pressing for repairs to the East Pier.

Damage was even being done by horses and carts passing over it and in 1876 the council stopped such traffic. It was, however, the stone-built section which partially collapsed.

Probably with their patience exhausted, the railway company, after offering to buy the pier, petitioned Parliament for powers to take it over and maintain it. They promised to reconstruct it and to relieve Stranraer of the original debt and also to pay £500 yearly in compensation for harbour dues, plus a percentage over a certain amount.

This offer, which seemed on the face of it to be most generous, having regard to the continued debt hanging over the council's head, led to fierce controversy. Many local people had to declare an interest; they had extensive holdings in the railway company. Stranraer Town Council decided to fight, but they lost and the Act was passed in 1877.

The defeat of the council might well have been a blessing in disguise, or as later events have shown, might have cost the burgh a considerable fortune through the establishment of the short sea route.

Of course, the council had still the older problem, the West Pier. In 1878 a sum of £8000 was borrowed for repairs; this was on the strength of the £500 annually to be received from the railway company.

Repairs and patching continued throughout the next ten years. Then came a bombshell from the railway company in 1892 when they asked the council to renounce all rights at the East Pier as they "will be forced to spend much money on dredging and alterations, and to provide a new covered station, platform and overhead platform-connecting bridge." The request was accompanied by a thinly-veiled threat that, if not granted, the company "would consider building a pier at Cairnryan for cross-channel shipping." The council had no choice. A public meeting was presented with the hard facts. Parliamentary approval was obtained.

As solace the railway company intimated they would help the council with their repayment of their 1878 loan of £8000 because of the cessation of the yearly £500 from them.

Work was started in 1892 on the pier improvements which were estimated to cost £32,000 exclusive of buildings and platform and in 1895 the *Princess Victoria* was berthed. By 1898 nearly 5000 tons of mud and sand were removed but the work was not nearly finished. Another 6000 tons was removed in 1901. A map of 1782 had shown that there was a wide bank of sand between the two piers. By 1898 the work on the pier was finished in time for the double run.

Both piers were extended and widened in the early years of the present century and dredging work continued until the decreasing traffic in later years led to a withdrawal of the subsidy for the work.

In 1938 the railway pier was considerably extended to accommodate a new steamer and in the years after the end of the Second World War many vast improvements were made to accommodate the increasing traffic.

A terminal was constructed in 1965 for the convenience of the half-million passengers who were being conveyed to and from Ulster and a large car park was laid out in what was formerly a pond for the hundred thousand vehicles which were carried.

... With free isch and entrie of ships

WHILE THERE WAS a fairly regular service on what has become known as the short sea route since 1642, it was not really until 230 years later that Stranraer became firmly established as the Scottish terminal.

Her position was challenged for many years by Portpatrick and latterly was threatened by Cairnryan, Girvan, Ayr and Troon. The basing of the service at Stranraer has meant incalculable good to the town and district. In 1692 the Magistrates were bemoaning to the Convention that "we have no ships, barks, or ferries, nor are we owners or pairtners in any."

There had been, since the middle of the seventeenth century at least, a service between Donaghadee and Portpatrick, run by a private company, but Portpatrick proved too stormy and too costly to maintain. An alternative was sought and in 1770 naval captains and engineers expressed the view that Stranraer was the more suitable. Captain Evans, R.N., in 1864, reiterated that opinion.

In 1836, however, a new short sea route was suggested by Captain Beechy, who favoured Cairnryan to Larne. Ten years later the same ports were approved by Glasgow Belfast Union Railway. Portpatrick was still served with the Royal Navy steamers, *Arrow* and *Dasher*. They were on the service from 1825 to 1837.

There followed the *Albion* (1844-60), *Scotia* (1845-63), *Caledonia* (1850), a second *Albion* (1860-65) and two ships named *Briton* (1860-62 and 1862-63). The second of these made the first official trip from Stranraer pier in 1862. Around 1860 there were a few sailings between Stranraer and Belfast by the Glasgow and Stranraer S.P. Company's *Briton* and in 1861 a private company was formed to run a Stranraer-Larne service to connect the Scottish railway and the newly-opened Carrickfergus and Larne Railway. They purchased the second *Briton*, built in 1862, but sold her the following year. Service reverted to the Glasgow and Stranraer S.P. Company until 1866 when Caledonian Railway, backed by L.N.W.R., put on *Fannie* and *Alice*, two former American blockade runners. They were withdrawn through lack of support three years later.

Despite efforts in 1870 to revive the traffic, it was not until 1st June, 1872, that the railway companies found third time lucky.

On that date, the Stranraer-Larne Steam-boat Company put on the iron paddle steamer *Princess Louise* (1872-90), a vessel of 497 tons. She was the grandmother of the Princess line and she introduced sailings which have been regular to the present day.

There was considerable excitement when the *Princess Louise* made her appearance, men and boys swarmed all over her decks. By the time of the out-

35

break of the First World War, six Princesses had been built and the service by then was operating a regular mail and passenger sailing.

Prospects appeared so rosy that in 1875 the three railway companies concerned put on a second ship, the *Princess Beatrice* (1875-1904), for which a loan of £6500 was obtained from the Carrickfergus and Belfast Railway Company. The *Beatrice* was a much finer paddle steamer and she, too, received a warm welcome at the pier when she made her first appearance the following year. The captain and his wife entertained a large company on board.

The company made a proud boast in 1879 that the profit from the short sea route was £2388 15s 10d. Not great by present-day standards, but sufficient for the company to embark on another ship, the first *Princess Victoria* (1890-1910). She was launched in January, 1890, and a new mid-day service was put into operation.

Two years later, the *Princess May* (1892-1914) was launched at Dumbarton. She was the last paddle steamer made for the Irish Sea. The condition of the pier was not to the liking of the railway company and in June of 1892 there was a strong rumour in the district that it was proposed to change the terminal to Cairnryan. This led to a special meeting of the town council which considered the proposal "unreasonable." At any rate, land was inspected; the excuse being that the pier would not carry the ever-increasing traffic. The double service was continued in July and it proved highly successful and in August the council conferred with the interested railway companies regarding the pier.

In 1890, the old company had been transformed into the Larne and Stranraer Joint Steamer Committee and had by then established a fine business as conveyers of cattle and sheep. Rather than build a new pier at Cairnryan, the railway company agreed to strengthen the Stranraer terminal but it was not until 1896 that Stranraer and Larne were finally settled as the ports. A claim was entered for Lochryan as the port for the Canadian mail service.

A new mail contract in 1902 led to the building of the first turbine steamer *Princess Maud* (1904-1932). The journey was speeded up considerably and the new ship was able to withstand the buffetings of the storms more effectively. The speed of the ships coming into harbour, however, was said to be the reason "for injury to Council property at Agnew Crescent Battery."

At the end of the 1911 season there had been created new records and this encouraged the building of the second *Princess Victoria* (1912-34). Like her predecessor her draught was shallow to suit the Stranraer terminal. There was no new ship until 1931 when the *Princess Margaret* took over and she ran until 1961 continuously and made the trip her very own. There were many sad hearts when she was sold to the Shun Tak Company of Hong-Kong. She had been named after the first Princess to be born in Scotland in 400 years and she had sailed as a commando ship during the dark days of war.

Her sister ship was the second *Princess Maud* (1934-39). The *Maud* did not resume the route after the war; she had been the last powered ship out of Dunkirk and played her part in the D-Day landings. She was sold to become *Venus of Famagusta* sailing from Cyprus.

The third *Princess Victoria* was the first ship to do away with the need for crane loading and the first to be specially constructed as a sea-going car ferry. A floating garage, she had space for 88 cars. One of the greatest single benefits was the introduction in 1939 of an adjustable ramp in order to use end-loading ships for wheeled traffic at all states of the tide.

Alas! She made little peace-time use of her facilities. Her special features were recognised when the Second World War engulfed Europe and she was commissioned as a minelayer. She was lost on war service when blown up by an enemy mine off the mouth of the Humber in 1940 with the loss of three officers and 31 ratings.

The harbour facilities at Stranraer were also brought in to play a part in the war effort. During the war years more than six million passengers, mainly military, travelled between the ports and more than 1000 special trains were run from Stranraer. The ramps were invaluable in transporting American troops, after their Ulster training, with their vehicles and assorted equipment.

After the war the service got back into full swing under the British Transport Commission and later the Caledonian Steam Packet Company (Irish Services) Ltd.

But even more tragic was the loss of the fourth *Princess Victoria* (1947-53). On 31st January, 1953, she foundered in the North Channel with the loss of 133 lives. No officers, women or children were saved. The bravery of radio officer David Broadfoot was extolled by the posthumous award of the George Medal while her captain, Mr James Ferguson, also worthily upheld the traditions of the sea.

Other ships on the route, mainly as stop-gaps, were *Hampton Ferry* (1953-61), *Shepperton Ferry* and *Twickenham Ferry*.

The coming of the *Caledonian Princess* in 1961 ushered in a new era. She was an ultra-modern vessel with room for 1400 passengers and more than 100 cars and she quickly made her own niche in the history of the service by being the first vessel to make the return journey regularly twice daily.

She was assisted for a time by the *Slieve Donard* in 1964, by the *Lohengrin*, a German charter in 1965, and by a Swedish vessel, *Stena Nordica*, in 1966-67.

Intimation of a sister ship, the *Antrim Princess*, was made in 1965 and it was expected she would take up the run later in the present year, 1967. She is the first railway vessel to be equipped with bow and stern doors to permit straight-through driving, experience having been gained with the *Stena Nordica*.

... *May be very convenient*

A LINK-UP BETWEEN STRANRAER and Ulster by tunnel is a dream which has been recurring since at least 1893 when an engineer considered it a feasible proposition. Three years later the locus had been shifted to Portpatrick but the scheme was abandoned when the promoters found out about the Beaumont Dyke, a ravine in the sea bed about 600 feet deep, running from opposite Corsewall Point to the Mull of Galloway. The scene shifted from Donaghadee to Whitehead, but again a part of the dyke had to be traversed. The cost was then estimated in the region of £10,000.

From Northern Ireland in 1906 came a proposal to have a submarine tubular bridge, floating at a fixed depth, and some 26 miles long. There was, however, no guard against the moorings or a ship sinking on top of it. Liverpool was next suggested, but in 1907 the talk was again quite cheerfully of a tunnel from Lochryan.

The scheme was mooted again in 1929 and in the late 'thirties when it was considered by Stranraer Town Council, though not seriously. Some impetus was given to it by a suggestion that it would save time for the rugby players who travelled to Larne and Stranraer in alternate years.

In 1966 there was an idea of linking it up with the Solway Barrage Scheme under which, according to the promoter, the whole of the South-West would have a far warmer climate. The question was raised again in Parliament this summer but the Government considered the time was not ripe for such a scheme.

... Ane Tolbooth

HIS MAJESTY'S SCRIBE who indited the Charter did not spare his quill in 1617. He made a lengthy list of what Stranraer's rights and privileges were to be, and mentioned "Ane Tolbooth".

Stranraer's first tolbooth stood in the centre of George Street at the old Mercate Cross. In it, in 1617, were imprisoned malefactors, miscreants, felons and those who had upset the Bailies. Jailers were the burgh officers.

Burgh Courts were set up by the Charter to be held thrice a week, on Monday, Wednesday and Friday. Serious offences were tried by the Hereditary Sheriff and in 1699 there is the only recorded instance of a sentence by execution. John McCracken was indicted for sheep stealing and the assize included three men from Stranraer, James McMaster, Robert Gray and Thomas Wallace. The accused was found guilty and the sheriff adjudged him "to be taken to the ordinar place of execution at Stranrawer and to be hanged upon a gibbet until he be dead."

It is thought that Gallowhill, which then belonged to the burgh, was "the ordinar place of execution".

Shortly after the Jacobite Rebellion an Act of Parliament was passed which abolished heritable jurisdiction and this probably transferred legal business to the local Burgh Court and J.P. Courts which were held in the Tolbooth.

The Tolbooth served as a council house as well as a jail and a centre for the market, and outside it were the town's weights and measures, and the stocks and gorgettes. There was no gibbet. The Tolbooth was a two-storey building with vaults beneath and in 1772 a prisoner begged the favour of being removed to the upper floor where he might have the benefit of a fire. In 1770, with no thought of preserving ancient monuments for posterity, the Civic Fathers considered the "ruinous building" should be swept away because of its condition and because " it impeded passage upon the maine street".

There was a rival claim on the civic purse, however, from the church, but the magistrates opted that things of the flesh were more pressing and they proceeded to erect a new Tolbooth, or Town House. The building was completed in 1776 and passed into use the following year; the magistrates later decided to build a new Market House.

By so doing they certainly cleared the street but created a headache for their successors in office, of such dimensions that the New Town House became the subject of considerable dissension not to be settled until a public inquiry had been held 186 years later. It was the cause celebre for a time and split the council on several occasions.

The Town House was erected "on a piece of ground at the side of the main street, at the head of the Middle Vennel, opposite the south-west corner of William McKelvie's house". The Middle Vennel was Queen Street and the Golden Cross was built on the site of McKelvie's house. What the councillors took over in 1777 and referred to as the Tolbooth, Courthouse, Tron or weighing place, had on its western march Mrs McKitterick's house; there was to be left a passage way between them "for all time coming". The original plan for the height of the steeple was altered as the Council had decided not to expend money on a church and four or five feet was added to the spire. In 1802 a new Market House was built behind the Town House at a cost of £146. John Hornsby, bricklayer, was the builder.

Laurence Crawford, clock and watchmaker, was appointed to keep the town clock, as formerly, for the sum of £1 10s yearly.

In the Market House all goods coming into the town were sold, and various charges were laid down on every item as a petty custom, swine 2d, sheep, goats and calves 1d, and lambs ½d. Twopence was to be paid on every stone of cheese, butter or tallow, cartload of salmon or other fish, except herring. Every boll of meal, barley or flour and every stone of wool or flax had a tax of one penny. A charge of sixpence per day was made for the use of the whole hall for the sale of goods. Curiously enough, nothing was charged for poultry or eggs. The practice of slaying animals ceased in the Market House in 1837 as it was considered a nuisance, though the previous year the shop below the Court Room was let to Mr John Todd, flesher, for £10 per annum.

In the succeeding years the two shops under the Court House were mainly occupied by fleshers including James Rodger and Andrew McHarg while the two shops or stalls in Church Street were occupied by James McMicking and Thomas Goodfellow. Mr James Byers was the tenant of the large store.

By 1790 it was found by the council "to their regret that the new prison is insufficient, as it has lately been broken into". It was ordered to be repaired. There was some trouble over the jailing of four seamen who had deserted from their ship, a brigantine, *Jean of Ayr*, which had sheltered in Lochryan while on a voyage from Liverpool to Quebec. Some of the townspeople who had had the temerity to shelter the deserters were most wroth when the four seamen were taken into custody.

James McNish, one of the burgh officers, was himself jailed for allowing a prisoner to escape from the low cell and this led in 1810 to new prison regulations. "The prison is not to be opened before 9 a.m. nor after 4 p.m. The cells only to be opened in the presence of two officers, one to secure the door, and the other to gradually and cautiously enter, both to take such precautions that it will be impossible for any prisoner to escape. Nothing to be allowed into the prison which would be injurious to the sobriety of the prisoners or aid their escape. A strict examination to be made night and morning to see that all is quiet and secure and that no operation has commenced or no instrument introduced to make any breach in the prison walls, doors or windows".

As a place of incarceration, the Town House had a short if not a merry life, but the hopes of the magistrates for a prison with walls 2½ feet thick were fulfilled as a result of the initiative of one, Bailie William Kerr, who in 1815 bought the Old Castle for a prison.

The council continued to use the Town House as a court room and for other municipal purposes. With the removal of the prisoners, advantage was taken of the space provided to utilise the old debtors' room by taking down the wall to give greater space to the court room. The stairway was also altered, in 1831, to make a small room for witnesses and to present a better situation for the bench. The public cellar was let in 1811 to Alexander Little for £3.

Paying for the jail was as big a problem. There were deficits in the burgh accounts in 1835 and in 1836 the council agreed to apprise the Lord Advocate, the Home Secretary, and the Sheriff Depute, of the burgh's heavy burden in alimenting prisoners after conviction with no revenue for this or any other purpose connected with the police or the jail. This was quite a serious state of affairs and in 1838 an attempt was made to milk the Harbour Account, but the Provost, who was acting treasurer of the Harbour Account, wisely stayed away from the meeting. The treasurer intimated he had had £2 0s 3d in the bank, but had paid 30s of that for aliment of the prisoners. The Provost refused to help out and by the end of the year the treasurer was broke and had no money to pay aliment of prisoners. In 1840 the building became known as the Town Hall.

Alterations did not wholly satisfy and there was a move in 1846 to erect a new Town House, but it came to naught.

In 1841 the council agreed to assess the Burgh for £190 as their share of the County Prison Board's expenses. There was a suggestion that the Board might consider building a new prison in Glenwell Park, but to this, despite the difficulties they had had with their jails, the council took umbrage. In 1845 they considered a better courthouse was needed in connection with the proposed new prison and when it was decided to deprive the Rhins and the Burgh of the new prison, which had by this time been agreed, the Magistrates protested to the General and Local Prisons Boards. The plans for the new prison permitted 15 cells within the bounds of Stranraer as had been suggested by the Inspector on his visit to Stranraer in December, 1840. A smaller jail was to be erected at Wigtown and Stranraer's share of the total expense was to be £24 4s 2½d. But even after the contract was signed there was a change of mind, this time by the Board who were said to have been "favourable to the local influence at Wigtown."

Stranraer's feelings were somewhat mollified by the payment of £100 from the County Prison Board which, no doubt, was sufficient salve for their pride when in 1856 the Sheriff intimated he would hold no more courts in Stranraer until a proper bench was provided.

The Commissioners of Supply wished the prison to incorporate the courthouse but Stranraer was having none of that. The Magistrates appealed to the towns-people to raise funds for a new courthouse on the existing site. Even when the prison was removed from their jurisdiction, more or less, they continued to use the Town House as a courthouse. The Town House was enlarged and the space under it was fitted up as a corn exchange.

The council agreed to improve conditions in the Courthouse and the Commissioners of Supply decided to contribute three-quarters of the expense if the total did not exceed £600. The council accepted, providing that their share would be no more than £400.

There was one drawback to the new edifice—its outward appearance; it joined the old building and had not the imposing effect desired, but, in the words of the council "it is hoped that in the course of time the public spirit in the place will step forward and remove the old dwarfish steeple and erect a suitable one in its place, and that the public will help to furnish the rooms with desks and benches."

During the next few years, until in 1874 the New Town Hall was occupied, the Town House was used for temperance meetings and by various other bodies, including the Athenæum Club, which had removed from premises in Castle Court. It was also used as a training ground for the Volunteers in 1887 by permission of the Sheriff. The council had still some pride in their former home for in 1886 the Coat of Arms was unveiled and a clock with a transparent face was obtained. In 1870 Dr Mackie left money for a new town bell, to be rung on Sundays when there was a service in the Established Church.

There were high hopes of a sale to the Post Office in 1892 but the premises were found to be unsuitable. It was put up for sale in 1896 but found no buyers. Alterations were made to it to permit of two shops and retiring rooms; the up-stairs premises were given over entirely to the Athenæum as a reading room and games room. In 1906 the practice of letting the stalls in the store room down-stairs ceased.

Its demolition was being proposed in 1961 and approved by Stranraer Town Council in order to permit a one-way traffic proposal. The council in 1962 reiterated their view, by a majority, that the Old Town Hall should go and they received a firm offer for its demolition.

However, there were many who felt it should be retained as the only building of architectural interest in the old town. The difference of opinion spread furth of Stranraer. Shortly after the council's view had been sent to the Secretary of State they received intimation that the building was classified as being of special architectural and historical value and he considered it should be retained. This decision was described as "incredible."

The Old Town Hall was one of the subjects of an appeal by the Town Council against the Planning Committee's proposals for the town, the council having in the interval changed its mind. The Reporter, who heard the appeal in 1963, refused to include the Old Town Hall in the list of buildings to be acquired and demolished. He stated it was one of the few public buildings left in Stranraer, indeed the only one of historical or architectural interest.

He made the point that the condition of it was far from perfect and stressed that the council had not fully considered what might be done about it.

The point was taken. Though it was estimated that it would cost between £6000 and £7000 to put it in order, the council, in April, 1967, carried out a scheme for utilising the building for something like its former purpose, a civic centre and a burgh courthouse, so the original Tolbooth remained.

...To imprissone

FACED WITH THE FAIT ACCOMPLI of the Bailie, William Kerr, who had purchased the Old Castle and a little house on the west side for £340 in 1815, the council approved and authorised him to borrow the money and asked him to proceed with his idea of asking the heritors of the county to join in the plan of using the Castle as a jail, they considered it would be useful to the county at large.

Five years later the council agreed to a resolution of the Commissioners of Supply regarding the use of the Castle as a jail. A Mr Kenneth Mathieson, architect, Glasgow, produced plans and specifications showing two cells for criminals, three rooms for debtors and a courtroom, all at a cost of £785. The Commissioners agreed to meet £600 and the expense of the courthouse was to be borne by the council which opened the subscription list with 20 guineas.

As a jail it was not a success. In fact, it was probably the first open prison in the country, though, as has been seen, the Tolbooth, its predecessor, had not been any more secure.

In 1826, Francis McKnight, one of the burgh officers, was dismissed for being drunk on duty, for taking drink to the prisoners, allowing people into the jail and for striking his fellow officer in front of the Buck's Head Inn.

His successor petitioned the council the following year for an increase in salary owing to the great number of prisoners in the jail and the trouble caused thereby in carrying firing and victuals up the long stair. The council was sympathetic and asked the Justices of the Peace for an increase from their funds. It was felt the town was not being adequately recompensed for the number of county prisoners.

However, the jailer rather blotted his copybook. He neglected to lock the doors on one occasion and the padlock of the main door had been burned off. As there were no other applicants, the Magistrates reluctantly continued the jailer and his assistant in office but advertised for successors and offered increased emoluments, eight guineas and six guineas, per annum.

Complaints multiplied. In 1828, for improper conduct, fighting and allowing unauthorised visitors of improper character, and taking spirits to the prisoners, the jailers were summoned before the two Bailies. They appeared and behaved in a most outrageous manner and charged one another with disgraceful practices and the Bailies had no option but to dismiss them. One of their successors, in 1830, was dismissed for being drunk and leaving the prison door open, but another jailer "of sober and honest habit and orderly conduct" was appointed.

And in the following year there was an attempted jail break in what was more modern style. Some person, or persons, it was reported to the Magistrates, had got on to the roof and had tried to liberate the prisoners. To guard against such happening again the Magistrates gave authority for the fitting-up of the large room below the prison as a temporary dwelling for the jailer.

The council must have been somewhat unfortunate in their selection of a jailer of sober and orderly habit, for prisoners continued to escape and in 1833 two new jailers were appointed owing to the intemperance and laxity of the former officers.

Escaping had become so common, however, that in the same year the council was served with a petition and complaint at the instance of the Lord Advocate, to the Lords of Justiciary, praying that their Lordships ordain the council forthwith to adopt such measures necessary to render the jail of Stranraer sufficient and secure. Six days were allowed in which to lodge answers. The council pleaded that the last two prisoners had not escaped by breaking out! They also intimated that the jailer had been dismissed.

However, the days of the council's travail were about over, for, in 1840, on the introduction of the Prison Act, the jail ceased to be a burgh responsibility. The council thereupon agreed to hand over to the Prison Board—on which they had two representatives—that part of the Castle which formed the jail, also books and other effects belonging to it, reserving the burgh's right to all other parts and retaining the title deeds. A motion that the room occupied by the jailer be handed over was defeated as was a suggestion that the "Black Hole" be given to the Board. However, later the council did agree to give the use of the rooms in the Castle, below the criminal cells, to the Board as well as the "Black Hole" and the Currying House adjacent. They emphasised this was only temporary. The Board were not happy about the offer but refused to accept an arbiter.

In 1843 it was quite common to find boys incarcerated with men and even in charge. The Inspector, in 1847, severely criticised the condition of the jail and reported he had found a boy in charge. On the other hand the authorities were boasting that there was not one boy under ten years in jail!

Prisoners were appealing for straw and oat straw for bedding and conditions were not improved when the tower of the Old Castle was brought into use as a police station in 1864, the prisoners who were accommodated two storeys up were reported to be emaciated. Though cells were made available elsewhere, in the New Town Hall from 1872, four of the cells in the Old Castle continued to be used, and were available until the present century but it ceased around 1907 for jail purposes. Workmen in 1904 found a note signed by David Guthrie asking for the release of two of the prisoners.

In 1853 the Castle belfry and bell were restored and the bell authorised to be rung at the same time as the town bell. The practice of the ringing of the Castle bell stopped and when it was sounded in 1918 to mark the Armistice it was the first time it had been heard for 50 years.

In 1801, Alexander Irving, William Gifford, Archibald Paterson, John McMaster and Thomas Sloan, with their wives and families and their servants, were all warned to flit from their respective houses and shops which were part of the Castle property; this at the instance of Alexander McMeikan, of North Cairn, who was sub-tacksman of the subjects. The old steading outside was let as a stable in 1874.

Apartments in the Castle were let by the council as late as 1907. The ground floor was leased until a few years ago to a nearby shopkeeper. In an upstairs room Stranraer Lodge of Freemasons had their meeting place, the Mechanics Institute met there, as did the Athenæum, their successors, and the Galloway Shepherds' Society.

With the ravages of time there has been damage to the superstructure and in 1952 the council decided the need to repair the bell tower had become urgent but they were advised they had no funds for the purpose; the money could only come from the Common Good account, which appeared appropriate.

In 1956 the estimate for repair to the tower was £400 and an approach was made to the Historic Buildings Committee who were sympathetic but had no money and advised the council to approach the Pilgrim Trust. The Trust could only give sympathy, not cash. When, in 1962, the council, again anxious about the Castle, made a request to the Ministry of Works, whilst the Ministry considered the Old Castle "could be an attraction for tourists" they would not give a grant for its repair or its maintenance.

Not everyone is enamoured of money being spent on the Castle, it has been described as a "monument to murder" with what justification it is difficult to ascertain. Certain buildings attached to it and adjoining were removed this year, in furtherance of a road improvement, but the Castle is still not seen in splendid isolation and there are no plans as yet for any restoration work.

In the last 50 years or so the Castle has been unoccupied. It was put to the more peaceful use of band practice, pipes and brass, and in 1965 part of it was let to the Royal Naval Auxiliary Service.

A reformatory was erected in Dalrymple Street in 1852 and had accommodation for 100 boys. It suffered from a disastrous fire in 1878 but was rebuilt two years later and in 1927 was closed. Its governor for 20 years was S. J. Ferguson, who died in 1929, and one of whose sons was Captain James Ferguson of the Princess Victoria.

The cost of keeping a boy in the Reformatory in 1902 was 2s per week.

The Reformatory site was subsequently given over to a picture house and a restaurant, while the houses in connection with it became private dwellings.

...Erections and creations

EVEN THOUGH THE COUNCIL had agreed in 1866 to have the court house extended their plans were not regarded in a very high light by the Commissioners of Supply urged on by the Law Officers.

The discomfort and want of accommodation of the existing court house had long been felt and had often been complained of by the Sheriffs and, moreover, had been condemned by Mr Mathieson, a Government surveyor.

The amount of civil business before the court was very much greater in the Rhins than in the Machars and the Machars already had a fine new Sheriff Court. There was no proper accommodation for the Rhins litigants.

In the Rhins also, Provost Guthrie ruefully admitted there was more crime and the Crown and the County were put to considerable expense carrying prisoners, witnesses, etc, to Wigtown in jury trials, simply because there was no accommodation provided by the Civic Fathers in Stranraer.

It was not proposed to build such a large court house as had been erected in Wigtown which cost £10,000. The one in the Rhins was to cost a mere £5000 or perhaps £6000 and the assessment for it, extended over a number of years, would not be, so the promise went, more than a halfpenny on the rates. This, it was claimed, would not be felt by anyone.

Although at a great distance from it, the Rhins proprietors had had to pay for the Wigtown court house and got little benefit from it. The proprietors were in favour of the new court house at Stranraer, but not the ratepayers of the town who were bluntly told by the Council that it was none of their business!

All the principal proprietors signed the requisition to the Secretary of State for the court house, as well as Lord Garlies, who represented the largest estate in the lower district.

Stranraer was not wholly enamoured of the proposal. For one thing, it was pointed out that the burgh would have only a third say in the running of the court house. Their main objection was that they would have a town house owned by the burgh and a court house owned by the county. This is what actually happened and it led to the very discord the opponents of the scheme foresaw. However, the state of Stranraer's exchequer and the combined might of Crown, County and Constabulary forced their hand. Accordingly, when the existing court house was condemned, the Magistrates somewhat reluctantly agreed to combine with the County.

In 1870 the Home Secretary at length gave his official sanction definitely to the proposal. The site was to be on the west side of Lewis Street and it was said "the building will give employment to a large number of masons, joiners and other tradesmen and labourers during the progress of its erection, and when completed will form an imposing architectural ornament to our town as well as afford a most needful accommodation to the Sheriff, the bench of the County Magistrates, the legal profession and the public generally." There was no mention of Stranraer Burgh Court.

There was a last ditch stand in 1871 when Provost Ingram, who was not so in favour of the proposal as had been his predecessor, requested the Prison Board and Police Committee to agree to a diminution of the ground on which the Burgh of Stranraer had undertaken to provide a new court house on condition that the present court house building be made over entirely to the Burgh. This was strongly objected to and the Commissioners eventually resolved to abide by the bargain made. The plans were sent for approval to the Secretary of State.

The ratepayers were still objecting but as they had not been asked to donate to the hall their objections were over-ruled. Work was started; it was preceded by the gift of a bell which in the next two years was lost so that the Trustees set aside a sum of £150 for a new one. It was not rung until 1878.

The new town hall was nearly complete with a Sheriff court house, offices, police office and cells, town hall and custodian's house in 1872.

And the official description was "a stately edifice, a great architectural monument to the burgh. It is a mixed style of architecture, the front being of a composite character with spirelets and crockets, while the rear elevations of the town hall and court house are in the Scottish baronial style. The buildings are situated on the west side of Lewis Street with the ground floor several feet above the level of the roadway. Internal arrangements are as excellent and commodious as its external appearance is handsome."

There followed a lay-out plan. From a passage, access was gained to the police office, prisoners' cells and constable's house and keeper's house. The new town hall was opened in 1874 by Sheriff Rhind.

As had been feared by the objectors, the new town hall was never satisfactory. It served as a prison only until 1904 for the jail was about as secure as had been its predecessors.

The cells were taken over as offices. In the ensuing years it was found that the divided responsibility and the claims of contending users made it almost impracticable.

As the main provider of the sinews of war, the Crown had first say, the County Council had second, and the Town Council had practically none. They had a town hall but did not own the steps from the front door to the entrance of the hall. The hall itself, commodious enough, was used for functions and various entertainments and the court house was used as a meeting place for the Town Council, for the burgh court and for the licensing court, both County and Town. If there was a clash of dates, as happened so often, then the Magistrates had to be accommodated in the town hall, and if there had been a let of the hall to some private individual or organisation, then the council was packed into a small room.

For many years the Dean of Guild Court was held in the jury room to which, strictly speaking, the Council had no right of use. Nor had they, of course, any jurisdiction over the lower rooms which by 1950 had been cleared of County Council clerk's offices but not until the early 'sixties had the Procurator Fiscal really a place to call his own.

Wigtownshire did not have its first full time fiscal until 1962 and he was preceded by a few years by the first full time Sheriff Clerk.

For many years the letting of the town hall was in the hands of the Town Council, by arrangement, but this duty was taken over by the County Treasurer in 1965. The untenable position of the Council was made clear in 1962 when they were informed there was no necessity for the court house committee to consult them in the matter of redecoration.

There were, in 1922, and again in 1962, plans for enlarging the hall, but these were not pursued.

Improvements to the acoustics were demanded by the Sheriff in the court house, while the residents nearby demanded that the noise created by the bands of the time using the town hall be muted! The committee would not permit bingo. So far as Stranraer Town Council was concerned the final blow to the esteem of the Council came in 1965 when they were informed they had no say in the income of the hall although they were responsible for expenditure on it.

This situation led the Town Council to consider a new town hall, or civic centre as it was talked about, and to enlarge their own council offices at Dunbae House which they had taken over in 1947. Also to consider re-furbishing and restoring their former Town House in 1967.

...For Civil Government

WHEN IT CAME INTO BEING in 1889, Wigtown County Council held its meetings alternately in the New Town Hall, in the Courthouse when convenient and not otherwise occupied by legal luminaries, and at Douglas House, Newton Stewart.

Offices for officials were utilised in the New Town Hall. The question of more satisfactory accommodation was raised in 1930 as local government work increased and again in 1938 when the medical officer and sanitary inspector condemned the premises in Queen Street which were being used by the welfare services. In 1939 the County Council purchased offices in Lewis Street opposite the New Town Hall for the sanitary inspector and the county architect whose department had been crushed into the Education Offices in Market Street which also housed the Library.

In 1953, a private house, Ashwood, was purchased in Sun Street and after alterations was converted into county council offices, the staff of Douglas House being thereafter accommodated in Stranraer, partly in the new offices but mainly in the part of the New Town Hall vacated by other departments. It was the first time the county council had an office of their own and it was opened, curiously enough, by the Valuation Appeal Court in 1956. A large U-shaped table was provided, with seating for 32 members, officials, and other accommodation for the Press and providing a measure of comfort and amenity. Subsequently, an adjoining property was obtained and demolished and this year there are being erected on the site offices for the Treasurer.

The county council's offices are used by various public bodies for meetings, but so far Stranraer Town Council has not accepted an invitation to make use of the facilities.

...To punish them according to the lawes

JUSTICE, IN THE OLDEN DAYS, was harsh and seldom tempered with mercy.

At times the biter was bitten. One of the earliest records of this sort of thing was on 15th August, 1617, when a Bailie arrested a man who was in bed and flung him into the Tolbooth where he was kept for 24 hours in the stocks. The Bailie failed to appear before the Privy Council when his victim accused him of "hamesuckin" and was declared a rebel.

Theft was common and, as is the case today, was regarded as more serious than assault. In 1688, James McCubbin and Alexander McClumpha were charged with stealing a barrel of herring from the shore, the herring belonged to William Symson. McClumpha confessed and when McCubbin attacked him in court for so doing he was fined £200. When McClumpha came up for sentence the Magistrates considering they had no executioner to " stigmatiz " him and that the lack was prejudicial to the burgh offered the job to McClumpha. "They doe hereby enact and ordayne Alexander McClumpha during all the days of his lyfetyme shall be oblieged to scourge and stigmatiz all malefactors and shall also put the sentence of death in execution against any malefactor the Magistrates of the burgh, for the tyme, shall enjoynd him." McClumpha, needless to say, accepted. He was paid a levy of 2s on every householder for his duties.

Meanwhile, the wretched McCubbin who had been lying in jail with no money to pay his fine, was released on condition that for the next two years "he repair all bridges and the Tolbooth and kirk walls whenever the Magistrates shall require him." At the end of each working day McCubbin received a drink.

Mercy was not strained when the weaker sex was involved. In 1699, Agnes McCallome and Janett Broune were found in possession of stolen goods. Miss Broune was sentenced to be "brunt" upon the face and "scowrgit" by the hangman while the husband of the other woman was fined £14 and she was ordered to be removed out of the burgh and the liberty thereof. For being a common scolder and slanderer of her neighbours, Issobell Fultoune was put in the high gorgetts for two hours daily, then taken to the Market to be exhibited publicly before being returned to prison. The taming of the shrew with a vengeance.

Banishment was a common sentence for both men and women for thievery.

In contrast, John Ross was, in 1710, fined £3 for committing battery on a ganger on the fair day.

Alexander Urrie was fined £2 Scots, plus expenses of victim's cure and loss of time, in a battery case. Witnesses deponed they heard "murder" cried.

But not all offenders were from the common herd of the time. One of the most outstanding men was Andrew McCredy, an ex-Provost. In 1718, he and a Mr Archibald Marshall, described as a minister in Kirkcolm, were in court for "barbarously fighting and wounding each other." McCredy was fined £15 and Marshall £10 in his absence.

It must be recalled that one of the duties of the Council was to have tradesmen as burgesses, and the responsibility for ensuring that there were no unauthorised tradesmen also rested with the Magistrates, so in 1712, Hugh White and James Kilpatrick, tailors, were before the Burgh Court for practising their trade as "unfree-men." They were admitted burgesses on payment of £6 each, before Martinmas.

The Magistrates guarded the privilege of admission of burgesses zealously. Anyone coming into the town had to bring with him a certificate and also one for his previous good behaviour. A pronouncement was made at the Mercate Cross to this effect.

A really serious offence in 1723 and for some years later was not to keep a sufficient peat or turf stack and kale yard for the family. The sentence for this offence was almost inevitably, banishment. Inspection of houses was carried out by the town's officers. Banishment was also asked for by the Presbytery in some instances.

The Magistrates also reserved the right to decree when houses were relet.

Complaints by neighbours against Andrew McCreadie, described as an indweller in Chappel, led to a warning by the Magistrates in 1729, to mend his ways or he and his wife and family would be banished, along with any idle persons frequenting his house.

Occasionally it was reported the wrong doer would not accept the punishment. For example, in 1731, John Gilmor, son of the late Burgh Officer, refused to go to jail and abused the Bailie who had sentenced him. He had to be taken by force but he broke the chains and bolts, threatened to set fire to the town and offered to murder the Bailie and the others who had helped to send him to jail. Banishment restored peace and tranquility. The calm of the council was rudely disturbed in 1776 when William Crawfurd, baxter, in Stranraer, intruded, uttered horrid oaths, abused the Magistrates and flouted their authority, and threatened their lives. He was bound over for two years. Crawfurd had attended a meeting at which objections had been taken to the quality of the flour used in baking bread and interrupted the clerk, Wm. McKie, when he was relating the terms of the petition from the inhabitants.

Obviously the Tolbooth, like the prison later, was not exactly secure. In 1776 a list of townspeople was drawn up for them to guard in pairs a prisoner, John Baillie, who refused to be incarcerated. After being twice on the run and recaptured he was set free on the third occasion; the complainer, from Whithorn, had not sent funds for his upkeep in prison.

There was no indication the rod was spared and the child spoiled but sentences on children were abnormally severe even for these early days. In 1777, following complaints about boys and apprentices playing ball and marbles in the sheds of the new Tolbooth, the Magistrates issued a public warning and indicated any offenders, when caught, would be imprisoned in the Laigh Tolbooth for 24 years, and otherwise fined.

An Old Luce woman was sentenced to death for murder and was ordered to be executed at Stranraer on 6th January, 1861, but a plea for clemency was sustained and the sentence commuted.

Sentence of death was also passed on one, Joseph Allison, in July, 1833, at Edinburgh. He was brought to Stranraer under strong guard and lodged in jail. The dread sentence was to be carried out on 7th August, between 2 and 4 p.m. and the Magistrates decided to execute the murderer on top of the Old Castle, which would save transporting him too far on the day. Bailie Thomas Taylor had the grisly duty of travelling to Glasgow to procure a gibbet and an executioner. A ballot was made of the burgesses so that watch and ward could be kept on Allison until the day of the execution. However, the sentence was commuted to transportation for life. The town council had incurred expenses amounting to £18 6s 9½d in preparation for the execution. No doubt it was charged to the Common Good.

Literally, burning of boats was a method whereby the people showed their resentment against authority. In 1844 the council paid £3 17s 6d to James Scott whose boat was destroyed by a mob at the Market Cross. Two years later the fiscal was inquiring into a similar circumstance, this time Samuel Roddan was the victim. Another boat was burned in 1847 belonging to A. Edgar. Over-exuberance appeared to be the reason for a claim to the council by Archibald McMeikan of damage amounting to £2 10s for broken windows, occasioned during public rejoicings when Mr Moorhead had fired a cannon in the streets.

With the setting-up of Sheriff Courts, the more serious offences were subsequently transferred to the higher tribunals and the Magistrates Courts, or Burgh Courts as they continued to be called, dealt with relatively minor offences. It is within living memory that a Bailie in Stranraer was wont to refuse to accept pleas of not guilty by accused persons on the grounds that "if you hadn't been there, you wouldn't have been here."

And in the earlier part of the century, the fiscal, magistrates and accused, at times, reached a level of almost personal friendship particularly when the offender was a person who was termed Scotch Jamie. Jamie looked upon the wine when it was red and made in all over 80 appearances in court; in the Spring and Summer he was given the benefit of a fine and in the late Autumn and Winter he went to prison. As a Knight of the Road he probably preferred the warmth of jail.

... Clerkes, serjeants and members of court

PRESERVATION OF THE PEACE, and prevention of crime, were responsibilities assumed by the Burgh Magistrates, as a result of the Charter. This was no light task. Alexander II, in the early 13th century, found it necessary to appoint a third Justiciare because of the wild men who roamed Galloway and because of the high number of murders, rapes, thefts and robberies which took place in that area.

The two original Justiciares, made three because of the reputation of Galloway, were added to, and by the time the Charter was granted they were termed Justices of the Peace whose main duty appeared to be to keep poachers in check and to provide for paupers. These Justices appointed two constables in each parish who were bound to serve for a period of six months under the penalty of a fine or imprisonment. In burghs the number depended on the population.

Because of the duties laid upon Magistrates, the power of police appointments was transferred to them. Conditions being what they were, offenders were usually chased out of town and into the country districts for the accommodation for prisoners was not exactly all that it might have been. However there were arrests made.

In 1714 the Magistrates issued an edict prohibiting the discharge of firearms within the burgh, on pain of forfeiture of the firearms, and warned the parents they would be held liable for damage done by children. This was repeated in 1732 when masters were held responsible for their apprentices.

The firing of guns or pistols within the burgh was again forbidden in 1776 because of "complaints given in of late wherein men's lives have been wickedly and wantonly made game of, and small shot lodged in their bodies is truth undeniable; therefore, it is expected that parents will take care of their children being deprived of firearms, and masters, of their servants, and that no person of any age shall in time coming discharge any firearms without liberty, except for the killing of a mad dog or such like."

Breaking of apprenticeships was a serious offence in those days. Magistrates were held liable to make good any damage done by wilful destruction. James McMiken, having retired as burgh officer in 1791, owing to age and infirmity, the council decided to pay his yearly salary for the rest of his life.

Magistrates, High Constables and several people of the burgh met and discussed incidents of stone-throwing whereby people coming into the town had been hurt. Parents and employers were warned to watch the conduct of their children, servants and apprentices. The Burgh Officers were instructed to patrol the streets. One of them, in 1814, expressed regret at being drunk on duty. As it was his first offence, the Magistrates agreed to overlook it but warned him as to his future conduct. He had held the position only for three days before his lapse.

For ringing the Castle Bell on Sundays, the constable, or burgh officer, was paid one guinea per annum.

An inhabitant of Stranraer in 1826 complained in a letter to the Lord Advocate that the police were in a defective state in the town. The Sheriff Depute of Wigtownshire was instructed to hold an inquiry and found, while the situation had been exaggerated, the Night Watch should be revived. The Council agreed and called a public meeting to see if the respectable inhabitants would be willing to subscribe towards this expense. They drew up regulations for a police system in 1827 on the lines suggested by the Convention. The "respectable inhabitants, however, were tired of subscribing and in 1836 the Council had reluctantly to inform the Lord Advocate, the Home Secretary and the Sheriff that they had no money with which to pay the police."

By 1838 the Sheriff Substitute was writing to the Council intimating that the whole question of the police was being gone into, with a view to better regulations and inquiring if the Council was willing to co-operate "in whatever measures will be adopted." He also invited their views on their proportion of the expense. The Council agreed to co-operate but cannily reserved judgment on the expense question.

What apparently was in His Lordship's mind was the effects of Robert Peel. Sir Robert Peel became Home Secretary in 1822 and after several attempts persuaded Parliament to form a police force, the Metropolitan Force, on the same lines as he had done when Secretary in Ireland and on 1st November, 1838, the new system of policing as devised by Peel was accepted in Wigtownshire. Stranraer's share of the force was a superintendent and a constable, because it was a port of considerable importance. The pay of the constable was £2 per month.

Between 1833 and 1837 ten trials had been held but in the 20-week trial period of the new Wigtownshire Police Force, 19 persons were brought to justice. Stranraer's jail was being taxed and in many cases the superintendent kept the prisoner in his own home overnight, or released him in the hope he would be apprehended in time for the court.

Wigtownshire Police did not operate without difficulty for no force existed in the neighbouring counties and criminals, after committing the offence in the county, simply fled over the border into the Stewartry or into Carrick. In the 20-week trial period 34 vagrants were arrested in the burgh.

Vagrancy had increased so much in the town that in 1849 the Council increased the number of burgh constables by appointing John Williamson. He was to receive £10 per annum and a suit—blue coat with red collar and cuffs, blue neck-tie with red edging and dark grey trousers, and hat with yellow band. The police superintendent, who had been appointed by the Rhins Police Committee was paid for keeping a horse.

Stranraer did not employ the policemen full-time; when not engaged on official business they were held responsible for getting pavements made and one of the constables, until 1869, doubled as a roadman. The force comprised a superintendent and five constables. The superintendent, Archibald Hutcheson, in 1867, was appointed governor of the Stranraer prison of which his wife was matron.

Under the Police (Scotland) Act, 1857, the Commissioners of Supply were required to establish and maintain a force. To do so they appointed a police committee on which served H.M. Lord Lieutenant and the Sheriff. They appointed the Chief Constable who, in turn, appointed his staff.

Stranraer had its own independent force until 1870. The proposed amalgamation with the County was strenuously opposed in 1869 by the publicans of the town not one of whom had appeared in court during the preceding five years. To force matters the Commissioners of Supply intimated Stranraer would require to pay one halfpenny more in assessment or amalgamate; if not the force would be halved.

Capitulation followed and the town joined with the county. Immediately they asked for a Sheriff Substitute for Wigtownshire as they had two courts and the

50

Stewartry had only one and they did not wish to be conjoined to Kirkcudbrightshire.

The Wigtownshire Police Force in 1908 comprised 24 men. Constables were paid 22s 2d weekly. There was a cycle allowance of 28s per annum and, in charge, a Chief Constable, Superintendent and ten Sergeants.

Functions of the Commissioners of Police had passed in 1870 to a joint committee with the County Council. In 1908 the council was asked to adjust the annual payment for the services of the police and a public inquiry followed the refusal. The committee claimed Stranraer had now six constables but the council counterclaimed that some of them spent their time solely on duty not in the burgh and that they had paid £40 a year more for the extra constable they had. They resisted, too, the argument that the old prison was acquired because of lack of cell accommodation by pointing out, fairly reasonably, that much of the accommodation that could have been used, was, in fact, used by private law practitioners. However, in 1910, the agreement was ended. In 1929 the County Council was required to appoint a Police Committee. The Wigtownshire Force, though it shared for some years a joint Chief Constable with the Stewartry, Mr Alex Donald, O.B.E., maintained its independence, and in 1939 Mr George Scott was appointed Chief Constable and was the first resident Chief Constable in the town.

In 1948 the three southern counties forces were amalgamated to become Dumfries and Galloway Constabulary with a committee comprising representatives from the three counties and the burgh of Dumfries and covering one of the largest areas in Scotland under one police authority.

Stranraer, since the amalgamation, as before, has maintained its position as a place of some importance and the Superintendent in charge of the Galloway Division is stationed in the town along with an Inspector who is in charge of the Stranraer sub-branch. There are, in addition, six sergeants, 16 constables, two women constables, two cadets, three civilians and two traffic wardens.

Prior to 1846, the burgh officer, or constable, was provided with accommodation in the prison but this was not satisfactory and in 1846 a police station was purchased in Lewis Street. Headquarters for the force were not considered of such pressing importance as the need for a jail and the two were again combined. The site was purchased from Mrs Jane Taylor and others and work started immediately and in 1847 the station and jail were ready to receive. The building was used as a prison for some years but it was decided to change to the new County Buildings where excellent cells had been provided and there was a modern house for the jailer. In 1884 the move was made and the old jail was purchased by Boyle Hill, though the tenant, John Craig, a dealer from Armadale, remained. He found the cells excellent stalls for his horses and as byres for cattle, using the fields to the rear as grazing grounds.

In the summertime he let part of the jail to boarders and visitors so that whilst some people had paid to get out of the building, others were paying to get in. No doubt the novelty appealed.

There was record of a honeymoon couple staying in one of the cells.

John Craig, who was a tenant for more than 20 years, became a personality in the town. Possessed of a stentorian voice, it was said his preaching—he was a member of the Plymouth Brethren Sect—could be heard from the Cross to Gallowhill. He vacated the station when it was repurchased for police purposes in 1904 by the County Council who had found the experiment of having a jail in the County Buildings very unsatisfactory.

A few years before 1958 the legalised cells were closed and all prisoners went to Wigtown. The space vacated was used as a photographic section and gave accommodation to the Inspectorate.

On ground, occupied partly by a bakery and fronting the sea opposite Portrodie and which, strangely enough, had also at one time belonged to the Taylor family, a new station was built by the Dumfries and Galloway Police Committee and to it the force was transferred in April, 1958. Their former station was demolished and made way for the Headquarters of the Fire Brigade.

History was made in the Sheriffdom in 1961 when Mrs Mari Mair became the first honorary woman Sheriff Substitute, an appointment made by Miss Margaret Kidd, the first of her sex to be appointed Sheriff Principal of Dumfries and Galloway, and in 1962 J. Hall Douglas was appointed the first full-time Procurator Fiscal for the County. He was succeeded in 1967 by Wm. Mair Morton.

... Shall in no wayes be diminished

STRANRAER MAGISTRATES REPRESENTED a scant 500 souls when the cherished Charter was obtained. There were prospects, however, of absorbing the two neighbouring villages, Clayhole and Hillhead.

Growth was not spectacular; in fact, at times there was a regression. By 1761 there were 1602 people in Stranraer, not a dramatic increase, but the natural growth over the century was nullified by emigration to the New World. In 1811 there were 1923 people living in 387 houses. There could very well have been a loss over-all had it not been for the Irish emigrants. These increased in number until by 1841 it was reported one-fifth of the population was either Irish born or of Irish parentage. In 1861 the population reached the high figure of 4002, a century later it was 9250.

Following the '45 Rebellion, the MacRoberts emigrated to the New World, and in 1820, because of distress after the Napoleonic wars, there was an exodus to South Africa. Among the later emigrants were the Cowans to Canada in 1879; Wm. Ross to Capetown where he became a member of Legislative Council, in 1874; Taylors, in 1888; William Todd to Yakima, Washington, in 1882. In 1900 the Medical Officer drew attention to the decline in population of persons under 35 years of age. At that time there were 6000 residents.

With the prospect of work upon the railway, the Irish crossed the sea in droves and in 1861 the town was heavily taxed by increased population. Active steps to discourage the flow followed in the next decade or two. The immigrants, it was said, were putting too heavy a burden on the public relief funds. They were most improvident and "they levied a very heavy contribution from the humanity of the inhabitants."

The policy was unsuccessful, for in 1871 the population had grown to 5939, of whom 1079 were in Inch and 1247 in Leswalt Parish. Thirty years later it had risen to 6036, including 2856 in the original burgh, of whom 1527 were females and, in 1911, there were still only 1535 females and 1339 males in the old part of the town.

There was another exodus overseas, particularly of young marriageable persons who saw few prospects at home. They had become better educated and, no doubt, were receiving information from those who had blazed the trail, as it were, of opportunities elsewhere.

Economic distress following the First World War and enticements by travel and emigration agents continued to rob the town of its most energetic citizens and the 6397 inhabitants of 1918 fell to a somewhat alarming 5695 in 1929. Grad-

52

ually the situation righted itself. By 1935 the council added considerably to the area of the town by extending the boundaries, to take care of the 6527 inhabitants. After the extension the population was 6635 and the road mileage increased from 14 to 16.176. Another extension in 1960 brought the population within the council's orbit to 9249 and at present it stands at 9365. The town continues to grow and is expected to house a population of up to 16,000 in the next two decades.

The population is not now so heavily weighted in favour of the Ulstermen. There is a considerable leavening of people from all parts of the country, particularly among the professional classes, and in recent years, thanks to the exigencies of war, there has been quite a number of English settlers. The people, generally, are more sophisticated than might be expected in a small burgh or town of similar size

Too much significance cannot be placed on the earlier figures, for the burgh boundaries did not result from an exact science. In 1802, for example, the council and several of the inhabitants met to ascertain the bounds of Royalty. They noted it was officially recorded, "that the old town beginning at the Burn of Peelker as the same passes in the fey beneath the Chapel and ascending up the said Burn as the same marches by the Mill of Chapel, up by the Old Croft of Clenoch, and therefrom as the same is stanked by the new arable lands called the Meadowlands of Ochtrelure, whilk it runs to the Dyke of Knockcally and therefrom passes to the March of William Gardener's feu lands, as the same is bounded in his insestment to the end of the yard occupied by David McWilliam and from the end of the said house to William Young's piece of feu land and passing therefrom, directly to a gray stone on the Braehead, and from the said gray stone, by the Water Drop to the march of William Young's croft, and therefrom down the fey by the tail of the Chapel Fey, as the same is presently marched and bounded."

Saint John's Croft was "bounded from the burn which comes from the Loch of Lochryan and the Lands of Aird on the East, The Tower, Fortalice, Manor Place and Yeard of Chapel on the West, the Water Gang which runs to the Mill of Chapel on the South, and the sea on the North."

The punctuation is modern and has been inserted to aid anyone interested in the exercise of just what exactly the town comprised in area.

In 1802, the study group, "after a careful study of the ancient charters and titles, found that the marches at present are — 'beginning at the shore upon the East, at the corner of Miss Susan Maxwell's dyke betwixt her property and the Ball Green and runs along said march betwixt the said Ball Green, Miss Maxwell's and James McClean's property, called the Glen, till it reaches Glenluce Road, at an ash tree about six feet to the eastward of William Ross's new Granary, where it crosses the Glenluce Road and runs along the march betwixt the Anti-Burgher Meeting House Green, and the land feued for the new Malt Kiln, called the Lands of Aird, and from the south-east corner of the said Meeting House Green, in a direct line till the south side of the Mountain Meeting House, and from the south-west corner of the Mountain Meeting House, until it joins Galla's Tenement, now called Little Ireland, in the Center, where the two burns meet and up along the said Burn in a north direction by Willi Young's Well, along Dr Taylor's march, till it joins Mr Patrick McKennal's Garden, by a large stone, and along the Braehead, till it joins the south-east corner of Robert Allen's Garden and from thence by the east end of the house formerly belonging to John Forrest, now to Thomas McCulloch and, along the east side of his garden, the east and north side of James Carnochan's Park till it joins the road leading to the Shore, which road it crosses and runs to the west end of John Semple's House and from thence to the shore'."

It is not surprising that a clearer definition was necessary and this was obtained through the Reform Act of 1832 which widened and more clearly defined the burgh boundaries within which there were 3329 people in 513 houses. Roughly the same ratio had been maintained, an increase of 300 in 40 years, but the accommodation was in a much wider area.

Definition was still not clear, for in 1841 the council authorised Mr John Emslie, land surveyor, to mark off the boundaries in a distinct manner, at a cost not exceeding £8. Three years later the Magistrates visited the bounds to ensure they had been correctly ascertained and marked off by the trigonometrical surveyors appointed by the Government.

In 1865, Stranraer Town Council gave serious consideration to a burgh boundary extension. Not that the council were imbued with illusions of grandeur; they were considering the rising costs of the poor relief. Many of the poor came into the burgh from neighbouring parishes and the townspeople felt the imposition too heavy. However, the hopes of relief by extension were extinguished by a change of Government which held up the scheme.

Stranraer Parochial Board had in 1894 attempted to persuade the council to embrace Inch and Leswalt Parishes for the purposes of poor relief, but Stranraer had changed its mind considering they would lose more than they would gain and emphasised the position should remain as it had been under the Poor Law Act of 1845. Representations by the council to the Secretary of State were unsuccessful. In 1896 the council decided to make the burgh as compact as possible.

Stranraer had become a police burgh in 1863 with the same boundary as the former Parliamentary burgh boundary. No question arose as to the demarcation until, in 1896, when Mr Peter Barr, a town councillor, induced the council to agree that his home, Duncliffe, Broadstone Road, was outwith the bounds. His reason was that the rates were lower in the country than in the town. In a dispute with the County Council regarding the repair of Cairnryan Road, the Magistrates appealed to the Ordnance Survey for a definite marking, on Cairnryan Road. It was given as it is today, but the Ordnance Surveyor pointed out that on the other side of the town the council had erred, and had erred for at least 50 years. Duncliffe was in the town, as was Larg Liddesdale. The council endeavoured to maintain that the term "due north-east" was synonymous with "true north-east" but without success, and to rub it in, Matthew Ewing, who had taken over Duncliffe in 1898, claimed compensation for a sea wall he had built and paid for, thinking he was outwith the boundary. The council paid up but ensured that boundary stones were set.

...For lodgeing of our leidges

STRANRAER'S POPULATION of 9365 lives in 2865 houses, of which 240 are in the original burgh, 1520 are in the part taken from Leswalt Parish and 1105 from what was formerly part of Inch Parish.

Of the total, 1644 dwellings have been built by the municipal authority which, in 1953, proudly opened its thousandth house.

The original pattern of settlement, not an unusual one in Scotland, comprised one main street with several offshoots. The town was divided by the burn in Strand Streets, which, in 1690, had several stone bridges built over it. John Kennedy had possession of Chappell in 1623 and was in 1635 styled of Stranraer. In 1668, Flora Kennedie, sister of Gilbert Kennedie of Arkletoune had sasine of the four merkland of Stranraiver, formerly held by Patrick Agnew of Sheuchan and later by Alexander Adair. In 1747 the sasines passed to Robert Vans Agnew of Sheuchan, who retained them until 1782.

54

Captain Andrew Agnew of Croach was given authority in 1700 to rebuild houses "upon the west tenement of ground lyand in the burgh of Stranraer, boundit betwixt the vennel which leads to the shore upon the East (Princes Street) and the vennel upon the West (King Street) commonly called Kledahouse tenement." The buildings were to be "free of taxation and ground burdens for seven years as an encouragement for his improvement."

Thus early was the council encouraging private enterprise and in view of the state of the town's finances this was hardly surprising. Mr Walter Laurey, minister of Stranraer, was given permission to rebuild a house on the south side of the close, which had fallen down. Mr Andrew Ross, factor to the Earl of Stair, was, in 1708, given "a portion of ground at the sea side bounded and limited betwixt the house and barne belonging to Hew Henry, on the East, and the tenement house belonging to Andrew Agnew upon the West, for building."

Adair's Land was sold by the council in 1711 to Sammy McMaster. This land was waste and was bounded by the Stinking Vennel, on the East by the tenement belonging to Patrick McMaster, and on the West by Baxter's Land. McMaster, who had been a dyar burgess of the burgh and burgh officer for 50 years or thereby, was given his land for £40 Scots. Andrew Ross purchased ten ells of land on the foreland in 1712 and Provost McCredie bought the piece of land next to it for a payment of 6d Scots yearly.

Other transactions around that time were in favour of Provost McCredie and Bailie John Gray who was, in 1724, permitted to build a stable as was Robert Wilson. All these developments were on the foreland which seemed to indicate that thus early the village of Clayhole was being brought into the scheme of things so far as the town was concerned. Despite these, there were still only 18 houses in the Clayhole in 1766. But by the time of the first statistical account, 1791, there were 50 houses, all on one side of the street.

At the beginning of the eighteenth century the Mid Vennel (Queen Street) was described as "one of our oldest streets." McDowall, laird of Garthland, had a residence there of considerable size, as had Lynn of Larg, Quentin Agnew (the Sheriff's brother) and Kennedy of Chapel. A writer of that time said that, these houses and a few others excepted, the town was composed of thatched one-storey cottages.

On the sea front, because of the presence of Lord Stair's Dragoons, more stables were built in 1725, Andrew Fyfe and James Baird receiving authority. In the same year, to encourage building, no doubt, the council set three years for lessees of land to build, otherwise the ground was to be sold by public roup. John McKie was given permission to build a "tenement" in 1731 on ground at the shore, next to that belonging to John Hunter Smith and in 1734 the energetic Provost McCredie was still expanding. He had permission to build a shop, stable and cellars next to John Dalrymple's house and yard and James McCoyd's little house while ground at Sarah McCane's house on the foreland in front of the Eastmost Vennel was given to William McCraken. Alexander Drenan, carpenter, and John McGill, shoemaker, were given ground for building, next to houses belonging to John Campbell and Mary Donald, and to Gilbert Drennan's byre. James Carnochan, school master, was given permission to build a house.

In the early 1770s the development began on the east side of the Burn of Chapel. Robert McCulloch and Adam Hanna, mason, Charles Baird and Alexander McWhinnie erected private dwellings in a new street in the Fey of Stranraer.

Building was booming, so much so that the Dean of Guild Court was called in to ascertain marches in 1769. They perambulated the marches of an old kiln, in the Bartey Fey and Glen of Chapel in 1773 when it was intended to rebuild. Wit-

55

nesses pointed out the boundaries, the northern one lying along the road leading to Glenluce, and turf "was nicked and turned up to mark these except where barley was growing."

Private houses, "reflecting the growing opulance of the town" had by 1777, become commonplace. Andrew McMaster, innkeeper, built a house on the east side of Castle Alley (Castle Street). The following year Mr Thomson was given permission to rebuild his peat house on his own ground on the west side of Castle Alley adjoining the Castle. By 1795 the survey of houses and tenements in the town revealed a valuation of £20,715.

One of the most significant additions to Stranraer's mansion houses was North West Castle, erected by Admiral Sir John Ross, the Arctic explorer, in 1820.

The less pretentious houses were, in 1836, mainly stone huts with thatched roofs.

A map of 1843 shows the town centre more or less as it has remained until the present day. The town was based on Hillhead Street (now High Street), George Street and Charlotte Street, with the vennels branching to the shore. There was a custom house in Princes Street and earlier in 1799 it had been established in the Chapel Fey. A courthouse in George Street, a tollhouse in Cairnryan Road and the Castle Prison in George Street.

Ann House and Ivy House were erected at the end of the eighteenth century. Houses occupied by Mr M. Gillespie, Mrs Captain Henderson and Mr Sprott in Bellevilla Road were separated from the corner property in Hanover Street by a house occupied by Mrs General McNair whose husband owned Ivy House. Around the first United Secession Chapel (St Andrew's Church) were a few dwellings. Dalrymple Street and Lewis Street were both built up but there was quite a cluster of homes in Little Ireland and Mill Street (Hanover Square), Little Dublin Street (Millhill Street) and Greenvale Street. Mr Thomas Taylor owned most of the ground in Lewis Street, from the corner of Sun Street to the Free Church. Neptune Street was part of the Clayhole. A roadway had been laid down in 1840 from the Quayhead to the Mill, the Lairey Burn was covered over in 1848 and the village of Clayhole had, to all intents and purposes, been absorbed in the town.

More substantial houses were built in 1852 at Ivy Place and at Broadstone. Castle Street was by 1865 almost completely built up, private dwellings replacing stores. Two-storied houses appeared in Bridge Street and unsightly buildings in Hanover Street were swept away.

Condition of Millhill Street and Little Ireland generally gave cause for public alarm (the area is at present the subject of a scheme of comprehensive development), and many of the inhabitants left to take up residence in Sloss's Close, and the Prettymill Close, both off Dalrymple Street; some went to Cance's Close and others to Cowan's Close in George Street. There conditions were but slightly better. These closes were wiped out in the nineteen-thirties by a more enlightened council.

Stranraer Building Society was formed in 1863 for the purpose of "supplying the working class with improved housing accommodation." This, the forerunner of municipal enterprise, was so successful that in 1869 there were houses to let in Hanover Street and in Glen Street, also in St Andrew Street, Market Street and the Backrampart. Hanover Street was widened.

Cottages were built in 1864 in London Road and on the west side of Queen Street and in Church Street. Streets were renamed, Academy Street was called after the school, in 1843, Lochryan Street, to a lesser extent, Station Street and Market Street came into being. Stoneykirk Road in 1839 had become Lewis Street, named after one of the residents who had fought at Waterloo. Glebe Street appeared, a continuation of the old village of Hillhead. Encliffe House was still, in 1869, on the outskirts of the town.

The last of the old thatched cottages in Hanover Street was pulled down in 1889 by Mr Andrew Wales, painter, who erected new and larger premises for his own business. In 1883 M. Penman had been compensated for the removal of his thatched house in Millhill Street and in 1903 a thatched cottage in High Street was removed. As late as 1917 thatched houses still stood in St Andrew Street and St John Street and in 1921 there was one in Sheuchan Street. There was a considerable improvement in High Street in 1910 when the wall at Mount Ryan was taken back. In 1913 the Council took action under the House and Planning Act of 1909 and condemned houses in Market, Fisher and Princes Streets and the Backrampart, 20 in all. They were not able to continue such action because of the war and in 1918 they estimated Stranraer needed 150 new houses under the Housing Acts of 1890 and 1918. Stranraer appointed its first Housing Committee in 1919 and it decided to build small schemes, at Broomfield and Marine Gardens. Stranraer's first housing list in 1929 showed 115 applicants. In 1931 it was reported there were several instances of gross overcrowding, two-roomed houses being occupied by 13 persons. A census taken in 1937 indicated that 304 houses should be closed. There were 1426 occupied dwellings in the burgh.

Private development was halted for many years, apart from a few houses in Royal Avenue and Cairnryan Road of the bungalow type, and, in fact, never again were tenements built, nor even flatted houses, except by the council.

Between 1935 and 1939 the local authority had built 274 out of a target of 400. In 1939 there were 1769 tenants in 1664 houses and 459 of the houses were reported to be uninhabitable. Squatters who took possession of former army huts in the West End in 1946 caused considerable embarrassment before they were housed in permanent dwellings. The council made excellent use of the areas awarded to them by the burghal extensions, of 1955 when 24 acres were purchased, and of 1960. The density of population in 1831 had been 8.60 persons per acre, rising to 16.86 in 1931. The town was bursting at the seams. The extension reduced the density to 10.44 per acre. The first municipal scheme had been at Broomfield in a triangle between Dalrymple Street and Edinburgh Road, in the south of the town. It was completed in 1920 and after the extension had been granted vast new areas were brought into the municipal orbit, mainly to the south-west and east, Murrayfield, Dick's Hill, Moorefield, Belmont, Sheuchan Park and Parklea; and the West End, a continuation of Sheuchan Street towards Leswalt, thus extending the Clayhole, and to the east at McMaster's Road. In 1916 the valuation of the town was £30,000 and in 1967 it was £268,309 gross and £225,250 rateable.

Although the development plan for the burgh indicated in 1952 that Stranraer needed 600 houses, the burgh had built and erected 1000 houses by 1953. A plan for the redevelopment of Hanover Square area was placed before the council in 1954 and was still under consideration in 1967.

By 1966 the council had thus provided 1644 of the 2865 houses in the town and had given every encouragement to the resumption of private building which resulted in small estates, at Sandyfield, Rowans Hill to the West and Ladies' Walk, London Road and Rephad to the East.

There are more schemes planned for it is considered Stranraer still requires 500 more houses. It was officially recognised as a growth point in 1966.

Through the extension schemes, the area of the town has grown from 59 acres in 1617 and the 387 of the Reform Act, to 625 in 1935 and 917 today and there is a prospect in the immediate future of more ground being taken in both to the East and to the West.

...Liberty and freedome for craftsmen

AUTHORITY WAS GIVEN under the Charter for the Burgh to have certain craftsmen considered necessary "pertaining to the liberty and freedom" of "ane free Burgh Royall and siclike."

Considered necessary, in 1617, were baxters, brewers, fleshers, fishers, fishmongers, cutlers, shoemakers, waukers, weavers, wrights, smiths and skinners.

Early in the burgh's history it was obvious her situation would be, with regard to the hinterland, a centre for commerce and the interchange of goods and services. Despite her excellent situation at the head of Lochryan, the sea was not regarded as of great importance. Earliest among the merchants listed were John Clark, Gilbert Adair and John Baird. John Knibloe was the apothecary, Alexander McCoune the shoemaker, Johne McCoslery the miller at Chappell, James McRyder the chapman, and William Colfine the cooper. All tradesmen had to be entered in the burgess roll.

A Customs Officer in 1655 who rejoiced in the unusual but later familiar name of Thomas Tucker, the first Englishman to penetrate as far as Stranraer—at least the first with peaceful intentions, wrote, "there is not, nor ever was, any trade to be heard of there."

With a population of well under a thousand there were not, naturally, any great centres of trade, but the people were busily engaged importing iron, tar, pitch, flax and hemp; from Ireland came cattle and grain. They exported skins — goat, rabbit and otter; also wool.

In their official return to the Convention of Royal Burghs in 1692, the Magistrates reported: "Forraigne trade they had none and their inland trade was most inconsiderable. They retaill goodes they bring from Glasgow, Air, Greenock and Kilmarnock. From Kilmarnock they import only knives and bonnets. They sell about seven hundred sheep skins and they had vented these fyve yeares bygone about half a tunn of wine, three last yeares whereof they had sold none. They also reported they had no ships, barks or ferry boats, herring fishing boats had since deaced and were lyen useless. The inhabitants are poor."

The Magistrates on oath declared in 1692 "they are not concerned in matter of trade with unfree burghs."

In 1686 the Council reached agreement with Hugh Sumervell and Thomas McCrakine, millers at the Mill of Chappell, that inhabitants "will take all their malt there 'to be grined'."

There were no incorporated trades in Stranraer. The Magistrates, however, had it in their power, and used it, to compel any trader settling in the burgh to enter burgess. The entrance money was not above eight guineas. A Trades Union Council was formed in 1939 but has never been active.

It was not only traders who were admitted to the Burgess roll. In 1701 James Agnew of Lochnaw, the Provost of Wigtown, was enrolled as were Captain Andrew Agnew of Croach, James Dalrymple of Dunragit and Mrs William Fuleartoune of Portpatrick, the first time a lady had been so named. John Hannay of Grenane became a burgess in 1714 and James Wales, a dyer, in 1713. There were also added — David McCulloch, baxter; William Saull, mason; Hew Sinclair, coatman; Daniel Turner, boatman; and William McKelvie, shoemaker. Francis Hay had been admitted a burgess in 1718 as a wigmaker. David McCulloch was apparently the first baker, registered in 1731, and there was a notary, in the person of Archibald Cowand, admitted in 1686, and a writer in Alexander McGuffock in 1731.

Because of the danger of fire, the Council in 1720 ordered that no lint be dressed in houses at night and much later, in 1779, prohibited anyone from dyeing clothes or wool in the town burn. The prohibition was the result of protests by many people and against William McHarrie in particular.

A century after Tommy Tucker's visit, Bishop Pocock of Meath had this to say of Stranraer, "the inhabitants live chiefly by the herring fishing and use boats of deal which last five or six years. They manufacture flannel blankets and frieze for their own use."

There were, however, in 1764 only two ships registered in Stranraer, but by 1790 the number had increased to 15, and one of them was of 150 tons burden.

Sea-going vessels were engaged in a fast growing trade with Gothenburg and the Baltic, bringing back timber and iron. Lime was imported from Whitehaven and Larne. Coarse fabric went to Virginia.

Stranraer had been warned by the Sheriff about her official weights which "were notoriously wrong" and in 1767 the Magistrates, ordered to make an inspection, found that most of the shopkeepers, too, had deficient weights.

Clothiers made their appearance on the Burgess roll in 1732 — Robert McMaster, Andrew McDowall; and tailors—Gilbert McTeir and Niven Agnew, while other shoemakers appeared in Andrew Ross, John McGill and Andrew Donald. James Dalrymple was the vintner and Anthony Ellies and William Lin the inn-keepers. Andrew McCulloch was the first barber so named in 1768, and Thomas McGraa the first butcher in 1771. Alexander Ross was registered as a shipbuilder in 1772, and Andrew McCready the horse hirer.

First intimation of a co-operative society was in 1771 when the townspeople, alarmed at the prices charged by farmers for their produce, formed themselves into a company, with a Deacon and twelve assessors, to enforce their own prices for farm goods.

Unfair competition in other directions was irritating the Burgesses and in 1787 the Magistrates agreed to enforce laws "regarding unfree trading by 'strowling peoples under the name of Uchoneers' who harm the traders of the burgh by selling all kinds of goods."

The chief fuel at the time was peat and turf, though some supplies of coal were being brought by sea from Irvine. Because of many complaints about the measure of the coal being sold on the shore, the Council in 1799 ordered the two bailies to obtain two tubs of 32-gallon Winchester measure to be used for all the coal sold from ships to the townspeople. Any loads found to be deficient to be confiscated and given by the Magistrates to poor families.

The Council also bought corn from neighbouring farmers and one was appointed to oversee the making of it into meal and the sale of it to the inhabitants. In order to finance this laudable project the Council obtained a credit of £1000 from the Paisley Bank in 1800.

Many more traders were being enrolled and in the latter part of the eighteenth century the first records of Shipmasters appeared — Alexander Agnew, James Murray, and sailors Peter Barkly, William McMaster and Maxwell McDowall. James McGill was registered as a doctor in 1784.

Described as a troggar, John McWilliam was elected in 1784. This was the first attempt to combat the Irish troggars who came over during the season selling linen and other articles and then returned to Ireland.

James McWhinnie was added as shipbuilder and William McNish as Surveyor of Customs. Samuel Maen was the kirk beadle in 1786 and a curious trade was that of landwaiter; John McMorland held that position. John McKie was the first banker, elected in 1791, and Isabella McMeekan was amongst the first of the women shopkeepers. In 1795 Benjamin Paterson was admitted as a candlemaker and James Saul as a currier. Weavers, tanners, saddlers, carters and cabinetmakers became numerous. William McNish became postmaster in 1799 and John Davidson the first of many watchmakers. Hugh Lewis Taylor was the first surgeon to be so registered in 1801 and he was quickly followed two years later by John Agnew, Hugh McKie and James McNair.

There followed a galaxy of inn-keepers—John Thorburn, James McColm, Mrs Taylor, John Drynan, William Hannay, William McMaster, and John and Thomas Agnew in 1804.

Later clockmakers included James Adair, Stair Adair in Castle Street, Andrew Davidson in George Street, Fergus Garrick and John Garrick in Castle Street.

More complaints by the townspeople led to the council in 1814 making regulations to try and regularise the size of loaves sold by bakers within the burgh. The peck loaf was to weigh 17lb 6oz.

Note was being taken in 1836 of the Lochryan sea captains, James Gillespie, David Kennedy, J. D. Haswell and Captain Douglas. In 1802 the Magistrates had convened a meeting of the inhabitants to decide the best method of erecting a harbour and Bailie John McKie was appointed treasurer of the fund.

Members of the legal profession, who doubled in eight years in number, led a writer to comment, "where the carcase is, there will the eagles gather." The eagles gathered in council for several representatives of the profession became elected members in the years which followed.

There were wrights and smiths at almost every street corner and with the coming of the railways there was naturally a big influx of railway workers around the middle of the nineteenth century. The transport industry grew in importance to such an extent that in the following hundred years it became second only, in terms of employment, to agriculture for the Stranraer townspeople. It was much larger than normally would have been expected because of the short sea route to Ireland. The distributive trades, too, loomed large as a means of providing work in the twentieth century, as did the establishment of creameries.

Zealous of the rights of their citizens, the Council in 1834 raised an action in the court in the name of the customer (the tacksman) against people coming into the Burgh and refusing to pay customs, so placing the livelihood of the tacksman in jeopardy. All "unfree traders who had set up shops were ordered to make payment for a Composition of Freedom."

Probably the first Labour Exchange started in 1836 when the Council adopted regulations for porters within the Burgh. These porters had to get permission from the Magistrates to ply for work and to register with the town clerk. Each porter was issued with a badge with the words "Stranraer Porter" and the same words were inscribed on his barrow or hurley. A scale of charges for the porter was fixed and he was given a copy.

All new councillors were elected burgesses but gradually towards the end of the last century the system of enrolling traders as such was dwindling. John Montgomery, grocer, was admitted in 1864 as was Mr William Wallace who on payment of £8 became bound to perform every civic duty incumbent upon him. Robert Dick, bookseller, David Easton, doctor of medicine, and William McGowan, saddler, followed as did John Orgill, surgeon, James Mitchell, draper, and Hugh McDowall, builder. When Mr Wm. Fawcett, grocer, was admitted to the roll in 1875 he was only charged £5 and the cost to Andrew Garrick, Balyett, in 1877 was only two guineas. There was a sliding scale, depending on whether or not one's father or grandfather had been on the roll.

In 1878 badges of licence were granted to chimney sweeps. An order of council in 1805 intimated that all chimneys must be swept every six months. They prohibited the practice of deliberately setting fire to them in order to clean them.

The council agreed in 1896 to spread the work over the various employers in the town, but the understanding was not effective and in 1898 a rota of tradesmen to serve the council's needs was drawn up.

By the twentieth century it was not considered necessary to enrol tradesmen as burgesses, though many trades guilds did spring up, chiefly among railway and kindred workers. Inclusion in the burgess roll was in later years conferred as an honour on some worthy citizens or visitors. Throughout its history, Stranraer has been singularly free of industrial disputes.

There was trouble among butchers in 1805. They leased stalls in the town's market house but withdrew their meat and intimated to the Council that, despite the regulations, they intended only to sell meat in their shops from then on, as people were selling meat outwith the burgh to the people of the town and advertising same, to their detriment. After taking counsel's opinion, the Magistrates reached an amicable agreement with the butchers. The Council had three years earlier laid it down that all goods coming into the town for sale be sold at the new market house, threepence was to be paid for every bullock, bull, heifer or cow sold except by butchers having stalls there.

Oysters were being sold at 6d for ten dozen in 1848. In 1872, bread cost 10d for a 4lb loaf, an increase of 2½d.

The tailors went on strike in 1898 and there was a threatened bakers' strike in 1904. There were disputes, few in number, among the local railwaymen but the only stoppages of work occurred as a result of differences at national level which were not really of great importance to Stranraer workers although they too had to withdraw labour in conformity with the national union's decisions.

Of purely local interest was the meeting in 1854 of shopkeepers who discussed early closing. They agreed to close at 8 p.m. but found, shortly afterwards, that many were not in favour and were remaining open until 9 p.m. and even 10 p.m., despite the agreement. In 1908 the practice of closing shops on Wednesday afternoons during summer time was severely criticised. In 1908 the Council agreed at the request of the shopkeepers that the fourth Wednesday of each month from April to October be a holiday and not until a year or two ago did shopkeepers agree to forego their monthly holidays in the summer months. An inspector was engaged in 1912 under the Shops Act and action was taken against shopkeepers who opened on Wednesday afternoons. A proposal for Saturday afternoon closing was mooted in 1947 but received little support.

... Goods and merchandise

BY THE CHARTER, the Magistrates were enjoined to have a Stand-mail, a Meill-Mercat and a Cloath-Mercat, among other things.

While there were no factories as understood in the modern sense, there was a "Meill-Mercat." In 1782 a successor to the original was built at Sheuchan.

To it, all the corn in the district was brought for grinding. The mill was rebuilt in 1895 after a fire the previous year which razed it to the ground. Damage was estimated at £3000.

It has been a family concern for almost a century. Millstones were rolled from Barhoise to Portpatrick in the early years of last century and the Hannay family, one of the oldest in Galloway, moved to Corsewall and subsequently to Sheuchan. The trade was built round the harbour at Clayhole where small schooners were loaded with oatmeal and taken to the West Highlands, the cargo being sold at various ports. Return cargo was mainly fish.

The Hannays, whose origins can be traced as far back as 1296 when they swore fealty to Edward I at Berwick, were millers at Kirkcowan at the time of the granting of the Charter to Stranraer.

There was a steill mill in 1723 which belonged to the burgh and which was rouped to Provost McCredie for 22s.

The Mill of Chappell was demolished on the expiry of the Multure Tack in 1725

The American Civil War put an end to the cotton trade in the town. Many people were employed as smiths and wrights from 1836 onwards, although both trades have now almost disappeared.

Printing works were established in 1843 when the "Free Press" was started in Castle Street. There was also a newspaper connected with it which in 1847 took over the former "Galloway Register," a monthly formed a few years earlier. In 1847 it was the only newspaper in Galloway. For a few years in the early part of the century a paper called "The Star" was published.

There was, in 1863, a boot and shoe warehouse in Hanover Square, a cooperage in George Street, and a grain market in Castle Street. Brick and tile works were started about 1860 on the outskirts, mainly in Stoneykirk Road, and there was an iron foundry in Sheuchan Street.

Bacon curing was begun in 1852, earlier the bacon was taken to Ireland for cure; in 1905 a factory was erected in Trade Street, and latterly another in St Andrew Street.

A knitting factory was introduced into Stranraer Academy in 1866 through the initiative of Miss Cunningham, North West Castle. It employed about 50 girls. Importations of elm, birch, yellow pine and spruce from Quebec were in demand in 1860 for local carpenters and joiners.

An effort to establish a shawl factory, made by Mr Robert Kerr in premises formerly used for coachbuilding in Sheuchan Street, fell through in 1860. There was a flourishing coachbuilder and a steelyard beside a coal business owned by M. Caldwell in Hanover Square and a dyeing establishment employed several in 1876.

Earliest mention of a milk factory was in 1882 in Trade Street and it was soon superseded by the Wigtownshire Creamery in Sheuchan Street and the Galloway Creamery in Stoneykirk Road.

The site of the Wigtownshire Creamery was occupied for a time by a weaving factory and a shipbuilding yard before being taken over by Mr James McHarrie in 1884.

One of the earliest local manufacturers of dairy equipment was John Gray of Stranraer, a co-inventor of the first milking machine in 1891. He employed a large staff at his premises in George Street, which are now occupied by Downie's Garage, and carried on a considerable export trade in cheese vats and allied equipment. He also had an ironmonger's shop.

In 1899 the Town Council passed a motion to attract industry to the town for the general prosperity and in the years after the Second World War a Transport and Industry Committee under ex-Provost Randolph E. Caughie was most active in this direction, and fairly successful.

Fishing was quite an important industry around the turn of the century and indeed up to the outbreak of the Second World War. In 1905, for instance, the landings at Stranraer were valued at £3120. Curiously enough in 1908 a fish curing business failed because of lack of water. A brewery in North Strand Street had a short life and ended in 1899. A hatchery was started in London Road in 1910 but it too did not last very long. An egg grading station was set up in 1940 ind closed in 1966. Efforts were made throughout the years to start a sugar beet factory but these came to nought, nor did a scheme to have a carpet factory meet with any more success.

More successful was the aerated water factory established in 1899 which moved in 1921 to Millhill Street, and a laundry in the same area in Trade Street lasted for some thirty years.

With the growing importance of the internal combustion engine and the beginnings of motor car traffic, a big business was built up from 1908 by another Mr James McHarrie in South Strand Street who extended in 1918 to Portrodie. Others soon followed, mainly Reid and Adams in Bellevilla Road and Inch Service Station in 1962 in South Strand Street.

Earlier the Downie family had a blacksmith's shop at the Co-operative Close in George Street and the two sons gradually extended their trade from building 'Lochryan' cycles to repairing cars. The business shifted along George Street to take over John Gray's premises and was taken over by a grandson who retired this year. The firm at one time built cattle floats which were exhibited at the Glasgow motor show.

One of the oldest businesses in the town is that of Thomas Harper and Sons, seed merchants, which was established in 1858 in Castle Street and removed to Charlotte Street and subsequently to St John Street.

Another one who took advantage of the changing times was Mr Andrew Sloss who in 1935 became interested in the cycle and radio trade and later made television aerials. But in the main it was to serve the farming community that most factories emerged, James Wyllie and Sons (Grain Merchants), for instance, from 1921 onwards built an ever-increasing business, as did A. McLelland and Son Ltd., cheesemakers and suppliers of farm feedingstuffs. After being established in 1871 in Kells, William McCormack and Son moved into Stranraer as coal merchants and suppliers to farmers and West Cumberland Farmers took over at Belmont.

Haulage firms proliferated, the largest of these became Agnew and Lithgow which has at present a nation-wide connection and one which extends to the Continent from Ulster.

There were still, however, no great strides in industrial progress. Cairnryan Knitwear was set up in 1956 and shortly afterwards moved to Portrodie. An effort to attract industry was given a shot in the arm by the establishment of an industrial estate in Stoneykirk Road near the Galloway Creamery. The ground, gifted by the Earl of Stair to the district, resulted in combined efforts by the two local authorities and with the co-operation of local businessmen, a factory for children's wear was opened in 1964. Shortly afterwards it was followed by Trimfoot International, a firm of shoe makers who took over another building for the manufacture of Baby Deer children's shoes and in 1967 they had engaged on an extension and removed all their interests from Walsall to Stranraer.

... *Sustentation of our Leidges*

WHILE THERE WERE COMPLAINTS in 1617 of the amount of whisky consumed in the town, there was little control over the matter, for the beverage was on sale in private houses, rather than in licensed establishments.

In 1692 the Magistrates reported to the Convention of Burghs that "we vent about half a hogshead of seck and a butt of brandie yearly, we consume about ten bolls of malt, Lithgow measour weekly."

Magistrates in the seventeenth century, however, started to grant licences to sell ale to householders and as the trade grew some of the private houses became public houses and hotels.

No-one turned up for their licences in 1766 and when an announcement was made by hand-bell only one person made application to the Magistrates. In the following year the town clerk was authorised to issue the licences on his own. There were complaints of too many retailers of whisky in the town in 1771.

Stranraer as the chief town in the district had a lot of visitors which perhaps was the root cause of the amount of drinking. In 1790 nearly 25,000 gallons of whisky were imported into the town and £5000 was drawn by the State. "The health and morals of the people are much hurt by the pernicious habit of dram drinking and they are of more importance than the proceeds of taxes", stated the writer of the Old Statistical Account.

Many of the early hostelries were around the sea front, such as the Downshire Arms which dated back to 1749. It was demolished in 1965 and replaced by a modern and up-to-date public house. In Fisher Street, the Crown Hotel was an unusually old establishment. It was closed in 1958.

Lord Stair had a town house at the corner of George Street which later became the George Hotel. Owned by Benjamin Patterson in 1835, it was modernised in 1967 and extensions are planned which will restore the ground used formerly for stables and yards. The hotel was sold in 1891 for £10,000 and improvements made in 1899. The stables became obsolete and were sold to a private firm for garage extension.

Oldest of the hotels still extant is the Buck's Head Hotel, which was rebuilt in 1762 almost in the same situation. It became ruinous in 1863 and was torn down along with several private dwellings nearby in Hanover Street and re-erected a few yards farther west. It was altered and extended in 1922 and is also undergoing reconstruction at present.

The old Bay Horse Inn, in Hanover Street, was pulled down in 1880 and replaced by the Royal Hotel, the name of which was changed in 1967 to The Robert Burns Hotel, and in the same year (1880) the County Hotel was built in Castle Street at the north end of the "Free Press" offices; it subsequently became a shop and offices.

Opposite was the King's Arms Hotel, formerly an old coach house which passed into the hands of the MacRobert family in 1847 and remained in their possession until a few years before it was demolished in 1959 and the site is now occupied by a large store. The Auld King's Arms was for many years the leading hotel in the town and its demise was a matter of considerable regret. There were no fewer than 37 feus connected with the site which in itself showed its antiquity as well as its inability to be satisfactorily modernised.

There were 23 licences issued in 1806 and in 1869 there were 51 licensed premises in the town, a number which again caused grave misgivings to those in authority as they considered "it is far in excess of the requirements". Sunday drinking increased to an alarming extent in 1884. A temperance poll in 1923 resulted in a substantial majority for "no change" and the poll was not repeated.

By the middle of the nineteenth century there were, in addition to these larger establishments, Meikle's Hotel, in George Street, and o p p o s i t e was the Albion; the Eagle Hotel, in Queen Street, which later became the offices of the Parish Council and subsequently passed into the hands of the County Council. In Market Street there was the Anchor Inn, and in Agnew Crescent, Lochryan Hotel which remained, as a non-licensed hotel, until the middle of the present century. The Queen's Arms Hotel was at the foot of Queen Street and became in course of time the offices of the Education Committee, and the Antrim Arms was opposite the Gas Works, in Harbour Street. The Commercial Hotel, in North Strand Street, was built in 1863, and other old premises were the Stair Arms Hotel at the corner of Bridge Street, the Grouse Inn in Church Street, and the Grapes Hotel which became a coaching house for the Portpatrick-Dumfries service. There were other public houses in various parts of the town.

A welcome addition to the hotels in the town came in 1962 when North West Castle, purchased by a local family of McMillans, was converted into the most modern hotel in the district. Subsequent additions were made and the hotel, fronting the Railway Harbour, became not only a landmark to visitors coming from Ireland but an important addition to the social amenities of the town.

There are 13 public house licences in the town, four licensed hotels and two licensed restaurants in 1967, five full off-sale and two partial off-sale licences.

...Increase and be made more

A N INDICATION OF THE TOWN'S PROSPERITY and its possibilities could be gained from the number of banks.

Longest established of these is the Bank of Scotland. Formed in 1695, it spread to Stranraer, as the Glasgow Union Banking Company in 1832. After a few months, owing to gross mis-management of its affairs, the branch was closed but was re-established in 1837 and became the Union Bank of Scotland in 1843 and in 1956 the Union Bank became one with the Bank of Scotland.

The year 1863 was the busiest for banking. Unsightly buildings in Hanover Street gave way to the Clydesdale Bank, "a decided novelty and greatest improvement in style of house building." The bank was built on the original site of the Grapes Inn which was removed to the opposite side.

In the same year a Savings Bank was tried, unsuccessfully, but its successor, the first bank to be built in Stranraer this century, was opened in Castle Street in 1964.

An old house opposite the court house in George Street was demolished in 1866 to make way for the British Linen Bank which had arisen out of the tobacco trade in 1740. Offices of the ill-fated City of Glasgow Bank which went into liquidation in 1883 became in 1897 the home of a solicitor who was subsequently town clerk. Between the King's Arms Hotel and St. Andrew Street there was for a time a branch of the Edinburgh-Leith Bank.

In 1874 the Commercial Bank building was erected in Bridge Street, permission being given to build over the burn; an amalgamation took place with the National Bank, in North Strand Street, but both branches have continued independently until the present. The Royal Bank is almost directly opposite the National Commercial Bank in Bridge Street.

... Let there be light

GAS PRODUCTION is one of the oldest industries in the town. Stranraer Gas Company, a private undertaking from 1826 to 1948, started off in humble circumstances and under grave difficulties. Gas works were created in Harbour Street and in 1829 the first gas lamps appeared. Land on the shore was sold by the Council to the company in 1839, Mr Alexander McNeel-Caird acting for the company, and in 1840 permission was given to lift pavements and lay down gas pipes.

By virtue of an agreement, the shareholders agreed to endow the new Academy School with profits in excess of 7½ per cent. This consumed for several years much of the income so that the company was not able to forge ahead, though progress was steady. The company in 1862 paid £500 in full discharge of the obligation towards the Academy. In 1845 the Magistrates agreed to put gas lighting in the court house. By 1846 the number of gas lamps in the streets had risen to 60 and more were added along the sea front, right up to Sheuchan Mill. The cost was met by public subscription. The improvement was considered most gratifying, "people could walk about the streets unmolested." The valuation of the plant was raised in 1871 from £90 to £200. In 1880 the Council appealed to the company to bring down costs and to some extent the company complied though they continued to erect more lamps in the streets. In 1885 they made a gift of all the gas consumed in the town during the visit of the Prince of Wales. There was a slight drawback to progress when in 1887 there was an explosion of gas in North West Castle, but in 1902 a big lighting scheme was carried through.

Money continued to be tight and in 1907 so many were the complaints as to the cost that people returned to paraffin lamps. There was a proposal in 1908 that the Council take over the works.

Public lamps had not been erected in Stranraer until 1802 when the council met in Mrs Taylor's house to consider the proper regulations to be adopted for erecting public lamps throughout the town.

Somewhat half-hearted efforts were made to improve the quality, without much success, and there were continued complaints up to and through the First World War years and, indeed, into the 'thirties. As nationalisation threatened, in 1939, the shareholders saw no reason for putting money into the undertaking which by this time had been challenged by electricity. Since 1948 and under nationalisation gas has been restored to a great measure of public approval though it is no longer used for street lighting, and only now to a limited extent for house lighting.

But gas has more than held its own with its younger rival in the matter of heating and cooking and a new retort house was built in 1950 and other improvements are at present in progress.

As early as 1883 lectures were being given on electricity and the possibilities of the new power for light and heat. In 1900 the Town Council agreed to a report that electricity was cheaper for lighting purposes than gas. There was considerable debate on the subject of introducing the new method, but as local people were shareholders in the gas company there was, to say the least, quite a formidable body in opposition. In 1929 it was tacitly decided to change over the street lighting system to electricity. The Council, exponents of the scheme at this time, were not concerned so much with the method as with the means. In 1931 electricity bought from the grid was supplied by a private company to Stranraer, Provost Waddell turning on the current officially at a public dinner.

This system was also nationalised and is run by the South of Scotland Electricity Board with much acceptance.

... And better service

WITH SO MANY SPRINGS and burns in the district, the problem in the early days of the burgh was not a water supply, but rather the necessity for getting id of the surplus.

From the earliest times the residents were ordered to keep the water courses :lear, though as the population grew, so did the necessity to bore more wells. In 1793 a spot was fixed at Burnside near the foot of Princes Street, for a well for he people of the area. The dues were paid off by the Council and amounted to ?9 16s 0d.

Stranraer's first gravitation scheme was at the West Vennel (King Street) vhere a fountain was found and Maxwell and Alexander McDowall, brothers and owners of the house, with a civic mindedness unusual in their day and generation, offered to sell the land to the burgh in order that a cistern could be built and a piped supply made available for the people in the neighbourhood.

They also permitted a lead pipe to cross their land. To pay for this boon the Council opened a subscription list with twenty guineas.

There were innumerable wells in the town, one opposite Backrampart was known as St John's Well and it served part of the Clayhole. There were two more at Foreland Place and Archie's Well at Hillhead lasted well into the present century. There was another at Elm House. Pumps were laid down in 1839 in the Far Fey (St John Street) and at McCulloch Place, in London Road, now the County Library. Perhaps the most famous and certainly the longest in use was John McWilliam's pump, in Sun Street. Like that gifted by McWilliam, the Council has preserved Bella Moore's Pump which stands in the front garden of a house n Coronation Drive. Her name is perpetuated also in the housing scheme of Moorefield which lies to the west. A pump in St Andrew Street was put in order and one at Queen Street, which was fed from McWilliam's pump, in 1845.

Despite the preponderance of wells, the douce, canny Councillors maintained in operation a water cart.

With the completion of a new water scheme from Spoutwells in 1850, the townspeople considered their worries were over, but the reservoir ran dry and the water cart was pressed into service two years later. A well in Charlotte Street and McWilliam's everlasting pump helped to stave off a drought. The cost of the Spoutwells Scheme was 2d in the £ in rates. The ratepayers were far from being satisfied and their complaints grew in volume as the water supply declined. They objected to paying for something they were not receiving, and they were at that time paying one penny for lighting and the same amount for police purposes.

Those resident in Hillhead, Sun Street and the Clayhole were most indignant, for they were not included in the gravitation supply in any event.

The Council had successfully appealed for a repeal of the Act of Entail in so far as it precluded landowners from giving permission to local authorities to cross ground with water pipes.

Many of the springs failed in 1865 and the medical profession expressed their anger in no uncertain terms. The Council considered going back to the original reservoir on the east side of Stoneykirk Road, but a gravitation scheme from Dinlinnie proved more attractive. Though water pipes had been laid out in London Road, the lack of drainage created difficulties and a petition was presented to the Council by thirty residents; nine in Sheuchan Street also lodged a protest.

Sun Street householders joined in the chorus in 1871 and a new well was installed, but the workers had to dig down 70 feet before striking water. Worse, at Dalrymple Street they had to dig down to a depth of 110 feet.

Ultimately an engineer was appointed in 1880 to make a survey of the Dindinnie Scheme and by 1882 the new water works, costing some £12,000, were opened amid great rejoicing.

The rejoicing turned to dismay in later years. Filtration difficulties resulted and in 1896 the situation was so bad there was a door-to-door inspection to trace leaks.

In 1903, though Auchtrelure and Clashmahew reservoirs were overflowing, the quality was not so good and the Council started consideration of an addition at Dindinnie.

There were troubles in other directions; the Town Burn was polluted. Ground for a new dam was purchased in 1905 from Sir Andrew Agnew, but, far from being pleased with the development, the ratepayers, led by James McHarrie, presented a petition with 470 signatories in protest, incidentally calling on the Council to resign. John Lithgow humorously moved that the motion be not accepted, but he declined to vote in the more important issue.

The Local Government Board, which had been closely following the shortage of water problem in the town, expressed their displeasure at the delay. Pressed on one hand by the Board and on the other by the ratepayers, the Council boldly took action and proceeded with the water scheme. The sequel was in 1906 when at election time four of the supporters of the scheme, by that time signed, sealed and nearly delivered, did not deign to face the electorate.

New filters and an embankment were erected; the cost was reduced to £6000. At the same time, no doubt playing it safe, the Council erected a handsome new pump at the old Golden Well, in Seabank Road. A new pipe was laid in 1912 and two years later filters were increased.

Expenditure at Dindinnie proved well worth while. The supply was in use in 1900 for the first time and in 1915 the level was raised. The water works there served the people for upwards of fifty years, even though at times there were complaints as to colour and odour. When the demands became heavier, however, as the population rose to the nine thousand mark, the filtration plant became over-burdened. In 1955 Knockquhassen was purchased to augment the catchment area. A reservoir there had been erected in 1939 at a cost of £10,542. By 1962 the consumpt had risen to 820,000 gallons and appeals were made for the exercise of economy. Despite impending threats of regionalisation of water supplies, Stranraer considered a £60,000 scheme of augmentation of filters was necessary and slightly to the surprise of the Council, the Department, successors to the Board, approved, even though in 1966 regionalisation of supplies had become more or less an accomplished fact. In 1945 the Council favoured a county scheme but in 1966 preferred a wider area if they were not to be permitted to retain control. In 1967 the supply was taken over by the South-West Area Regional Water Board.

Flooding was a major problem until the 1950s but after several remedial measures were taken with the Black Stank or Bishopburn, the Town Burn and the Laundry Burn, the situation was eased.

... *And to collect*

STRANRAER'S FIRST POST OFFICE was in Lewis Street. Established in 1833, it was managed by Miss McMeekin. There was one letter carrier, William Buchanan McWhinney, who charged one halfpenny for delivery but nothing for reading the contents to the recipient.

McWhinney's livelihood was threatened by the penny post in 1840.

From Lewis Street the Post Office shifted to South Strand Street, then North Strand Street and thence to more commodious premises in Hanover Street in 1857 and later to Bridge Street. In 1879 it was on the move once again, this time to Princes Street. Whilst in Bridge Street the telegraph came and the Post Office engineers were blamed for damage to the Old Castle when putting up the poles. A subsequent move in 1898 to Charlotte Street saw another brush with authority for the Dean of Guild was unhappy that the Postmaster intended to live above the office. A joiner's workshop on the site was pulled down and a new building, erected by private enterprise, was let to the postal authorities. In 1964 the Post Office had its first home of its own when a corner site in Hanover Street was obtained and a new building erected in keeping with the importance of the service.

About 1890 when public demand was insisting on a better Post Office, the Council offered the Old Town Hall, but the postmen objected to working so near a graveyard.

The postal service in the area went back to 1662 when a sum of £200 was granted the people of Stranraer to build a sailing packet to maintain communications between Portpatrick and Donaghadee. The subsidy was later increased to £800 and Stranraer had the best cross channel service of any.

In 1836 a mail coach was started between Stranraer and Newton Stewart. It took eight hours for the route. The system gave way to the railways in 1861. The mail to Ballantrae and Glenapp was carried by gig and foot until 1869 when a three-wheeled velocipede was introduced. The remainder of Ayrshire was covered by rail. The rider of the velocipede, M. McNeillie, tried it out to Cairnryan then resigned and went back to Glasgow.

Stranraer became the most important telegraphic centre on the west coast, for all the wires from Ireland came through the Post Office. They were tested each morning and in 1932 a Repeater Station was erected on the Cairnryan Shore road for the receipt of Atlantic telephonic communications. They are descrambled and relayed.

A new Telephone Exchange was erected on ground at the head of Clenoch Street and behind Ivy Place in London Road in 1963 and in 1964 the service went over to the S.T.D. system.

... *Other things necessar*

FIRE WAS ALWAYS a hazard in the town in the early days, but it was not until 1878 that the council seriously considered setting up a voluntary brigade. In the following year a suitable fire engine was obtained and stored in the Old Town Hall in what had been the former exchange or market.

A raging fire in the Reformatory in 1878 found the hoses inadequate and the water supply insufficient. Workshops were destroyed and the houses opposite were threatened.

Among the first volunteers for the service was Mr Henry McPeak who gave over 40 years' service to the brigade as did his two sons, John and Douglas, and the latter, like his father, became Officer-in-Charge of the Stranraer Station.

Bellevilla House, then occupied by Peter McClean, Duchra, was burned, fortunately not seriously in 1880, in a year of outbreaks which included a warehouse in Bridge Street and Meikle's Hotel in George Street, and following a fire in a bakery in Castle Street, the firemen, a voluntary body, started to practise. Considerable damage was done to Sheuchan Mill and the Academy in 1894.

Additional hydrants and a four-wheeled manual fire engine were purchased in 1905. Mr Wm. Downie was appointed fire master at a salary of £5 per annum. The brigade was still accommodated in the store under the Old Town Hall. A serious outbreak in 1913 in the King's Arms Hotel, Stranraer, tested the equipment which was found wanting and again a fire at the Greenvale Laundry in Greenvale Street showed the inadequacy of the preventative measures.

The council committee examined one of the places which had been burned and another which had been so much damaged as to be a danger. The owner of the damaged property, John Hood, was hard to convince so the committee gave him "a few shillings so that he could get it sorted himself."

A new convener, in 1928, elected to test the efficiency of the Brigade and staged a practice at a house in West End. When the engine and apparatus arrived, however, the men were so exhausted by the haul that the convener decided the "fire" was out of control and suggested that the town and county get together and purchase a mobile unit.

An unsuccessful attempt was made in 1937 to have the brigade housed in more suitable premises but all that transpired was the purchase of a new tender and in 1939 the two councils came to an agreement that the Stranraer Brigade would attend outbreaks in the landward area of the Rhins as well as in the town; this was not an agreement reached without some dissentients. The brigade had moved to Ashwood Drive.

Subsequently more up-to-date equipment was purchased by the Joint Fire Brigade Committee when, in 1957, all fire-fighting equipment came under regions, though when the firemen moved to their new premises in Lewis Street, formerly the old jail and police station, in 1960, they were still a voluntary body.

... *And to contryve wayes and streets*

OBVIOUSLY, FROM THE WORDING of the Charter to the town "from the burn which comes from the Loch of Chappell to the Loch of Lochrayane on the east to the water gang which runnes to the Mille of Chappell on the south," the Magistrates could look forward to consider building of bridges if the burgh was to grow. That was one of their many functions. As early as 1693 James McMaster and James Lavor were hired to repair bridges upon the "Walk Mill Wattirgate" and upkeep same.

In many instances when houses were being erected the builder was permitted to arch over the burn or to erect a bridge. In some instances there were reports of people building bridges for themselves and being ordered to remove them.

Coincident with and complementing the improvements that had to be made to the roads, streets and bridges, was the necessity for improving drainage.

In 1704 "the magistrates and advisors of council ordayned the water coming down the Hill of Park to be diverted to come down the westmost side of the town and to prevent same from running down the High Street in respect of former times. The Westmost Vennel was the old race."

Dykes found wanting in 1720 were ordered to be secured by the inhabitants.

In 1725 the Council decreed that the Upper or Westmost Vennel (King Street) must be paved or court fines would have to be paid.

King Street was also known as High Vennel and latterly as School Vennel in the 18th Century. In 1774 mention is made of Burnside and Fey and Castle Court was termed Castle Alley until the end of the 18th Century. The district around the road to Portpatrick was known as Townhead and Swan Isle was mentioned in 1790. Bridge Miln was named in 1793.

Charles Robison, mason at Cairn of Lochryan, was employed by the Council in 1730 to rebuild the Bridge of Stranraer called the Bow Bridge. The bridge had fallen down and been totally ruined in the previous winter by the frequent excessive floods of rain. Robison, who "had the character of an honest, faithfull and diligent worker" offered to do the work for half-a-crown per day and to find sufficient caution to uphold the bridge for seven years thereafter, or at twenty shillings Scots per day without caution. The council had to provide all the materials, and pay the other workers. Robison was simply overseer, the first clerk of works. Efforts were made to obtain a grant from the Commissioners of Supply.

In 1781 an estimate of £5 15s was accepted from Andrew McComb, mason, for building a bridge at the foot of the burn and paving part of the street around it and Edward Wallace was appointed to make pavements at 2½d a yard, particularly in 1790 to the top of the main street leading to Portpatrick, the Council considering it to be in a ruinous state.

In addition to agreeing, in 1782, to make up the side of the burn at Little Bridge with large stones to keep up the road, the Council agreed to repave the Cross Street from Mr McKie's house to the East Vennel (Princes Street) and they also accepted another estimate for another bridge and pavement at the Widow Mathison's. Alexander McKinzie in 1789 was ordered to clear away stones he had dumped in the Town Burn which had caused a spate and damaged the bridge and burn-race. McKinzie had to pay for the damage. Other people were ordered to stop forming banks in the harbouring places of the burgh, it being noted that three convenient banks had been decided upon for the purpose of ease of access to vennels. The Water Bailie was given authority to remove all stones for the town's use. He was later authorised to remove all stones within the high water mark of Stranraer's shore as being hurtful to shipping.

A map of 1782 showed there was a wide expanse of sand from Balyett to the Broadstone. There was only a track round the east shore on the Cairnryan Road and there was no road after the Mill.

John and Peter McMiken were hired by the council in 1804 to widen, strengthen and generally repair the Town Bridge by Thomas McCree's house, leaving four feet open at McGrigor's corner for a passage. The passage around the bridge was to be levelled and the old street lifted from the east end of the bridge to the head of the East Vennel (Princes Street), the rise to be lowered to fill up the low ground as far as it would admit for levelling, and the new street to be paved anew. For all this the council paid £66 16s.

Roads into Stranraer in 1762 were almost impassable but the Carlisle-Portpatrick route, thanks to Oliver Cromwell, was in good condition. They were for the most part unbridged. The London-Portpatrick road, however, ran through the town.

A petition was sent to the Road Trustees in 1827 asking that they open up the Shore Road to Leswalt and Kirkcolm and repair it; the council pointed out the propriety of maintaining this road as a toll road. There were various other tolls around the town, but farmers in these two parishes apparently managed to get round both the road and the toll.

A new street was made when property on the "way to the shore" in Princes Street became available between property owned by Miss McMaster and Sir William Wallace.

71

In reply the County Road Trustees asked for a grant of £250 to assist in creating a battery at the Clayhole and to restore the road leading from the Quay to Leswalt. Stranraer objected vigorously to their road fund being used for a road outwith the boundaries, but they did in 1831 agree to the Road Trustees withdrawing a sum of £25 for the purpose of repairing the battery and the road at Ballgreen, the cost of which was £70. The council pointed out that the burgh was not bound to contribute.

A new road was laid leading from the Glenluce road to the brick kiln in 1841, later becoming known as Dalrymple Street. Mr Robert Brough, paviour, was given permission in 1842 to raise the leaden pipes from under the streets and to have half of them for his trouble of repaving the streets to the satisfaction of the council.

Stranraer planned the Breastwork between Fisher Street and Princes Street in 1864 and by 1902 had it completed, so far as the wall was concerned.

During the 1830s there was a scavenger in the town who was paid 3/- a week. By 1841 there was complaints about the lack of scavengers. In 1907 a street cleaning machine was bought.

A protest was made to Parliament in 1845 on behalf of the burgh and Clayhole concerning the Road Act. In the town itself there were by this time New Dublin Street and Millhill Street, also St John Street, St Andrew Street, Charlotte Street, Harbour Street, Chapel Street, Glen Street, Thistle Street and Rose Street. These all required repair.

Arching over the burn was a popular pastime around the middle of last century. A subscription was raised in 1847 to arch the burn between the two bridges in North Strand Street, the council offering to contribute £10. They afforded the same privilege to Alexander Rankin, in Stoneykirk Road, but did not pay anything towards the cost though they did gain some yards of public road as a result. They were more generous later when they gave the balance of £25 towards work at the foot of North Strand Street but they had obtained the money from a legacy of £100 from Provost McDouall. With a rare burst of generosity they agreed to contribute £20 towards the coping and cementing of the Clayhole Battery and granted £100 for the repair of the road between the Quayhead and Leswalt. The council had also given the freestone for the battery. In 1861 they extended the road from King Street to Queen Street, laid down earlier, to North Strand Street. In 1857 the Magistrates had acquired ground on the shore which they let to Thomas Adair for a ship-pond. Adair later created a saw mill at Burnside which in the twentieth century became a garage.

Stranraer made application in 1864 to the Roads Committee to manage the streets in the town and a rate of 3d in the £ was charged for upkeep. In 1865 James Millar was appointed Roads Surveyor and three other men were engaged to do the work; the police officer, John Wilson, was relieved of the duty as it was felt he had enough to do. Tarmacadaming was done to the road from the prison to Portpatrick Turnpike Road and from the railway station to London Road and Hillhead to Foulford (Glebe Street), altogether a total of six miles.

Later, in 1898, tarmacadaming was considered too dear. All the streets in the old town were re-cobbled at a cost of just over £2000 of which sum the Improvements Committee met £875.

Widening took place in Leswalt Road and at the Bridge at Sheuchan in 1875. Bridge Street was widened by taking back the Church wall four feet and a similar improvement was made at Ivy Place by the same means in 1897, and when property belonging to A. Alexander, draper, was obtained in George Street, the roadway was widened also. But the people were against tarmacadamising the streets and forwarded a petition to that effect to the council of 1875, and because proprietors of similar causeway might want the same, the council turned down a proposal to lay down granite sets between Castle Street and Church Street.

Storms had created havoc at Cairnryan Road in several winters and in 1873 washed away the original toll house at the bottom of the bowling green and in 1877 the turf dyke was removed and a wall erected. As damage had also been done to the road near the railway bridge, in 1870 the railway company were asked to bring up stones from Glenluce for its repair, free of charge.

After doing considerable work, Stranraer was claiming in 1875 to have the best paved town. It appeared an empty boast even at the time, even though in 1871 pavements between the burgh and Academy Road, in Lewis Street, had been made. For, so far as the streets were concerned, the council had to pay for a wag-gonette damaged in Lewis Street in 1883 and in 1887 for a pony which was hurt by putting its feet through a hole in Princes Street. They were also taken to the Court of Session over the death of a boy and while they were assoilzied the expense was quite considerable in defence of the action. A man was appointed to look after the roads and streets, in winter time, in 1888 and the following year John Nish, mason, was appointed Roads Inspector and Sanitary Inspector.

Petitions were presented to the council in 1885 for what were termed level crossings. Mr John Gordon, London Road, asked for one opposite the Original Secession Church; ratepayers in McCulloch Place wished one also across London Road, and the congregation of the West U.P. Church in Lewis Street asked for a similar convenience. The council's answer was to put a crossing opposite Stair Arms Inn, and one in London Road opposite Mr Rodger's house.

Broadstone Road was deviated in 1884 to the south of the works at Sheuchan, later the creamery; previously the road had run on the north side. A sea wall was erected at Portrodie, between the slaughterhouse and the pier, in 1890.

Cairnryan Road suffered considerable damage from high tides and a wall was erected to replace the fence. The road was practically reconstructed in 1898 and by 1902 was a new thoroughfare almost altogether. Lord Stair donated £200 towards the cost but there did not appear to be any approach to the County Road Trustees. A pavement was also made.

Cyclists found the new road a boon. Repaving was carried out in 1898 in the main streets, the contractor starting opposite the George Hotel and thence to Castle Street and Hanover Street. Despite a dispute as to the quality of the work, it was continued practically throughout the whole town. Stair Drive was created in 1890, and at the other end of the town improvements were made to the sea wall at Agnew Crescent and concrete footpaths, "a great attraction to the tourists," were laid. To the Railway Company, in 1895, there was a request to widen the sharp corner at the entrance to the pier opposite North West Castle. The request was granted but not until 1966. In 1895 the council was concerned with the con-siderable amount of damage done to the shore road from one burgh boundary to the other. They accepted an amicable settlement with regard to Broadstone Road, undertaking to make it up, if the proprietors provided and maintained a sea wall.

After the council had invoked the 1892 Act, new pavements were laid in 1911 but in 1920 the condition of the streets was said to be terrible. Many were tarmacadamed in 1926.

In 1932 the council agreed to rename certain streets following the erection of houses to the east of the Rock Garden, the street from Stair Drive created in 1900 and Royal Avenue, a much later adjunct was to have been called "Ross Drive" but it has remained Royal Avenue. The ground was used for many years as a market garden. In 1967 Ballgreen Cottage, the last remaining building of the original croft and one of the oldest in the town at that time, was demolished.

Vast new housing schemes, mainly in the perimeter, which resulted in the population being decanted from the town centre, kept the council busy laying many new roads and streets and fixing pavements.

With the passing of the Town and Country Planning Act the responsibility for improvements, not only to the classified roads, but to all roads in Stranraer passed to the new authority and a planning consultant was engaged, Mr Richard E. Moira, who made exhaustive surveys of the town and produced a report in 1955.

This formed the basis of vast schemes of redevelopment as a result of which there was a danger of the old town centre almost completely disappearing.

The characteristic of the shopping streets, which still roughly paralleled the old form of settlement was one of houses above shops, with a small number of offices. The side streets, King, Queen and Princes, had properties which were generally bad and in the neighbourhood of Hanover Square the situation was reckoned to be so poor that a huge area was scheduled for demolition and redevelopment. Sweeping changes were in prospect elsewhere.

Naturally there was a public outcry only allayed after many serious discussions between town and county authorities and representations from the residents affected. Generally the plan was approved in principle but certain modifications were made before that state of affairs was arrived at.

Public inquiries were held and the objectors hotly contested each item with which they were concerned giving ground only grudgingly. Throughout the early 1960s the topic was one of considerable speculation and agitation.

Compulsion had to be resorted to in some instances before the scheme of improving the town could be proceeded with, and the upshot was that certain properties were to be demolished in five years, others in ten, and the remainder in from 15 to 20 years.

In the midst of much welter and confusion the town council had their own schemes, one of which was to demolish the houses in Sheuchan Street on the seaward side, but this the Planning Authority was not prepared to accept. The council's view was that it would open up a promenade from the Breastwork to the Creamery and provide an outlook for the town as had been dreamed of for centuries.

Five properties in George Street-Charlotte Street between South Strand Street and Castle Street were demolished in the early summer of 1967. This was the main objective of the planning authorities for the immediate present.

...May not be hindered

THERE WAS AN IRREGULARITY about the pattern of Stranraer streets which, because of traffic problems, raised major questions of reconstruction and redevelopment in the old town centre.

Unilateral waiting was introduced in 1952 and superimposed in 1960 was a one-way system which was to be extended this year. A suggestion at a later inquiry for pedestrian precincts in the old part of the town has not, as yet, been followed up.

These problems could not have been foreseen in the early days, although there were problems of another kind. Bye-laws were passed by the council prohibiting horses being tethered to buildings and thus impeding the footpaths; but these were minor irritations.

When, in 1899, the first motor cycle sped through the streets of Stranraer it created considerable stir but nothing to the excitement engendered by the first motor car.

In 1905 the first motorist to offend the law was charged, a year before the registration for the town and county was officially fixed as OS which has remained the basic since. The County Council, as Roads Authority, imposed a ten miles speed limit (which was reinforced in 1916) and a census of 1909 showed there were 251 vehicles daily on Stoneykirk Road and 335 on Leswalt Road. In 1922, 278 cars were counted in one week on Cairnryan Road, compared to 37 in 1913, and in 1925 there was a 25 per cent increase. Apart from the two war periods, the numbers steadily and sometimes alarmingly increased. By 1952 there were 4631 vehicles registered, in 1965 there were 8014. Many of these were, of course, farm tractors which do not normally frequent the town, but private cars in ten years rose from 2765 to 4851.

To cope with the issue of licences, a taxation office was built at the New Town Hall in 1931 and by 1960 it was obvious it, too, was too small to cope with the immense amount of work. It, therefore, was removed to a building in Ashwood Drive which had been the former school and was subsequently the Labour Exchange.

Parking was a problem as early as 1929 when many proprietors were encouraged to cut away dangerous corners. Vehicles were prohibited from remaining in the streets and were directed to the Breastwork. A one-way system was inaugurated in 1930 on a small scale and later developed, and after an attempt to have 'Halt' signs in 1938, a waiting time restriction for vehicles in the streets was enforced in 1939. This was rather more rigidly observed in 1950 and in the years following.

Extra parking spaces were provided by the Town Council in 1950 at Hanover Square and North Strand Street, but these were being taxed beyond capacity in later years and the problem was met, in a different way, by the provision of garages when municipal housing schemes were being erected in the 1960s.

... For commerce and traffique

STRANRAER WAS SWEPT into the vortex of the railway mania which roused the country in the middle of the nineteenth century.

At the outset the burgh was rather bypassed but when the first train steamed into the Town Station in 1860 the excitement was intense. The first engine had arrived in Stranraer in 1859, prosaically, brought by sea. Portpatrick was the terminal for the Carlisle route to Belfast but it was obvious that Stranraer would soon make a claim. The potentialities of Lochryan were very much in view.

In 1845 the Council had petitioned Parliament in support of the Glasgow, Dumfries and Carlisle railway line and the following year plans for the British and Irish Union Railway were shown to the council who sent a second petition to Parliament.

At the outset, the line from Castle-Douglas was to end at Cairnryan and throughout the 1850s the track was being laid. Belfast had considerable interest in the venture and a party from Ulster visited Lochryan in 1856 to see how the proposed line was progressing.

While it was agreed that Portpatrick, being the nearest point to Ireland, should be the terminal, there were promises that the new means of travel would not interfere with the direct steam communication between Lochryan and Belfast and the deputation was convinced it would be important to have the railway touch Lochryan.

Progress was made in 1857 both from the financial aspect and the actual work. The Belfast and County Down Railway Company had an interest to the extent of £15,000. Landowners were subscribing, as were the public, and an application was made to the South-West Railway for aid.

The first engine by rail came from Glenluce in 1860 and it was hoped that the line to Portpatrick would be completed that year, but bad weather halted progress. In February, 1861, the first train from Castle-Douglas arrived in Stranraer. A few days later it went on its journey to Portpatrick. On the outward journey the initial service to Kirkcowan was in October, 1860.

Stranraer had its bridge erected over the shore road in 1861 and there was considerable stir with ships arriving in the loch with cargoes of logs for the pier. The line to the harbour was inspected and passed a year later.

An amalgamation of the Midland and Glasgow and South-West Railway Companies was mooted in 1872. The South-Western, Portpatrick and Girvan Railways had been in existence since 1869.

But Stranraer had borrowed trouble. Portpatrick Railway Company asked the council to carry out repairs on the railway pier, and the council asked a higher annual payment to carry out the work. The wrangle which followed lasted until nearly the end of the century and resulted in heavy costs to the council who protested in Parliament against a Bill brought in on behalf of the Railway Company.

The council agreed to a motion in 1876 that a line should be built to Chapelrossan. Without funds, their support was only tacit for the proposed Rhins of Galloway Railway, a scheme which was not pursued.

Round-robins were held in the villages of Stoneykirk, Sandhead, Ardwell and Drummore. Naturally the people were in favour, but while the spirit was willing, the purse was weak. The income for produce and passenger traffic was estimated to be £3000 which was insufficient.

The Girvan-Portpatrick Railway was ready by 1877 but there was a hitch. The Portpatrick Railway Company, owners of the track between Challoch Junction and Stranraer, would not permit their rivals the use of the line to come into Stranraer. The Ayrshire venture was supported by Stranraer who wished two strings to its bow. They had favoured a line via Ballantrae and Colmonell.

Portpatrick Railway won its fight with Stranraer, the issue being settled, so far as Parliamentary action was concerned, in 1884. As security for a loan to fight the company's Bill the council pledged the Old Castle and the Old Town Hall.

Cheap excursions were run and there was considerable public support for the railways, so much so that in 1891 it was suggested there be a double line from Stranraer to Castle-Douglas. The traffic for the short sea route made heavy demands on the rolling stock.

Time-tables came under fire on various occasions. In 1898 the council agreed to request an alteration whereby a traveller could get to Edinburgh via Dumfries and back on the same day. There is no record if anyone did so. Other efforts were made in the 1950s for special trains, particularly over the New Year holiday time. The company obliged and six persons travelled! Following the change in system there were many objections to the difficulties of travel in the South-West and for the most part these were overcome by synchronising bus and train times.

For some years the Railway Company ran a coach to Drummore, a poor substitute for the earlier much-vaunted Rhins of Galloway Railway, but, as events showed, one fully justified, for in 1950 the line to Portpatrick, rather derisively termed a branch line, was closed.

Nor had the Company its troubles to seek on the Ayrshire route where the cuttings at Glenwhilly and Barrhill proved danger spots when there were heavy snowfalls. The worst of these occurred in 1895, 1908 and 1947. Horses were replaced in Stranraer for delivery of goods by the Scamel, an iron horse of much less personalised appeal. The last horse in service was named Clown.

After a long, drawn-out public inquiry in Stranraer following a report on the state of British Railways by a Dr Beeching who recommended closure of both lines from Stranraer, the decision in 1964 was to close the Dumfries line from Challoch Junction, thereby effectively putting an end to the Portpatrick line which had litigated so successfully against Stranraer.

The last train from Stranraer to Dumfries, via Galloway, ran in 1965 and the line was not restored even though agitations were stirred up in some parts of the Province for a reprieve. These lasted until this year when plans for lifting the track were completed.

Meanwhile diesels had been put on the Stranraer-Ayr route; the Dumfries train branches off at Ayr; and these, after birth pangs and troubles, settled down to provide a reasonable service.

After a hundred years, however, the railway bubble had burst and from a wide network created in the mid-nineteenth century was reduced for the most part to a system serving large cities and centres.

... *Better service and ministring*

CIVIC CONSCIENCE was often stirred at the poverty of the people, but not always shared by the public at large.

As early as 1720 the officers of the town were instructed to inspect houses to see if any of the families had not sufficient peats, turf or kale yard for their families during the winter and in 1724 the Dean of Guild was ordered to impound a cargo of meal from a ship lying in the harbour and to pay for same, because of a scarcity of food owing to the drought of the previous summer.

In 1767, the Magistrates met other persons and subscribed money to purchase meal for the poor of the burgh. They also obtained authority from the Justices of the Peace of the neighbouring parishes to impound meal in cottages and farmhouses in the district, on behoof of the poor of the town.

Vagrancy was common in 1800 and the burgh officers were ordered to patrol the streets leading into the town and "to apprehend all such who do not possess the town badge. Any inhabitants found serving beggars not having the badge are to be fined 5s and the town officers are to receive sixpence for every beggar they commit to prison." In view of the cost of keeping a prisoner the effort did not seem value the result.

Meal had to be purchased for the poor in 1801 and the council agreed to advance £50 for the purpose of relieving the distress of the necessitous inhabitants. There were other ways of raising cash. For instance, in 1806, because of the great nuisance existing of pigs roaming around the streets, the council agreed that "in the future the owners be fined 2s 6d for each transgression, one half of the fine to be paid to the informer, and the other half for the use of the poor."

Naturally enough, the Kirk was concerned about the condition of the poor. Rev. Mr Wilson, who was also an ex-councillor, presented an account in 1834 for £122 5s 4½d that the Kirk Session had expended on the needy. The council were not exactly overjoyed. They instituted an investigation to ascertain the state of the Poors Fund and the number of vagrants within the burgh who were getting permanent relief from the Session. Two councillors were appointed to act as burgh representatives in the distribution of the Kirk Session's Poor Fund. They also called a meeting of all the parishioners and laid the facts of the case before them. The council also agreed in 1840 that the poor "had enough to contend with in the high prices of victuals, without being cheated in weight and measure."

In 1843 the condition of many was stated to be desperate, they were ragged and destitute. Nevertheless, there were upwards of 50 appeals handed in against the assessment for the alleviation of suffering, by parties aggrieved at the higher imposition levied by the council. The numbers assessed totalled 500 and the rate was tenpence in the £ of valuation.

So desperate were the people at this time that in 1847 a lawless mob, as it was described, assembled in the streets and forced proprietors to sell them oatmeal at prices below market value. A proclamation was issued against such lawless behaviour.

"Martin's annuity" of £10 for the poor was vested in the Stranraer Parochial Board. Dr Robert Martin had been educated in Stranraer and on his death in 1773 had left the income from land in the Stewartry for the annuity.

A Stranraer surgeon, Robert Wilson, was presented with a testimonial in 1848 and £1000 for 35 years' service to those in need.

Soup kitchens had been established and were widely supported, presumably even by those who resisted the tax, and gifts of coal were being made. A clothing society was formed in 1856 to lend blankets to the poor in the town for use in the winter months and in 1865, in Stranraer, a further step was taken by the society which decided to supply the needy and aged men and women with clothes for half their value.

From 1878 onwards, 120 rations of soup and bread were handed to the poor every day, also coal and money donations and on New Year's Day there were special treats. This form of aid lasted throughout the whole of the remaining years of the century.

Houses were almost indescribable. Asses and horses were kept in the dwellings, deep litter for poultry had started, though not officially. Under such dreadful conditions it was hardly surprising that whisky was said to be the beverage not only of saints but of sinners. Stranraer Presbytery petitioned in 1847 against whisky and other refreshments being supplied at funerals.

Little action appeared to be taken under the 1895 Paupers Act apart from holding concerts for those in need. The Parochial Board did in 1884 raise funds to help to provide clogs and stockings for poor children attending public schools in town.

The county medical officer wrote in 1894, "The life history of the people can be summarised as follows—first, they are decimated on the threshold of existence, next, great numbers of the healthiest and in the most productive time of life leave the district, and some of the remainder live to a great age."

An instance of the latter was reported in 1862 when Archibald Nibloe's grandmother, who had reached 110 years, told her grandson she recollected her grandfather saying he had seen the fleet of William III sailing down the channel after leaving Lochryan previous to the Battle of the Boyne. A more remarkable instance was that of James Garrett, born in Innermessan in 1811, who was still at work at the Breastwork with his son, grandson and great-grandson in 1911. His father and mother had lived for 100 years and 103 years respectively.

An indication of the conditions in "the good old days" of our grandfathers is shown by the fact there were ten applicants for the post of roadman in Stranraer in 1888 and thirteen applications for three vacancies in the sanitary department of the town after the council had sacked four men to be replaced by three as an economy measure.

In 1902 there were 15 applicants for the post of lamplighter, and 28 for the job as slaughterhouse superintendent for which the wage was 18s per week. There were 23 applicants for the post of cemetery keeper in 1913; in 1921 there were 39 for the keeper's job at Stair Park.

By the turn of the century there was a considerable improvement, if not with regard to the conditions of the poor, at least in regard to their treatment.

Amongst the remedial measures which afforded relief, from a health point of view at any rate, was the establishment of District Nurses in 1905, a year after the Children's League of Pity had been inaugurated and which did much good work the following half century. Because of the high rate of infantile mortality, in 1910 the medical officer insisted on a link with the District Nursing Association.

A suggestion that there be medical inspection of schoolchildren in 1906, however, roused resentment and was not followed up until many years had passed. Dinners for necessitous children were started in 1907 by the School Board.

Ambulance funds were set up in 1915 and in 1919 a maternity and child welfare clinic was opened in a building to the east of the Academy.

Though conditions had vastly improved, still the medical officer was reporting in 1930 that there was worse poverty in Stranraer than for 16 years. Milk and meals were being supplied to schoolchildren, some of whom had not before tasted milk. The necessitous children created a big problem and the Provost of the Burgh set up a relief fund which, even in this day of Social Security is still considered necessary. The fund was augmented considerably by a bequest from a Mr John Simpson whose name is commemorated in the housing schemes to the south of the old town.

Free meals and free issues of boots and clothing were continued during the peace years between 1918 and 1939 and indeed since, for in 1944 the School Meals system was put into operation. The Milk in Schools scheme was started in 1922.

Aid was also given towards payment of rent and in many cases assistance was given towards rate relief, in some instances tenants and occupiers were relieved altogether of rates.

Stranraer had been declared an unemployment area as early as 1923 and various schemes of relief were started under the Ministry of Labour. Conditions were a repetition of the experiences after the Napoleonic Wars more than a century earlier.

As late as 1940 there was concern in the council at children being found begging in the streets.

Ground had been leased to Captain Alexander Gordon at Bellevilla in 1871 on which he erected a house. This became in 1962 the first Old Folk's Home in the town. It is under the auspices of the County Council. A club for old folk had been provided in 1956 at Coronation Park in Lewis Street by the Town Council.

Stranraer's economic situation, in 1967, was not, however, by any means rosy for there were in the area covered by the Employment Exchange one in ten of the insured population out of work.

...*Zeal and dilligent care*

STRANRAER WAS FORTUNATE in that, whilst only a small burgh, they had had the advantage of the presence of the Knights Hospitallers of St John whose self-imposed duty it was to look after the sick.

Following their disbandment there was no settled place for hospitalisation in the town until 1891, although the Public Health Act in 1867 empowered local authorities to establish hospitals. Patients in need of treatment received it, if they could afford the expense, at the Edinburgh Royal Infirmary. Glasgow Royal Infirmary accommodated the sick poor and, at times, complained that contributions from the Rhins were not commensurate with the costs involved.

Thanks to the initiative of Miss Cunningham, North West Castle, a small beginning was made locally in 1892 when a house was obtained at 68 Dalrymple Street for the treatment of injured persons and those suffering from non-infectious diseases.

It was most successful and soon the demand exceeded the supply. Largely through the beneficence of Mr George Garrick, Mount Vernon, a Provost of the town, a new hospital was built in Edinburgh Road, the name of the donor being commemorated. It is thought Provost Garrick's son was a doctor. At any rate when, in 1896, the Provost had reached man's allotted span, he died, and left £1200 to the treasurer of Stranraer Cottage Hospital for the purpose of buying or obtaining a new hospital. Stranraer Town Council made an annual contribution to the funds.

Provost Garrick was apparently a man of forthright character and speech and was not an endearing personality but his deeds far outweighed his speech. Work began immediately and the Garrick Hospital was opened in 1898. It was emphasised it was not to be used exclusively for Stranraer.

In a few years it was obvious the hospital had not sufficient accommodation but nothing was done until 1935 when a new wing was added, the money being raised by voluntary subscriptions and handed over at a fete at Lochinch to H.R.H. The Duke of York, later King George VI. More than £30,000 was raised.

It became apparent that a regular income was required to maintain the establishment and Rev Eric M. Nicol, then minister at Inch, suggested a scheme whereby a levy of one halfpenny per working person in the Rhins be collected. This led to the formation of a subscribers' scheme which worked very well until with the National Health Act, 1948, the administration of the hospital passed into the hands of the Dumfries and Galloway Hospitals Board. During its few years of existence the Contributors' Association had a membership of 36,000 in the South-West and contributed £150,000 to the hospitals in the area.

Local medical practitioners presented a scheme to the Department of Health asking for an extension to the hospital, particularly in the surgical wards and after interminable delays this was started early in 1967 when a new ward wing was agreed to contain 20 beds. One of the oldest houses in the town, dating back to 1700, Clenoch Cottage, was razed to make way for the extension. Earlier, in June, 1964, the first phase of the extension was carried out when a new kitchen was built at the Garrick.

In 1955, Stranraer took a big step forward in the treatment of the sick when a Health Centre was opened, on ground adjoining the Garrick Hospital. Included in it is a child welfare and maternity clinic, a function which had been inaugurated in Stranraer by the council in 1919 in a building in the Academy grounds.

It was only the second Health Centre to be established in Scotland, the first being in Sighthill, Edinburgh, and the example was copied in the succeeding years by many other burghs.

The clinic combined surgeries for all the medical practitioners, public health services and hospital out-patients' services under one roof. It remains unique in that it is attached to a hospital. Five consulting suites were provided as was accommodation for the county medical officer and county dentist.

...To combat disease

FROM TIME TO TIME, throughout the centuries, Stranraer had been subjected to outbreaks of cholera, there is a record of an epidemic in 1690, and of small-pox and fevers.

Patients were treated at home more or less, even in the years between 1840-49 when there were recurrent attacks. In 1849 when cholera claimed 300 victims in Stranraer, particularly from the Little Ireland district, there was an isolation hospital opened at Ballgreen. Objections were lodged by those who resided around Glenwell.

Under the Public Health (Scotland) Act town councils were empowered, in 1867, to build hospitals, but it was not until towards the end of the century that the Infectious Diseases Hospital was opened, and it was closed in 1894. Three years later it was reopened as Stranraer and Inch Hospital for infectious diseases. The Stranraer hospital was only half the size of that at Newton Stewart and it contained eight beds. It was meagrely furnished and had an uninviting appearance. There was a strong local prejudice against sending patients to hospital.

By a Sheriff Court decision the hospital was limited to patients from Inch Parish in 1895 but the medical officer of the time merely commented, "It is very little service to the district anyway."

Nor was it in demand despite a serious epidemic of diphtheria, the source of which was reckoned to be contaminated milk.

Incidentally, the appointment of a medical officer in 1891 showed that in some respects at least the county was not too far behind; only some 50 years after the Act was passed.

Negotiations for a new hospital dragged on for several years. The Upper District presented four sites—Rephad Farm, one in south, one in mid- and one in north Stoneykirk Road. The council wished the "present site." The Local Government Board became tired of "the excessive delay" and ultimately the issue was forced by an unprecedented action by the Burgh Medical Officer. The Council had thought the cost, £5000, was excessive but they later considered it would be better to spend another £500 and have a brick structure instead of the corrugated iron building proposed by the Upper District. The deadlock which had existed since 1900 was removed by the Board coming down with a hard and fast ruling.

There were difficulties of management and of payment, only solved by an approach to counsel for a legal opinion, a favourite method in those days.

Outbreaks of typhoid were alarming the medical officer, so much so that he made a direct approach through his profession. He complained bitterly about the state of the Town Burn at the north of Dalrymple Street, blaming it for the epidemic and also pointed out strenuously that there was no provision for smallpox cases. A minor irritant was that the burgh chamberlain would not give him access to official figures for his annual report unless he paid a fee.

The Board's complaint about excessive delay led in 1907 to a happy solution to the intractable problems, and the Clenoch Infectious Diseases Hospital was built.

There were difficulties for a few years afterwards, allegations being made of mal-administration and of parents unwilling to permit their children to go to hospital. In 1910 and 1911 epidemics of measles and scarlet fever closed the infant schools and taxed the Clenoch Hospital. A case of typhus was reported in 1927, the first for thirty years.

With the gradual improvement in conditions, and the removal or closure of old suspect shallow wells, the incidence of infectious diseases fell and the hospital was run down. A recurrence of minor infectious disease in 1939, due to environmental changes, wrought by the evacuation of schoolchildren from Glasgow, caught the authorities out. There had been few cases reported for several years. After a brief busy spell Clenoch was closed as an infectious diseases hospital in 1946.

In 1947, despite an objection by the doctors in the town to the site being used as a maternity hospital the Dumfries and Galloway Hospital Board decided to utilise it for that purpose. Stranraer Town Council had pressed for such a hospital since 1940.

Since its erection it has proved most successful and an extension to it is eagerly awaited and has been promised for 1970.

...In one whole body

CARE OF THE SICK, the needy and the poor, traditionally the responsibility of the Church, after the granting of the Charter, came more and more under the civil authority.

Alarmed at the condition of the poor, Stranraer Town Council in 1843 decided to erect a Refuge. They took over premises in Queen Street as a burgh poorhouse. A suggestion was made in 1846 by the Parochial Board of Old Luce Parish that all parishes in the Rhins should unite, along with Stranraer, to build a poorhouse, to be used by them all as the most economical means of relieving want and distress. The council agreed and petitioned the other Rhins parishes on the subject but it was not until 1849, largely through the instrumentality of Sir John Taggart, that a meeting of public-spirited citizens was called to consider what had to be done for the destitute. Mr George Guthrie "moved that the meeting approve, in principle, of a poorhouse for the Rhins".

All nine Parishes in the Rhins took shares in the laudable venture, later Colmonell and Ballantrae Parishes were included, thus encompassing the ecclesiastical area. Subsequently the Machars Burghs were embraced, which parallels the present Presbyterial bounds of the district.

Siting of the poorhouse was a problem. For a time the "Graineries" in London Road were favoured; others considered the Gallowhill was more suitable. No doubt the situation at the Gallowhill appealed to those who smarted under the imposition of a tax for the relief of the poor. However, by the casting vote of the chairman the present site was accepted. There, in Dalrymple Street, which was then sufficiently far out of the main stream of the town as not to give offence to many, the poorhouse, then termed a workhouse, was built in 1850 at a cost of £4209 including furnishings, which was based on £10 a billet. Very few of the livingrooms were plastered. It was run by a united board.

Accommodation was provided for the industrial schools for both boys and girls until 1859. There was room for 300 inmates but in 1854 there were only 30. But after harvest there was usually an influx.

More enlightened people considered the poorhouse had the appearance of a prison, a view emphasised by the decision to erect a high wall around it, for the purpose, it was rather ingenuously said, of shielding the inmates from the sun!

The wall, erected in 1871, remained for many years.   At least none of the inmates suffered from sunstroke, but when it was lowered considerably, there was revealed to the public an excellent garden, carefully tended and one of the sights of the town in the middle twentieth century.

By 1906 there were 134 inmates; the average cost of their keep was 5s 3½d a day.

With the passing of the Local Government Act of 1929, the administration of the Home, which had been the responsibility of the parochial boards until 1895, and the parish boards subsequently, became a matter for the Wigtownshire County Council.

Public opinion was slow to change, however, and the Home for a generation or more later was still not exactly enticing.   The old stigma was hard to remove despite the fine work by successive Governors and Matrons.   The poorhouse gradually has been used more and more for geriatric patients, those suffering from mental ill health had been removed elsewhere to Dumfries.   Within prescribed limits the conditions at the Home were gradually improved, until at present, largely through the insistence of the medical profession, there are plans made for extensive alterations and improvements to bring the Home, now termed Waverley Home, into line with modern thought and views.

... For ease of our leidges

PUBLIC HEALTH did not become a matter of great concern until 1848 when a new Act promised to sweep away nuisances; it was repeated in 1867 when more stringent powers were given to local authorities.

In the meantime the Magistrates had been taking whatever steps they could, using their own powers, and occasionally that of the Dean of Guild, to remove the more offensive matters affecting the town.

Ex-Provost Andrew McCredy was given permission in 1712 to stack gritts and turf on waste ground next to John Ross's house on the foreland and to build a house.

There were complaints in 1724 of a midden opposite Dr Crawford's door and the council decreed that no one was to put ashes or dung opposite the surgery. In 1767 they ordered all peat and turf stacks and dung to be removed from the streets and decreed that no rickles of stones or heaps of ashes were to be left. The Magistrates expressed disgust with the dirt and nastiness of the burgh caused by slovenly people.

New orders for carting of coal and peat within the town were posted at the pump well at the Cross in 1795.

Mr Colin Ritchie, Culmore, bought the right to the town dung for £5 in 1802. The council were rather more concerned about keeping the streets clean rather than making money. They did, maintain, however, that the wrack remained the property of the townspeople. Shaking of carpets upon the streets of the burgh was prohibited in 1808. In 1844 a committee was appointed to remove nuisances and to promote the cleanliness of houses in the burgh, thus preventing the spread of contagious disorders.

The Act of 1867 also empowered the council to supply proper water and drainage. Curiously enough, the number of scavengers in the town was reduced to two. Their job was to clear away ashes and manure. An Inspector of Nuisances was appointed in 1875. By 1905 the medical officer was able to report that the condition of the houses of the working classes had greatly improved and that their sanitary arrangements were better than some of the more commodious and self-occupied villas. He did complain, however, that the practice of feeding cake to cows was having a deleterious effect on infants.

Disquiet was caused by the condition of Stranraer's Town Burn. In 1848 a petition of complaint was presented to the council about the effect of Messrs Rankin's farina mill on the burn. For many years at the turn of the century the council and the Galloway Creamery were at loggerheads regarding the discharge of whey and other effluent into the burn. This, in fact, led to a Court of Session action and interdict being granted against the Creamery. In 1900 it was stated the burn was filthy. The medical officer approached the medical board on the matter.

This bother was not cleared up entirely for 30 years until Stranraer had laid down more sewage pipes. A big sewage scheme was carried out in 1952.

Pigs were ordered to be removed from near dwellinghouses in 1903 but in 1927 there were still 100 pigs kept in the burgh. From the turn of the century, until Stranraer put on hand its own cleansing department, the cleaning of the streets was done by private enterprise, the council employing a man, his horse and his cart. The burgh surveyor produced figures in 1928 to show it was 6s 7d a day cheaper to have two horse refuse vans, rather than one motor vehicle.

... As shall be needfull

WITH RISING POPULATION, Stranraer was soon faced with the necessity for extending burial grounds. The oldest was, naturally, that at the Old Parish Church in Lewis Street and as other churches were established there was normally a cemetery in the vicinity — at Thistle Street, London Road, Dalrymple Street and Bridge Street.

In 1729, however, before the churchyards were provided, Lord Stair, when approached, gave ground lying between two fields at Ballgreen. Voluntary contributions were to be made by the inhabitants. Each person who paid 5s or delivered two boatloads of stones would be given a piece of ground therein. For 2s 6d and one boatload of stones a slightly less area was to be provided. A dyke was to be built and faced with stones and pillars for a gate. Any deficit was to be met by the town. Part of the cemetery was to be laid out for strangers whose friends paid for the burial and a free part was for the military. A part was also to be left for the poor who were to be buried gratis and if any inhabitants buried strangers in their burial place they were to be fined £3 Scots.

Plans of a new burial ground were laid before the Council in 1788.

Lord Stair granted a piece of ground on the new road (Dalrymple Street) leading from the Glenluce Road to the Brick Kiln for a burying ground. He also gave ground, in 1848, at Clenoch Hill and Mr Agnew gave a piece of ground just north of Sheuchan Church for the same purpose, a condition being that the view of windows of Park House be not obstructed by trees or buildings. Fees were fixed for the new cemetery in 1850. John Hood, church officer, was appointed sexton and William Galbraith, session clerk, registrar. Mr Galbraith later became registrar for the whole district, under the new statute of 1854.

The cemetery at Sheuchan was extended in 1893.

A new cemetery was suggested at Springbank Plantation-Liddesdale but the Council in 1910 agreed to use the kirk field at Gallowhill mid-road, opposite the Trotting Track. The Glebe Cemetery, as it is called, was extended in 1965.

...In favour of whole communitie

READINGS AND RECITALS formed the main cultural activities in the early days of the town's history as a burgh.

Public announcements of these were made from the old Mercat Cross. Stranraer had its first band in 1840. By 1855, with the increase in literacy, more interest was taken in world affairs. So much so that there were complaints from the public that the only place where there was a newsroom was in connection with a billiard saloon. This saloon, however, was the forerunner of the Athenæum which started in 1850 when the Mechanics Institute was taken over. The meeting place was the Old Castle. A new reading room was set up in 1857 in North Strand Street following the removal of the Post Office. It was mainly for the working classes. Newspapers were provided and the charge was one halfpenny per visit, or 2s 6d a quarter.

When the Athenæum amalgamated with the Popular Lectures Committee and the Theological Library Committee, there was a much stronger body which removed to the Old Town Hall. The Athenæum remained there until 1966 when it ceased operations.

A coffee house for Stranraer workmen was opened in 1878 and the following year penny readings for the poor attracted large attendances in the Old Town Hall; each person who paid was contributing to the poor. Seven years earlier the Good Templars was formed. They met in the Old Town Hall and paid one shilling for the use of gas. Latterly they had premises of their own in Bridge Street but the branch has not functioned since 1946. The Good Templars were preceded in 1863 by the Band of Hope.

The Y.M.C.A. had a branch in 1883; but neither of these organisations has been active for many years.

Stranraer Dramatic Society was formed in 1891 when a Burns Club was also born. The Burns Club has long since disappeared but the Dramatic Society continued until the Second World War and after a few years in abeyance was resuscitated in 1966.

In 1898 a Literary Association came into being and continued intermittently during the next 50 years when it was superseded by the Stranraer Literary and Debating Society.

For a time after 1899 there was a Fife and Drum Band but it was connected with the Volunteers and it vanished before 1914. A Town Brass Band was formed with 15 members under Aaron Sisson in 1910. Five of the members resigned after the first practice. It was disbanded during the war. It is again in operation.

Attempts were made in 1904 to revive the Choral Union which had lapsed some years after its origin in 1883; there had been a Choral Union and Orchestral Union ten years earlier. In the years before the First World War, and afterwards, there was a revival in the Orchestral Union and again after 1946 there was considerable interest shown, so that in 1967 there was a membership of 40.

Spurred on by the Wigtownshire Musical Association, reformed during the years of the Second World War when "Let the People Sing" became a happy phrase, and by the Stranraer Music Association, also a revival of an earlier body, the Education Authority gave music a fillip by the appointment of music organisers. One result of these appointments was the Music Festival in the town which, though aimed mostly at schoolchildren, was not without its attraction for adults.

At present the Festival runs for seven days and two evenings. Stranraer Music Association were surprised and gratified when in 1945 every available seat was taken for a performance of the "Messiah."

In 1908, with the growing interest in the theatre, St Andrew's Hall became the mecca, and local pantomimes and other entertainments therein were largely patronised for many years. The hall was closed during the years of the Second World War and never reopened. During its comparatively short life before the war years, Stranraer Amateur Operatic Society, which has since been revived, performed "The Mikado" and other Gilbert and Sullivan works.

An event of some importance was Pinder's Circus which appeared at the Breastwork in 1889 and a visit of Buffalo Bill's Wild West Show around the same time created considerable stir. At intervals since there have been other circuses but the only one of note was Bertram Mills which drew large attendances when it pitched at Stranraer before making a tour of Ireland in 1960.

Whilst the live theatre, as it became known, and the Amateur Orchestra faced competition from the new-fangled radio, there were more insidious and fearsome competitors. Animated pictures were first shown in Stranraer by a Mr Green in a tent on the Breastwork around the beginning of the century and eventually there were two picture houses, one in Queen Street and one in St Andrew Street, both one-storied.

The Empire in Queen Street became a theatre but for various reasons was closed, but the New Kinema, as it was termed, after it had been rebuilt in St Andrew Street, had opposition from a rival in Dalrymple Street, the Regal. It was erected on part of the site of the Stranraer Reformatory and was opened in December, 1931. It had the latest talking picture installation, the New Kinema having been converted to the remarkable new technique earlier in the same year. Four years later the New Kinema was modernised and enlarged. In 1966 it was closed so far as pictures were concerned. The Regal still remains.

Main reason for the closure was the big change in habits of the people, by the progress made with television which from its reception in Stranraer in 1951 has grown to such a stage that it is the exception not to have a set installed.

For a time the new medium threatened to overwhelm all other forms of entertainment but again largely because of the interest of the Education Authority and the teaching of music, singing and dancing in schools, new generations of entertainers have arisen to fight off the threat of total extinction of cultural activities in the town.

Having overcome the bogey of television, local cultural associations found another enemy, that of a game of chance termed Bingo, based on an old Army game, which became a craze in 1962. This attracts hundreds nightly to various halls in the town and withdraws their support for things musical to a considerable extent. In the early 1950s, it appeared for a time as though the people had lost their interest in reading. A County Library, with its headquarters in Stranraer, had been started in a small way in 1921. A mobile library was put into the country districts, not served by any of the many sub-branches, in 1963 and in 1964 the library had to be extended so great had the demand become for reading material.

The library is now one of the main centres of the town and caters for all tastes, from the very young to the elderly. It has, too, a most interesting museum attached which contains relics of the town and district in profusion.

...And to collect, intromitt with, and apply the customs

STRANRAER HAD NO LITTLE DIFFICULTY collecting and intromitting the customs of the burgh, particularly in the early days, nor was the town exchequer ever in a prosperous state, except for once.

In their report to the Convention of Royal Burghs, in 1692, the Magistrates intimated their common good amounted to yearly, £143 16s 8d, and that their debts amounted to two thousand and five hundredth marks of principall, the annual rent whereof "is payed by a tax on the inhabitants" and that they had no mortifications belonging to them.

They also reported that "all their publict works, commissioner's charges to Parliament and Conventiones, were all payed and maintainit by a tax on their inhabitants and that the two pairts of the tenements of the town belong to the heretors in the countrey and that the rent of their houses will extend to twixt thertie pound and fourtie shillings Scots."

The council paid yearly 400 merks, with four bolls of meal, for which the inhabitants were taxed, to the minister; the school master and precentor "hath two hundred merks yeirly out of the Common Good, and all other public servants are payed by a taxation on the inhabitants". They "had no casuall common good".

Five hundred pounds was the tax imposed for school master's salary, minister's stipend and other burgh debts, by the council of 1716. Two years later there was an increase of £100 but in 1723 the burgh had enough on hand to forego taxes; reason being there was sufficient funds to pay for the minister's stipend.

Repeated demands on the treasurer in 1833 led him to report he had not liquid cash to pay all. He was authorised to yield to the most pressing demands and the council decided to take action against certain unfree traders as an example to the rest. A committee was appointed to look into the burgh funds and when it was found there would be a deficit of £171, it was agreed to call a meeting of the inhabitants to put this to them. At the meeting in 1834 it was decided unanimously the stent master should ingather the funds. He was instructed to take extreme steps and to make no exceptions. In 1835 the treasurer was due £177 7s 7½d and the other debts amounted to £210 16s 2½d. A levy of 2½d in the £ was imposed on the inhabitants.

There was trouble in 1839 when Provost Morland, who was in charge of the Harbour Account, refused to hand over the money to the treasurer, claiming it was a separate account and also claiming that the account was indebted to him. A compromise was reached, the Provost receiving £60 and handing over the balance of £75. Curiously enough, the account had worked the other way; for many years, both before and after, the Harbour Account was aided by donations from the Common Good.

Though it was prescribed, an account 20 years old was considered by the council in 1871 and a compromise reached, half of it being paid.

There was a no-nonsense decision when the bank refused to carry an overdraft on the Harbour Account in 1875, the council simply changed the bank.

In 1832 the council instructed the treasurer to draw up an account of the burgh's income and expenditure so that the clerk could prepare a memorial on it for counsel's opinion as to whether or not the burgh had the right to impose a stent for the exigencies of the burgh upon the inhabitants.

This would appear to be the first budget. The reason was that "several in the town allege that we do not have this right and great difficulty is being experienced in collecting same."

Public conscience was stirring in the 1840s. An officer was appointed to look after the records of the poor, at a small salary, and the council met many of the inhabitants to consider the poor when it was agreed to levy an assessment of 8d per £ on means and substance for this purpose, one half to be paid by the landlord and the other by the tenant. But in 1844 it was found the amount gathered for a year had been spent in six months and the sum included £60 from the burgh funds. The council gave £40 to keep the fund going. The assessment was raised to 2s. A new method of stenting the inhabitants was adopted in 1845. The town was divided into five districts with councillors as stent masters in each, and the valuation was fixed on heritable or moveable property, capital or money, profits of trade or professional income, vested or realised.

... *Buying and selling*

STRANRAER HAD TO PROVIDE "ane market" for the benefit of "our subjects resorting thither, very convenient for the frequent trade, and also to others in buying and selling of all sort of victuall, merchandise and other things necessar for the commoditie and sustentation of our leidges".

There was an ordinance forbidding any others from holding public or private markets within the "space of four myles in circuit." The Charter also expressly indicated the market was to be held on Sunday, and that together with it, were to be held "two frei faires, twice a year, one of the twenty day of June and the first day of August".

Reporting to the Commissioners of the Convention, in 1692, Stranraer Magistrates indicated that they "have two yearlie fairs, each of one dayes containwance and a weekly flesh mercat on the first day of November to the first of January and no longer, and that the customs of both are a pairt of their common good".

With the closure of the Tolbooth and the Old Town Hall, markets were transferred to the Breastwork, and there for a time two auctioneers had their premises, on let from the council. Horse fairs were a regular feature and remained so until the mid-thirties of the century, still at the Breastwork.

In 1827 the Council agreed to a petition and prohibited the exhibition of cattle, horses or swine for sale on the streets of the burgh, but intimated that a piece of ground lately taken in by the town on the shore, opposite Milroy's Smithy, might be used for the purpose.

Glenwell Park had been tried without success and it was given over for a playground. In 1834 the Council, who still let the stalls under the Old Court House, were of opinion that these were bringing in too small a rent. Fleshers had combined and formed a cartel not to raise rents against each other. The Council's retort was to advertise the lets in newspapers in Ayr, Glasgow and Dumfries.

Subsequently the market was removed to Charlotte Street where James Craig was auctioneer before going to Bellevilla Road where John McDowall had been carrying one on in part of Glenwell Park and complaining of the children coming through from the playing field adjoining. Later the mart was settled in Bellevilla Road as its permanent home. In that year an attempt was made to change the market day, which had been discreetly shifted from Sunday to Friday. Thursday was the day suggested to make a straight run through for farmers, whose only occupation it appeared was to go daily to market.

The two free fairs continued on the dates allotted until 1829 when on the motion of Rev David Wilson the Town Council agreed that St John's Fair be changed from the first Friday in August to the third Friday of that month, to keep it clear of the week of the Stranraer Sacrament.

When it was revived in the 1960s, St John's Fair was brought forward to the last week of July. It had then passed into private hands.

The June fair became more and more a horse show and parade and was held at the ground offered by the Council right up until after the Second World War.

From 1896 onwards, what became known as the October Fair, has been held at the Breastwork, but it is a fair of a different kind, being maintained by travelling showmen.

The old feeing fairs on term days started to fade away with the mechanisation of farms in the district; a farmers' exchange vied with the auction mart as the gathering place for merchants and customers, in the twentieth century. It was situated in South Strand Street and replaced, in a way, the facilities once offered by the Council underneath the Old Court House.

Mr William Black, in 1835, proposed to build a weighing machine for the convenience of merchants, and farmers, at the Breastwork. The Council, who gave the site free, became owners of the machine as soon as Mr Black had received back in dues the cost. The revenue, so far as the town was concerned, was to be put to lighting of the streets and public places. James Craig, the tenant of the Market, used the machine in 1905 and for some years afterwards.

The Council provided a new slaughterhouse in 1870 and in 1905 closed Glenwell Park which thereafter they used for storage of vehicles and equipment belonging to the town. Glenwell Park, in Bellevilla Road, was one of the subjects of an inquiry in regard to town planning and the town's yard will shortly be removed to the industrial estate created in Stoneykirk Road in the 1960s. The slaughterhouse will probably also be taken to the same area.

...Granted all and haill that croft of land, with all fermes

SUPERIORITY WAS GRANTED STRANRAER, by the terms of the Charter, over the Merk Land of Marslawe, Saint John's Croft and all "fermes and feu fermes" lying within the bounds.

Holdings were small and mixed; oats, coarse barley and flax were the staple crops. The best field received all the manure. Though Galloway Nags were even by then famous, most of the farmwork was done by oxen.

While in the main the farmer's dwelling was better than many of those who lived in the built-up part of the town, their houses comprised two-roomed single-storey dwellings with bare earth and trampled heather for flooring. Thatch was removed at flittings but the wooden beams were often offered to the incoming tenant.

In 1684 the oat crop was almost completely lost and there was near famine in the land; money was scarce.

Sheep worrying was a problem as early as 1704 when John Lin complained to the Magistrates "that he had great loss and damage of his sheep in Refad by the inhabitants keeping dogs and these dogs going out and killing sheep." The Magistrates ordered all dog owners to kill their dogs unless they could prove they had use for them. Similar drastic action had to be taken in 1896 when sheep were being lost to dogs and foxes.

Nine-tenths of the land was still moor and moss in 1707. Fields were ploughed three years and rested for three years; barley and oats alternated as the main crop. Horses, sheep and goats were exported; sheepskins were a valuable by-product. Corn was thrashed by flail; when these were introduced in 1720, ministers preached against them as implements of the devil.

In 1723 the landlords threw crofts together to make for larger farms. While no doubt this increased productivity it rendered homeless 1000 people. Many of them emigrated, Australia being the most popular. Grass and clovers were sown and fields were fenced. This did not apply as much to Stranraer as to other parts of Galloway. Married men who occupied clay hovels were paid £7 per annum and single men could be hired for sixpence a day.

It was recorded in 1766 that 600 to 700 bolls of oats and bear were exported from Stranraer to Greenock, Port Glasgow and Ayr. With the population of Stranraer at near starvation point, the town council took strong action. They suspended the town's customs until Martinmas because of the "terrible scarcity of meal" and enjoined the neighbouring Justices of the Peace for warrants to search houses where it was thought more meal was being kept than was strictly necessary for the farmer, his family or his servants. The Magistrates themselves purchased the meal and distributed it to the needy.

The farmers who had been forced to pay fairly substantial tolls were no doubt selling in the most lucrative market. The townspeople retaliated in 1777 by forming a co-operative. The tax on the boll of meal, weighed in the Tron House, was fourpence.

Turnips were introduced by Lord Stair in 1766 and he later encouraged the farmer to grow field cabbages. Potatoes were still practically unknown in 1786. Lime, bone manure and guano were being used fairly extensively by 1814 but the system was to manure only the best field. The importance of the introduction of turnips was almost equalled by the start of dairying in 1814. By the mid-century it was growing fast and excellent cheeses were being made by 1836 and Mr W. H. Ralston, Culmore, gave dairying impetus by setting up an advisory service.

A recession in the cheese trade in 1860 led to a second exodus of young farmers from the area; many emigrated to New Zealand.

Stranraer Town Council decided in 1802 to enclose 25 acres of land at Gallowhill which had reverted to them from Mr Agnew of Sheuchan Estate. Alexander Gibb of Little Mark obtained the let which was for 21 years at a rent of 15 guineas yearly. The tenant was obliged within five years of entry to lay down 1000 barrels of lime. The council agreed to fence off the road running through the land to the farms of Marks, the march along the burn to be a stone dyke and the farm to be called "for all time" Greenfield. Charter of Confirmation and Precept was given in 1821 by the Magistrates to various people renting lands at Glenpark, now called Springbank.

Mr Gibb was succeeded by Thomas Adair who, in 1825, was warned to be removed and the farm was advertised. It is not surprising that "Thomas Adair, present tenant, secured the let." The rent was raised to £19 10s. In 1829, to liquidate a debt, the farm had to be sold by the council.

Stranraer and District Agricultural Society took over the smaller shows and fair day competitions in 1832 and staged what has become an annual event. It has been held during the second week of the Glasgow Fair and in the early days took place on Tuesday or Friday or on a Saturday but latterly on Wednesday. Entries were not confined to members and landlords did their utmost to encourage house gardens by naming special awards. They complained, however, that no sooner was a shrub planted than it was uprooted; whilst it was almost impossible to grow trees so opposed were many people to them.

Nor was that the only difficulty; the old struggle between the town and country came to a head again in 1852 with the exaction of taxes, the root of the matter. The farmers claimed the tacksman was exceeding his rights. For milk carts, the toll was threepence, turnips were charged at threepence a load. So irate did the farming community become they suggested a harbour at Soleburn or Innermessan to cut out this iniquitous tax. In 1908 Kirkcolm farmers obtained their supplies by sea, goods being unloaded at Wig Bay, but this practice ceased in 1912. There were tolls at Cairnryan and Bishopburn. In 1866 the council considered it inexpedient to raise charges to farmers for the use of the weighing machine.

Stranraer Cattle Show was held in various fields in the town but after 1869 it settled for a time in a field, Ballgreen East, east of North West Castle. There was considerable interest at that show for Messrs J. and A. Douglas presented a reaping machine they had had patented. A few years earlier the Auction Mart had been established by a private firm, the Magistrates having until then provided the facilities at the Breastwork where the Horse Show and Fair continued for 50 more years. Peter McCulloch and Peter McCaig were given authority in 1869 to erect a mart in Harbour Street at the Breastwork on the east side opposite the gas holder and M. McDowall was in 1884 given permission to have a second mart.

Bone ash was in demand, it was exported from Australia in 1876. Agriculturists were becoming increasingly interested in fertilisers and Stranraer Harbour had a record number of ships in 1897 when cargoes were being landed in preparation for the sowing. The coming of the railways had greatly assisted the potato trade and crops were most profitable around the turn of the century.

Another relief was in 1903 when the Magistrates found that the income from the Customs was insufficient to meet the expenses of the tacksman and the duty was withdrawn. The custom had gone back to the seventeenth century when it was necessary to raise money "to pay the police, build a jail and fight the English."

More important, from the farmers' point of view, was the establishment of two creameries in the town. In Sheuchan Street a small establishment was set up by a group of local businessmen and farmers and it handled the milk, turned it into cheese and butter, and provided an outlet for the farmers' produce. It remained in private hands from 1884 to 1918 when it was taken over by the S.C.W.S. and considerably enlarged and vastly improved.

In 1899 the Galloway Creamery was erected on ground purchased from the Earl of Stair in Stoneykirk Road. The Galloway Creamery Company Ltd. became an incorporated company under the Companies Acts of 1862 and 1898 and the company reformed itself as the Galloway Creamery Ltd. With two outlets for milk, dairying became more profitable and more intensive, but led, incidentally, to fewer and fewer cheese-making dairies until in 1967 these had almost completely disappeared. In 1906, one of the foremost cheesemakers, Mr Henry McFadzean, took up a post with a Kilmarnock firm.

Life was becoming more endurable as a result of the introduction of the milking machine which was first displayed in the district at Glengyre in 1907. Forty kye were milked in 50 minutes.

In 1927 the farmers formed a milk pool and in 1933 the Scottish Milk Marketing Board was set up with Lord Stair as chairman. The Galloway Creamery passed into ownership of the Board at that time. Whilst dairying became more profitable other branches of the industry did not and there was a huge protest meeting against dumping held in the town in 1930. It might be added that before the coming of the Board the income from dairying had also fallen to a most uneconomic level.

Both creameries absorbed, in some small measures at least, many of those who were deprived of work on the farms with the changing of dairying and with increased mechanisation on the land, a change which was accelerated as a result of war-time which, paradoxically, but understandably, led farmers to go back to the horse for transport to a greater extent because of the shortage of petrol.

The Rhins of Galloway became quite famous for Clydesdale breeding but, as early as 1920, there had been a dispute as to whether or not the horse would be supplanted by the tractor and except for a short period during the Second World War the Clydesdale gave way to mechanisation.

Considerable alterations have been made of late at the Galloway Creamery and it is claimed, with some justification, that as a result of these it is now the foremost creamery in the country, if not in Europe. Alterations are not yet completed.

Part of ten farms are still included in the burgh boundaries and 95 acres are under cultivation whilst 78 acres are in permanent grass.

There is also a piggery within the town boundaries.

... *Slaughter, shed blood, or do injurie*

COMING FROM AN AREA which was wont to send its serving men into the van of battle, it was not surprising that in the intervening years Stranraer should worthily support the King's Colours, in peace, and in war.

An aftermath of the Bothwell Insurrection in 1683 led to fines and imprisonment on local participators and among those imprisoned was Sir John Dalrymple of Stair.

The fleet of William of Orange took shelter in Lochryan on the way to the Battle of the Boyne in 1690. The presence of the Navy gave cause for rejoicing in Stranraer but unfortunately a fever epidemic broke out among the soldiers and deaths were so numerous that it was said a man could scarcely walk from Stranraer to Cairnryan without stepping all the way from grave to grave of King William's men. For some time following a permanent Army was maintained in Ireland and soldiers were continuously arriving at Stranraer and by way of Knockglass to Portpatrick by way of the Old Portpatrick Road. To provide lodgings for the soldiers, many houses were built and the Earl of Stair had one on the site of what is now the George Hotel at the corner of Church Street.

For many years Lord Stair raised locally companies of Dragoons and these were accommodated, and their horses stabled, in premises along the shore front. On 24th March, 1725, sensible of the trade accruing to the burgh, the Magistrates considered the benefits and advantages to the inhabitants of the continued quartering in the town by the Earl of Stair of his Dragoons.

They noted that a great many of the inhabitants sold ale or liquor and could give accommodation to the soldiers, but had no stables "to entertain the horses." As there was waste ground lying at the shore opposite the tenements belonging to Andrew Fyfe and James Baird, the council decided to grant portions of the land for stabling. This was ground at the junction of Fisher Street and King Street.

John Semple and Gilbert Drennan, John McCaul, a boatman, Patrick Gibson, cooper, and David Ross, a ship's carpenter, all took advantage of the offer but none more so than Bailie William Ker who rebuilt the old house at the foot of King Street, a pretentious building which had double steps leading up to the entrance. Patrick McQueistone owned the house next door.

Some time in the 18th century, Alexander Kerr took possession of Andrew Fyfe's property and it became in time the Crown Inn.

Stranraer was not seriously affected by the 1715 rebellion, in fact, Lord Stair made representations to the French Government to prevent despatch of shiploads of arms and ammunition and other military stores from French ports for the use of the Pretender in Scotland. There was more excitement between the risings, for in 1733 there were so many troops in the district the council ordered people with horses for hire to make them readily available. Hiding the horses away was considered a reflection on the burgh.

The people of Stranraer had ringside seats on 20th April, 1778, but the expected naval engagement in Lochryan did not materialise. John Paul Jones, who, earlier in the month, had created havoc in the Solway Firth, brought his ship round to the Firth of Clyde and around a dozen merchantmen sought safety in the loch. The American captain, at the last moment, declined to follow them in where he could have created havoc, owing to a change in the wind which might have bottled him up in Lochryan and left him at the mercy of naval vessels known to be farther up the coast.

The townspeople showed concern when the French Revolution broke out in 1793 and when there was another uprising in Ireland the Wigtownshire Cavalry was raised, fife and drum recruiting 28 men in Stranraer. The Hon. Keith Stewart commanded the *Berwick* and raised 70 volunteers in the district.

By Act of Parliament, in the late 1790s, Stranraer had to raise ships' companies for the Navy because of the situation in France. The council decided to offer each man in the burgh who would serve, a bounty of 15 guineas. They appointed a committee to interview the men in the court house for enlistment purposes and authorised them to adjourn to any public house, if they so wished, while treating with the men. Another committee was appointed, cautiously enough, to assess the value of property in the burgh so that the cost could be equally spread over all the property owners.

For land purposes, the Galloway Militia was raised "to meet Haughty Gaul's invasion threat" and it was McDouall of Logan, the descendant of that doughty opponent of Bruce, who raised the standard. Lieutenant-Colonel Andrew McDouall kept his militia in being until after the Napoleonic Wars.

The militia was resuscitated in 1843 when volunteer companies were raised by the Earl of Stair and representatives attended the reviews in Edinburgh by H.M. Queen Victoria in 1861 and 1881 and by King Edward in 1905.

Stranraer Company was known as the 2nd Wigtownshire Rifle Volunteer Corps. They had a shooting range on the foreshore. In 1880 there was an amalgamation which led to the formation of the Galloway Rifle Brigade.

In 1855 Sergeant John Ross brought ever-lasting fame to his native town when he was awarded the Victoria Cross for bravery at Redan in the Crimean War. Sergeant Ross was born in Glebe Street.

Stranraer Old Town Hall was the training place for the Artillery and Rifle Corps; the Volunteers had used a field on the Shore Road, which became known as the Volunteers' Green. It was hoped it would later become a public park but it was lost in building operations.

The age-old connection with Carrick led to a unit of the Ayr and Galloway Artillery in 1892. They took over the Drill Hall in Bellevilla Road, the former U.P. Church in 1800. The Galloway Rifle Brigade had a big review at the Jubilee of 1897 and took part in the South African War. In 1900, troopers back from the campaign were honoured as were other returning soldiers in 1902; they were all admitted burgesses. In 1908 the Territorial Force came into being and the Royal Scots Fusilier Company was centred in the town.

At the outbreak of the First World War, a unit of the 5th Battalion the Royal Scots Fusiliers went from Stranraer and the town raised the first detachment of The King's Own Scottish Borderers. Volunteers for civil defence were enrolled in 1917 and again in 1939 when the Local Defence Volunteers, subsequently the Home Guard, did much good work. There were objections to the limited form of black-out in 1915 but none, curiously enough, in 1939-45 when the regulations were more vigorously enforced.

An air base was opened at West Freugh during the First World War and operated spasmodically until 1929. It was reopened in 1935 and two years later became a bombing range. There was a move by the Air Ministry in 1947 to close it but this was successfully resisted by the Town Council which feared the effect on the economic life of the burgh from which many of the employees were drawn. In the immediate pre-war years and, indeed, afterwards, an Air Display at the station attracted thousands of spectators but such displays have not been held for some time. The station was adopted by the council.

In the peaceful years between 1918 and 1939, Stranraer became firmly attached to The King's Own Scottish Borderers and maintained a unit until the call to arms in September. Through the Volunteer Army Reserve instituted in 1967 the name of the local regiment lives on in the Reserve Unit in Stranraer.

Before the cessation of hostilities in the First World War it was estimated that 1000 out of Stranraer's then 6000 of a population were in uniform. The percentage was no less in the Second which affected the town to an even greater extent, except, fortunately, in the matter of casualties, as the various war memorials indicate.

Not all who served, by any means, were in the local regiment.

In fact, Stranraer's first casualty was a boy from Princes Street who lost his life in a sunken ship and when the *Princess Victoria* went down, a victim of enemy action, there were five Stranraer men missing. By 1942, with many Stranraer men in captivity, the local council raised a prisoner-of-war fund, some of the men were prisoners for more than three years.

Meantime on the home front various funds were raised, the most popular being for Spitfires and War Weapons and Warships. The "Wings for Victory" and the "Salute the Soldier" Campaigns were most enthusiastically supported.

A canteen for servicemen and women was set up near the Harbour Station and the playing fields and golf course were taken over for a transit camp. Various detachments of the Army and Air Force were stationed in the district, and perhaps most important in the long run was the fact that many of Glasgow's schoolchildren were evacuated to the town and district. The experience was one that was long remembered both by the evacuees and the hosts, principally the hosts. An air raid warning was given in the town as the children were being accommodated in various halls prior to being introduced to their new homes. There were 1491, including teachers and helpers.

In general, Stranraer rallied magnificently to what proved to be perhaps the most trying of all war-time emergencies.

Various "Welcome Home" efforts were held after the cessation of hostilities and twelve Stranraer men, who had been honoured in war, were honoured in peace by having conferred on them in 1947 the right of burgesses. This followed the practice after the First World War.

...In no ways inferior

NOT UNTIL THE CLOSING YEARS of last century did the council consider Stranraer's natural amenities qualified it as a "holiday and health resort." There had been placed down bathing machines in Lochryan in 1864. Bathing boxes were provided at the east embankment of the East Pier and a bathing ledge was constructed in 1889, but in the same year the council prohibited bathing from the west wharf.

A guide, forerunner of the information bureau of 1967, was appointed in 1897, but his main duty apparently was to inform visitors of the beauties on the road to Portpatrick. In order to attract tourists, the council, in 1889, also decided to advertise in Scottish and Irish newspapers. But when a committee of the council was set up, only four of the 18 members thought it important to attend. The nucleus were, however, keenly supported by the Improvements Committee. This committee was revived for a time in the 1930s and did much excellent work before giving way to Stranraer and District Development Association which carried on for some years and in turn ceased because of the activities of the Scottish Week Committee which revived St John's Fair.

Little use had been made of Lochryan until the 'nineties but a slipway was thrown across the sawmill on the sea front and a concrete pavement laid down at Portrodie which were considered to be a great improvement to the amenities. A continuous promenade from the railway pier to Sheuchan Buildings was considered as early as 1906. In 1907 Sheuchan Land Company claimed the foreshore at Sheuchan Buildings and fenced it off; the council agreed to feu it.

But even earlier than that was a motion by Wm. Hay that Clayhole Bay be reclaimed. He wished it turned into a sports park but was slightly before his time and received little support. He tried again, three years later in 1896, but again failed to capture the imagination of the majority. Very much alive to the possibilities of the town, he was undaunted and in 1896 forced a vote for a golf course in the town. Again he was before his time. However, he did manage to get the town advertised as a health resort and a summer residence.

By this time a Bailie, Mr Hay came back in 1900 with a scheme for reclaiming the foreshore, still wishing it to be a public park. He attacked the smell which even then was emanating from the foreshore at Clayhole and which plagued residenters for several years in the 'thirties. As a result of his perseverance he did manage to get an active "Summer Visitors and Bathing Accommodation" Committee formed.

Music for the public was provided in 1902 officially and in 1932 the town band gave concerts in the Garden of Friendship while local pipe bands also provided music. The council borrowed £200 in 1906 to start the brass band.

Reclaiming Clayhole Bay remained a dormant dream until 1923 when serious consideration was given to a suggestion that it be enclosed by a concrete wall, the cost was estimated at between £6000 and £10,000. While no official decision was made, residents were encouraged to get rid of their rubbish and rubble on the shore at Clayhole, the slaughterhouse and Ballgreen on Cairnryan shore. Despite considerable opposition, reclaiming was started on a fairly extensive scale in 1928. The objections were more to the method, not to the principle. Agnew Crescent residents put up with a lot during the next few years until the work was stopped because of the strong odour emanating from the part being reclaimed. More sanitary steps were taken and a considerable portion of the foreshore, which had been a fairly extensive layer of sand, covering clay at one point, and at one period, was added to the town limits.

On part of it was created a Marine Lake, first suggested in 1930. After the council in 1957 had made big plans for tourism the Agnew Crescent Bay scheme was revived in 1959 when it was estimated to cost £77,000. The major part of the work was completed in 1962 and was added to as the years went on. Earlier the council wisely laid down a paddling pool on the reclaimed land portion, a small thing but their own, which became the happiest place in Stranraer for many years and still remains so. A proposal for a bathing pool was made in 1923 but abandoned.

So successful was this comparatively small improvement that it recalled the proposal of 1938 to have such a facility on the East shore and a second pool was laid down there in 1965 to be accompanied shortly by a shelter. The old bathing boxes fronting the diving board opposite Ladies' Walk had long since disintegrated and those at Broadstone and West End had been removed in 1927. Changing trends in fashion had probably rendered them obsolete in any event.

... *Being of deliberate mind*

CURLING AND FOOTBALL are the oldest games played in the area. Unlike curling, however, football waxed and waned.

First organised games were played in 1873, though Stranraer Football Club had been formed in 1869. In 1879 they met Cree Rovers in a first round Scottish F.A. Cup tie. The game was played in a field outside town, for until the early 1920s, the club had no settled ground.

The new body faced opposition in 1880 when Stranraer Rangers were formed but the youngsters were squashed in a match which ended in a ten-nil win for the official club and little more was heard of the side. A visit in 1886 of some famous footballers in a Glasgow Select sharpened the public interest. A regular pitch was found necessary and in 1896 ground at Sandmill on the Cairnryan Road was secured; in 1898 the club moved to the Trotting Track, now King George V Playing Field, James McHarrie permitting its use. The next move was to Rephad.

Lack of interest and difficulty in travelling caused the club to go moribund at the turn of the century, only one match was played from the New Year of 1903 to March. Thanks, however, to the indefatigable efforts of George Wade it was resuscitated. George Wade was still trainer in 1935. In 1908, when the council agreed to fence off a portion of Stair Park and permit a charge to be made, re-admission to the S.F.A. was obtained. When the enclosure was completed in 1932 they moved back to it, from the playing field across the road.

There was a flourishing period during the 1920s and in 1927-28 seven trophies were annexed in a season when Dundee played at Stair Park in the Scottish Cup. Dundee were the first of many well-known teams to visit the ground, Partick Thistle in 1938 were held to a draw and, ten years later, Glasgow Rangers won only 1-0 amid scenes of feverish excitement, and in 1964 the side made history by defeating Third Lanark, then in the Scottish First Division, by two goals to one. An Austrian team visited Stranraer in 1954 and a youth international also took place at Stair Park.

Stranraer made progress in the football league ladder moving through various grades into the Scottish Second Division but all through the years maintained their contact with the Southern Counties Football Association.

Their future was threatened in 1964 by a movement to cut down the number of teams competing in the national league and a legal action regarding league membership is in course of being heard. The club is run voluntarily by a committee with which James Murray has been connected for fifty years.

During the war years when so many servicemen were established in the district, and in the years immediately following, several players of renown played on Stair Park but without being invidious, and paying tribute to many stalwarts who had gone before, one of the most outstanding was a local lad, John McCutcheon, whose terrific shooting power earned him a fearsome reputation throughout the country. Unfortunately he was in his prime during war-time conditions but he gave many marvellous displays during the decade before the present one.

Apart from the senior club, and its reserve side, there was considerable interest taken locally in Summer Leagues, and latterly in Amateur League football. But the enthusiasm of the 1920s when there were competitions throughout the whole of the rural area was not recaptured after the Second World War and the game is in a slump at present so far as interest is concerned.

Cricket made its appearance in Stranraer as early as 1856 when membership was high, but was confined more to landed proprietors and professional classes. It died away in 1869 but in 1880 had a new lease of life. A pitch was obtained at Bowling Green Park in 1903 but again the game suffered a recession and it was not until 1930 that it was resumed.

By the introduction of cricket in school there was a resurgence in the years after the end of the war and there is at present in the summer an interesting league held at King George V Field. Games are also played against visiting clubs.

Bowling has been a popular pastime for more than a century. In 1845 games were played on almost any piece of flat ground available and in 1859 Stranraer Bowling Club was formed, playing in the east end of the town. Stranraer West End Club was formed and had their green in 1876 on a piece of ground in Sun Street, now occupied by the tennis club. There was considerable interest in 1879 when the first open tournament was played. Stranraer Bowling Club opened a new pavilion in 1903 but the West End Club were undergoing a period of difficulty, having lost their green. However, after a lapse of some years a new green was obtained in a field adjoining Sheuchan School and since its reformation in 1924 the club has had a fairly prosperous existence. In 1949 the members won the South of Scotland Championship. In 1950 an Australian touring team visited Stranraer and in the following year one came from New Zealand.

Golf was much later to appear on the scene. Proposals for a club were first mooted in 1893. There was an amalgamation between Stranraer and Glenluce golfers in 1896. Stranraer players soon found the journey tiresome and approaches were made to the Town Council which led to a motion in 1896 that a search be made for a site, but it was not until 1905 that a course was laid out, over nine holes, on ground given by the Earl of Stair and lying between Cairnryan Road, Ladies' Walk and London Road. It was later extended to eighteen holes in 1911 when the membership had grown to such proportions that the original three fields became insufficient.

The course was requisitioned in 1940 and was built upon in the years following the end of the war. Meantime, Stranraer had been left, by Major Garroway, ground at Creachmore and Drums Farms, to the west of the town for a golf course and after protracted negotiations between council and club the ground was finally laid out in 1951, the architect being James Braid, one of the greatest golfers of all time. The club owed much to Lord Stair for a very satisfactory financial settlement from the War Department, which was given through the Stair Estates although the club had been tenants only of the previous course. In 1967 they owed another debt, this time to Stranraer Town Council which provided funds for a new clubhouse.

Rugby, the carrying code branch of soccer, has been enjoyed in the town since 1873 although it was not until 1922 that an official club was formed, it was called Wigtownshire Rugby Club.

They opened with a fixture with Larne thus establishing a precedent which has been maintained for 45 years. They have their ground at what is now part of the senior school playing fields, opposite Stair Park, in London Road. A seven-a-side competition was inaugurated in 1926 and proved most successful.

The game was introduced into the senior school in the years between the wars and is still organised but travelling distances militate against many fixtures though the Stranraer High School proves a very happy breeding ground for the senior players.

It is true to say, however, that it has never caught on as a spectator sport in the town.

Tennis became popular in Stranraer in 1886 when the Stranraer Lawn Tennis Club took over the former bowling green in Sun Street and by 1897 championships were held. In 1906 the grass courts gave way to blaes. Municipal courts, built in 1923, aided the popularity of the game and the number of its devotees. Stranraer High School, when in Lewis Street, had also a court but it was seldom used. There is a growing interest now among schoolchildren with the facilities available at the new site of the schools.

Curling, which equals football as the most ancient pastime, by its very nature was not played regularly. In 1854 Limekiln Loch was the club formed for Stranraer and in 1871 a curling rink was laid out in Stoneykirk Road, but it fell into disuse and for a time was used for quoiting matches and for archery which had a short life in the town.

Trotting was at its zenith at Cults in 1885 so much so that a track was laid out to the south-west of Stranraer and both during and immediately after the First World War it became a rage, superseded by straight-forward horse racing for a time. The trotting track, was, however, lost to the sport when it was turned into a playing field for the town.

Despite the advantages of the loch there was never a swimming club formed though, in 1897 and onwards, aquatic sports were held, including rowing matches. Lochryan Rowing Club was started in 1910 and annually held swimming competitions, but it was not until a few years ago when, as a result of the persistence of Provost A. A. Walker, a practice swimming pool was included in the facilities of the new schools, that swimming became really popular. There had been proposals to have an out-door pool at Agnew Bay in 1923 and again in 1930 but these did not come to anything.

Athletics had their hey-day in 1897 but again lack of organisation and difficulty in competition led to a falling away until, in 1927, Stranraer Harriers was formed with the Stranraer family Robertson being the mainstays. This form of activity is on the decline. The Cycling Club, formed in 1900, is defunct. A hockey team, organised by Stranraer High School, played on Stair Park in 1911 and in recent years has grown tremendously in strength. Motor cycle scrambling did not catch on in the district though races were held in 1952. There was a roller-skating club in 1909 which had a short existence. For the past 50 years there has been much interest in pigeon racing with two clubs in the town.

One of the oldest indoor pastimes is carpet bowling but until the last twenty years it was more or less confined to the country districts and only latterly has it been possible to play in the town where several halls have been pressed into use.

From 1918 until after the end of the Second World War, the Town Council organised the annual sports day, but with more and more physical training teachers being appointed by the Education Committee, this duty was taken over so far as the youth was concerned, by that authority. School sports are held at every scholastic establishment followed by inter-school and inter-district events.

Badminton was introduced to Stranraer in 1917 in the Drill Hall when the presence of troops gave the game a fillip, and later the club transferred to premises in Castle Court, in the building which was demolished in 1967. After Castle Court, Queen's Hall was in use, Stranraer High School gymnasium and the Masonic Hall, as well as the Town Hall, but the promoters had always difficulty finding suitable premises in the town.

Table tennis, started in the early 1930s, reached its peak before the outbreak of war and during it, when many servicemen's clubs took part. There were various centres throughout the town. By 1953 there was a decline in interest and it was not until 1962 that the league competition was restarted.

One of the exceptions to the normal graph of rise and fall in popularity was the sport of angling. There had always been anglers in the town but it was not until 1947 that they were gathered together, under the aegis of Stranraer and District Angling Association. They were fortunate in that the Earls of Stair permitted them to use stretches of water round the town and several of the lochs. So great was the membership that the initial fee of £2 has remained constant for 20 years.

...In great tempests

STRANRAER'S STREET PATTERN was laid down by the earliest inhabitants to avoid, so far as possible, the effects of the northerly winds and high tides, so that George Street was set some distance from the shore.

On the seafront, the large expanse of sand militated against the most severe results of storms being felt, and the town planners of early days ensured that there would be blockages of streets by buildings so that there was not a danger of the winds blowing through the whole town from north to south.

There were many occasions when, despite such precautions, Stranraer was visited by great storms and considerable damage was done. Several of these occurred between 1813 and 1839 and in May of the latter year the Town Clerk reported snow on the ground. This followed the "greatest storm ever to strike Galloway."

In a "terrible gale" in 1894, 9 seamen were drowned in Lochryan, lamp-posts were torn down in Stranraer and the streets left in darkness. A severe snow storm the following year created much damage and another violent storm in 1896 flooded houses on the seafront.

Cairnryan Road was on several occasions practically washed away. In contrast, there was a heat-wave in 1900.

The year 1928 saw the worst gale since 1894 and in 1929 blizzards again swept the town. Similar disasters followed in 1933, 1938 and 1940, when Stranraer was under a thick blanket of snow, as it was again in 1947. Serious floods also took place in 1950 and there was an 83 m.p.h. gale in 1952, followed by a heavy snow storm. Blizzards of 1963 and 1965 are well remembered.

On the other side of the coin, Stranraer claims a high place in the sunshine records and has a rainfall below average.

... *Other cause or occasion*

SPECIAL DAYS OF CELEBRATION in the burgh mainly concerned Royal occasions. Visits from reigning monarchs were, however, few and far between. In the main it was the Coronation of a Sovereign that was the occasion for rejoicing.

The visit by King James VI to Lochryan and Castle Kennedy towards the beginning of the 17th Century was, of course, the most momentous. King William of Orange also stayed at Castle Kennedy in 1690.

In 1850, Admiral Sir John Ross was greeted by his excited townspeople when he returned after an absence of sixteen months' search of the Arctic for Rear-Admiral Sir John Franklin.

Queen Victoria was presented with a loyal address in 1847 when the Royal Yacht put in at Finnart. The Prince Consort, the Prince of Wales and the Princess Royal were also in the party and came ashore for a short time. In 1885 the Prince and Princess of Wales and Prince Albert Victor were given a tumultuous welcome when they arrived from Larne. Prince Albert Victor repeated his visit in 1889.

A trades procession was held to celebrate the Queen's Coronation, and a fountain was unveiled at The Cross to mark her Jubilee. Motions in the council to have the fountain removed were made in 1958 but it still remains.

In 1911, Provost Young gifted a bandstand for Stair Park to commemorate the accession of King George V.

King George VI and Queen Elizabeth showed a particular fondness for the district. In 1924, when Duke and Duchess of York, the Royal couple visited the town on the way to Ulster and came back by the same route. Thousands of people turned out. Ten years later they again were in Stranraer, His Royal Highness to attend a reunion of the Scots Guards, and in 1935, at Lochinch, the Duke accepted purses for the Garrick Hospital. Nearly the whole populace turned out to watch. In 1936 the Duke and Duchess of Gloucester were Royal visitors and they have visited the district on other occasions since. The Duchess of Gloucester accepted the Freedom of the Burgh in 1953 on behalf of the K.O.S.B. at a ceremony in Stair Park.

A trades procession in the burgh in 1936 was an outstanding event of the summer season.

After the Coronation the King and Queen were greeted by thousands of loyal subjects in 1937. During the war years the first ship to sail from the new port at Cairnryan carried Their Majesties to Canada on a secret visit, and the Prime Minister, Winston Churchill, was another outstanding figure whose short stay in the district was a closely guarded secret. Her Majesty, then Queen Mother, returned in April, 1955, for a short holiday at Lochinch and paid a visit to Stranraer where she was greeted by the Provost and Councillors at Dunbae House.

In 1955 Queen Elizabeth and Prince Philip visited the town. Her Majesty graced the Stranraer and District Agricultural Society's annual show, accompanied by Prince Philip, while Prince Charles, Princess Anne and Prince Michael of Kent spent the afternoon at Lochinch.

Her Majesty and the Duke of Edinburgh were accorded a civic reception at Stranraer and signed the Visitors' Book. On the same day Her Royal Highness Princess Margaret arrived at West Freugh in an aircraft of the Queen's Flight and joined the remainder of the Royal Party at Lochinch. The next Royal occasion was in August, 1958, when the Queen, Prince Philip, Prince Charles and Princess Anne landed at Wig Bay during a cruise up the west coast. The party was met by the Earl of Stair, then went to the House of Knock. They left the next day. Prince Philip, when touring Galloway in 1965, embarked on the Royal Yacht.

During the war years the Princess Royal visited Stranraer in connection with a Forces Club which had been established in the former Ritz in Dalrymple Street.

Other distinguished visitors to the town included the Earl of Rosebery, the Earl of Hopetoun, and the Hon. William Ross, M.C.P., J.P., V.D., of Cape Town, who were made burgesses. Dr Jameson, of the famous Jameson Raid in the Cape Colony, was offered the freedom of the town, but was never able to come to Stranraer to receive the burgess ticket. His father had been editor of the "Free Press" during the time of the Crimean War. General Sir Ian Hamilton addressed a British Legion parade in 1923, and earlier visitors included the poet Keats in 1818, George Borrow in 1866, and Robert Louis Stevenson in 1871.

In later years Sir Harry Lauder, in 1942, came in connection with a war effort and Lady Baden-Powell, the following year, made a short stop.

The King's Own Scottish Borderers were presented with a banner in 1961 on an official visit.

Stranraer has three memorials, the first, unveiled in 1922, commemorates those who fell in the two world wars, the figure of a Royal Scots Fusilier, and, in 1951, as a tribute to the British and Allied servicemen, a memorial was unveiled in the Glebe Cemetery, and the third is a peace-time memorial, crowned with an anchor, in Agnew Park in tribute to those who died in the Princess Victoria Disaster in 1953. It was unveiled in 1962.

... Haunts, uses and exerces

IN THE NINETEENTH CENTURY Lord Stair had given the council Glenwell Park for a playing field attached to a school, but it was not until 1904 that there was a really settled place for recreation for children. Another gift, this time of Stair Park, was put to much better use. In 1931 a small piece of ground on the seafront, opposite the Railway Pier, was given by another Lord Stair and converted into an attractive garden, and, in 1939, when work of reclamation at Agnew Crescent Bay was completed, the Council were able to formulate plans for an addition to the play space in the town, even although it was not completed until 1959.

A most important addition was made as a result of a decision of 1946 to create out of a former Trotting Track and Archie's Bog in the south of the town and near large housing schemes, a spacious playground, and a delightful addition was ground at Park House, at the former Hillhead district, opposite Sheuchan Parish Church, gifted by Lady MacTaggart Stewart in 1950.

Most in use for recreation was, of course, the vast new playing fields laid out in conjunction with the secondary schools in London Road in the near neighbourhood of which an area of ground had earlier been acquired by the Education Authority and is in use as pitches for rugby, hockey, and for track racing. This ground which had been provided by the Earl of Stair to the Stranraer and District Agricultural Society is used annually by that body for the cattle show, one of the main events of the summer season.

An open space was created opposite Hannay's Mill in the West End which was laid out in seats, and there was for a time a children's playground at Marine Gardens, on the Cairnryan Shore road.

... *Good, true and thankfull*
service

STRANRAER HAS BEEN FORTUNATE in attracting so many voluntary workers for the public weal. Among the Provosts were Patrick Kennedy whose services covered more than 25 years in the latter part of the seventeenth century; Patrick Patersone, whose service spanned the end of one and the beginning of another century and covered 49 years to 1722; Andrew McCredie, who had 21 years' service from the beginning of the eighteenth century; and, of course, the Earls of Stair whose services, broken by other commitments, covered more than two centuries. Dr Orgill was 30 years a councillor in the nineteenth century and John Campbell served for 27 years. In later days the Dyer family, which provided two civic heads, had between them three generations, 92 years of public service. John Waddell served for 34 years, and Robert Murray for 31 whilst of the present council, R. E. Caughie has 22 years and Tom Dunbar the same number with a break.

Among officials, the Black family, father and son, looked after the town's affairs from 1841 to 1913. John Bradford was chamberlain for 42 years, John Bennoch, clerk for 25 and W. Millar Wilson, chamberlain for 21 years. The Lock family were burgh officers from 1872 to 1960. Dr. Thomas Harper was medical officer for 40 years and Wm. McDowall was an employee of the cleansing department for the same length of time. Miss Ella Torrance, the present assistant town clerk, has been in the burgh service for 37 years.

CLACHAN OF CLERKS

1692 S. Paterson.	1780 John McKie.
1712 Alexander Patersone.	1799 Gilbert Nish.
1720 Robert Ker.	1841 Will Black.
1729 John Smith.	1883 William Black.
1734 Thomas Naismith.	1913 W. G. Belford.
1768 Thomas Naismith and	1918 John Bennoch.
Alex. Ross.	1943 C. D. Smith.
1772 Robert Ker.	1945 R. McInnes Wilson.
1776 Wm. McKie.	1963 Roland M. F. Thomson.

POSSE OF PROVOSTS

1617	William Agnew of Crooch.
1628	Sir Patrick A g n e w of Lochnaw, Kt.
1653	Thomas Adair.
1664	Hew Kennedy.
1672	Patrick Kennedy.
1674	Andrew Cowand.
1678	Patrick Kennedy.
1679	James Johnstone.
1681	Patrick Patersone.
1683	Alexander Baillie.
1684-86	Patrick Patersone.
1688	John Row.
1689	William Torbrane.
1690-92	Patrick Patersone.
1693	Patrick Kennedy.
1695	Patrick Kennedy.
1696-98	Patrick Patersone.
1699	John Dunbar.
1700-02	Patrick Patersone.
1703-04	Andrew McCredy.
1705	Patrick Patersone.
1706-07	Andrew McCredy.
1708	Andrew Fordyce.
1710-11	Archibald Primrose.
1712-13	Patrick Patersone.
1714-15	Andrew McCredy.
1716	Patrick Patersone.
1717-18	Andrew McCredie.
1719	Patrick Patersone.
1720-21	Andrew McCredie.
1722	Patrick Patersone.
1723	Andrew McCredie.
1724-25	John, 2nd Earl of Stair.
1726-27	Captain John Dalrymple.
1728-29	John, 2nd Earl of Stair.
1730-31	Captain John Dalrymple.
1732-33	John, 2nd Earl of Stair.
1734	John McDowall of Freugh.
1766	John Hamilton of Bargany.
1767	John Dalrymple.
1768-70	John, 5th Earl of Stair.
1771-72	Viscount Dalrymple.
1773-74	John Hamilton of Bargany.
1775-76	David Leggat of Barlockhart.
1777-78	Viscount Dalrymple.
1779-80	John Hamilton of Bargany.
1781-82	John, 5th Earl of Stair.
1783-84	John Hamilton of Bargany.
1785-86	The Hon. Major-General Wm. Dalrymple.

1787-88	Viscount Dalrymple.
1789-90	Thomas Smith.
1791-92	John, 6th Earl of Stair.
1793-94	Patrick Heron of Heron.
1795-96	Thomas Smith.
1797-98	John, 6th Earl of Stair.
1799	Patrick Heron of Heron.
1800-02	John, 6th Earl of Stair.
1803-04	The Hon. General William Dalrymple.
1805-06	John, 6th Earl of Stair.
1807	Thomas Smith of Edinburgh.
1808-10	John, 6th Earl of Stair.
1811-12	Thomas Smith.
1813	Sir Hew Dalrymple-Hamilton, Bt.
1814-15	John Smith Cuninghame of Caprington, W.S.
1816-17	Sir Hew Dalrymple-Hamilton, Bt.
1818-19	John Smith Cuninghame of Caprington, W.S.
1820-21	Alexander Smith, W.S.
1822-23	William Kerr.
1824-25	John, 7th Earl of Stair.
1826-27	Alexander Smith.
1828-29	John, 7th Earl of Stair.
1830-31	John Smith Cuninghame.
1832-46	Charles Morland.
1847-51	Alexander McDouall.
1852-57	Alexander McNeel-Caird.
1858-70	David Guthrie.
1870-74	Alexander Ingram.
1875-81	John Campbell.
1882-84	William McGibbon.
1885-87	George Garrick.
1888-93	William McGibbon.
1894-00	William N. MacRobert.
1900-09	Viscount Dalrymple, 11th Earl of Stair.
1909-14	Robert Young.
1914-16	William Fox.
1916-28	R. B. Dyer.
1928-33	John Waddell.
1933-38	Robert Murray.
1938-47	George W. McDowall.
1947-51	Andrew Ewing.
1951-54	William Dyer.
1954-60	A. A. Walker.
1960-63	R. E. Caughie.
1963-66	Alex. Murray.
1966-	Jas. Brown.

ADDITIONAL INFORMATION

List of books for further reading, available from Wigtown County Library:

Agnew, Sir A. N.—Guide to Wigtownshire. 1908. (illus.)

Commission on Historical Monuments of Scotland — Report on Wigtownshire. 1912. (illus.)

Dick, C. H.—Highways and byways in Galloway and Carrick. 1916. (illus.)

McIlwraith, W.—The visitor's guide to Wigtownshire. 1873 and later editions. (illus.)

Mackenzie, W.—History of Galloway—2 vols. 1841.

McKerlie, P. H. — History of the lands and their owners in Galloway — Vols. 1 and 2. Wigtownshire. 1870-78 and later edition 1908.

MacTaggart, J.—The Scottish Gallovidian Encyclopaedia. 1824.

Maxwell, Sir H.—History of Dumfries and Galloway. 1896 and 2nd edition 1900.

Robinson, S.—Reminiscences of Wigtownshire about the close of last (18th) century. 1842.

Symson, A.—A large description of Galloway. 1684.

Wood, J. M.—Smuggling in the Solway and round the Galloway seaboard. 1908. (illus.)

Acknowledgments

This history of the Royal and Ancient Burgh of Stranraer is respectfully dedicated to the Provost, Magistrates, Councillors and Officials of the town, both past and present, in token of gratitude, on behalf of the townspeople.

In its compilation, invaluable assistance has been rendered, among others, by Sir James Fergusson, Keeper of the Records of Scotland; Roland M. F. Thomson, Esq., M.A., LL.B., Town Clerk of Stranraer; Alastair Wilson, Esq., County Librarian; Inspector Wm. F. Russell, Dumfries and Galloway Constabulary; former Editors and present Editorial Staff of the "Free Press", and, above all, by A. D. Nelson, Esq., without whose aid this book would not have been possible.

John S. Boyd.

SUPPLEMENT

FOR THE YEARS

1967 – 2000

In 1967, to mark the 350th anniversary of the elevation of Stranraer to the status of a royal burgh, a history of the town was published entitled "The Royal and Ancient Burgh of Stranraer 1617-1967; History and Development". It was written by J. S. Boyd, Editor of *The Wigtownshire Free Press*, as the newspaper was then known.

It seemed appropriate to the Stranraer and District Local History Trust to mark the new millennium by republishing this well known and much consulted work. The Trust is greatly indebted to Mrs Boyd for giving permission for the history to be reprinted. The original text is reproduced here in facsimile form. However it was also felt desirable to bring the account up to date by adding a short section covering the period from 1967 until early 2000. This was written by Jack Hunter, Donnie Nelson, and Christine Wilson. The authorship of each chapter in the new section is indicated by the initials at the end of the chapter. It is worthy of note that Donnie Nelson also played a major part in the compilation of the original history, as J. S. Boyd acknowledged.

In the compilation of the new section the assistance of a great many people was sought and willingly given; the Trust wishes to record its gratitude to all of those.

An imaginative and attractive feature of the original work was the use of quotations from the charter document of 1617 as chapter headings. While these have obviously been retained, the topic of each chapter has been added in brackets after the chapter quotation. This has been done for ease of reference as it is hoped the new edition will be of use to those interested in the history of the town, the original having been out of print and unobtainable for many years.

Any opinions expressed or implied in the following chapters are those of the individual authors and would not necessarily be endorsed by the Stranraer and District Local History Trust.

Contents

LOCAL GOVERNMENT

In the 33 years since the History was published two major changes in local government have occurred. The first took place in 1975, when county councils, town councils, and old-style district councils were abolished and replaced by a two-tier system of regional councils and district councils. In addition community councils were created, without powers but to act as a conduit for local opinion. Most functions were allocated to regional councils with district councils having as their main responsibilities housing and leisure and recreation.

Stranraer, which had been the seat both of Stranraer Town Council, at Dunbae House, and Wigtownshire County Council, with its headquarters in Sun St, lost both those roles but instead became the meeting place and administrative centre of the new Wigtown District Council. This body covered a larger area than the old county council, extending in the east to Ravenshall between Creetown and Gatehouse. However, the original proposal, that it should extend as far north as Girvan and be consequently known as Merrick District, was dropped after opposition from some quarters in south Ayrshire.

Departments like Education, Roads, and Planning were now based in Dumfries, seat of Dumfries and Galloway Regional Council, but some retained a branch office in Stranraer. Stranraer museum was forced to vacate the building in London Road it had shared with Library Services since the former was now a District function and the latter a Regional one. The District Council took over Dunbae House and the Sun St complex, the latter being significantly extended.

In 1995 another radical reorganisation of local government in Scotland took place with the two-tier system replaced by all-purpose councils although community councils were retained. The body responsible for this area became the Dumfries and Galloway Council with its headquarters and meeting place in Dumfries. So Stranraer ceased for the first time in over fifty years to be the centre for any statutory local government body. However, the West Galloway Area Committee, one of three such groups set up by the new council, meets in Stranraer. Its secretariat is based here and several council departments have local offices here.

When the present structure of local government was instituted in 1995, Stranraer and the immediately surrounding area were allocated 7 seats in the 72-seat Dumfries and Galloway Council but in 1999 that number was reduced to 5 in a 42-seat council.

JH

POSSE OF PROVOSTS PROLONGED

James Brown 1966 - 69
James Wales 1969 - 72
Molly Murry 1972 - 75

CLACHAN OF CLERKS COMPLETED

1963 Roland M. F. Thomson
1971 Edward J. Hendry

EDUCATION

The second half of the twentieth century brought many changes in the organisation and provision of education in the area.

In 1970, Stranraer Academy and Stranraer High School combined to form one comprehensive secondary school, in keeping with Government policy. It was now one of only two secondary schools in the county. The older name - Stranraer Academy - was kept, while pupils dressed in the uniform of royal blue with gold and saxe blue of the former Stranraer High School.

Within a short time the school leaving age was raised to 16 years, involving curriculum changes both in practical and theoretical ways in order to interest those students whose school days were compulsorily extended.

The new school maintained a role of more than 1600 pupils, with a staff of around 100 to cope with the increased numbers. C Block was added to the rear of the school site to provide necessary accommodation.

In time the Scottish Leaving Certificate changed its format. Higher and Lower Grades were replaced by Higher and Ordinary Grades in 1962 then by Higher and Standard Grades.

A further Certificate of Sixth Year Studies stretched the curriculum for some senior pupils. Standard Grade exams were structured to provide three levels of attainment - Foundation, General and Credit. Modules for classwork were included in the examination results. In the year 2000 a new certificate - Higher Still - is being introduced.

At the starting rung of the education ladder, privately run and voluntary play groups were set up in the town to help little ones to develop and to socialise with others by participating in group activities such as games, listening to stories and poems and drawing and colouring

In the eighties, the first nursery class was added to Park School, with children under five years attending several sessions in a week. Nursery classes now thrive in four of the town's five primary schools.

The formality of primary education changed. Tiered classrooms of the old days with rows of desks with tip-up wooden seats were replaced with groups of children sitting round tables on more comfortable moulded chairs. Furnishings moved to suit the lesson and eventually wooden floors were carpeted. Children moved about to find equipment and often sat on the floor to listen and discuss. Blackboard and chalk were replaced for much of the day by modern teaching equipment and classrooms became light, bright and colourful with displays of work. Specialist teachers visited the schools to teach art, music and physical education. Support has been provided for children with learning difficulties by Specialist Teachers at all levels of the child's school career on a short term or on-going basis, depending on the problem.

Stranraer for many years has offered evening classes in academic and interest subjects. Many adults took their Highers also at these classes before moving on to college. Subjects such as typing and book-keeping, motor mechanics and nautical subjects were taught, and there were leisure classes in art, dressmaking and woodwork. Many a nest of tables, table lamp,upholstered chair and dress and jacket were produced over the winter.

As to the buildings, Dalrymple School, housed in the old Stranraer Academy, moved to a new building to the south of the town in the 70s and was renamed Belmont. In the last decade of the century, flat roofed buildings of the 60s - Sheuchan and Rephad (and even twelve year old Belmont) Schools - were renovated inside, and pitched roofs, more suitable for a Scottish climate, were added.

Aird Special School, for Children with Special Needs, built in the 60s, was eventually integrated into the Academy, catering for children with severe learning difficulties, as current thought believes in integration of most children with learning difficulties into their local primary classes.

In the early nineties the Regional Council agreed to rebuild Stranraer Academy on its present site. At the time of writing this project has been partly completed, with new and old buildings in use. Progress has been hindered by soaring costs, but hopefully the new century will see completion of the new school.

In 1990 the site of the old Stranraer Academy was used for yet another educational purpose when the old building was razed to the ground. A magnificent college was built on this convenient central site - an out-station of Dumfries and Galloway College. It was named The John Niven Centre after the farmer whose service to the community was enormous. He had spent many years as councillor and Convenor of the County of Wigtownshire, and thereafter as Convenor of Dumfries and Galloway Regional Council on the reorganisation of local government in 1975.

The John Niven Centre offers courses throughout the day and some classes in the evening. These can be certificated vocational courses in such subjects as catering, hair dressing, motor mechanics, building or computing, or leisure interests such as Italian cooking. Ample opportunities are open to all in Stranraer and further afield to pursue their interests and inclinations in furthering knowledge and experience.

Glasgow University offers extra-mural classes each year during the winter evenings, and also Saturday one-day courses. The class " Discovering Galloway from Books" held in Stranraer Library attracts a particularly large group. This class has continued for many years.

1975 saw the reorganisation of local government. County councils vanished from the scene to be replaced by Regional Councils. Director of Education for Wigtownshire, Douglas Gunn, retired and his Depute, Neil Macdonald, became Area Director of Education based in the Education Office in Market Street, supported by a team of Advisers in Primary Education, Art, Music, and Physical Education, the School Meals Organiser and support staff. During the 90s the Area Education Office was closed and the building became the home of The Children's Panel.

At the end of the century Stranraer Academy educated 1152 pupils, while the Stranraer primary schools had roles of :-

Rephad	236 + 73 (Nursery)
Belmont	226 + 60
Sheuchan	299 + 61
Park	260 + 73
St. Joseph's	63

The John Niven Centre had 320 full-time and 930 part-time students.

CLW

CHURCHES

In 1967 the writer of this history remarked that away back in 1893 it had been stated Stranraer had "ten churches in the town, a supply far in excess of the population" and went on to note that seventy years later the number was exactly the same. With the new millennium drawing near the number of places of worship has now increased to eleven.

For some churches in town the period from 1967 to 2000 has simply been a quiet time, with few changes in buildings or purpose, but it should be noted that the ecumenical movement has been more marked, particularly with the advent of a strong Christian Aid committment which has seen a sharing of both service and services which would have been unthinkable half-a-century ago.

Stranraer Old Parish Church still presents the same external appearance but had a massive stone-cleaning exercise on its Church Street frontage and the entrance had two of the former "Provost's Lamps" added in the 1980s, a gift from Wigtown District Council which ensured the continuance of these reminders of burghal status. It might be noted that these lamps now have plain glass in them but one of the original etched pieces showing the old coat-of-arms has been preserved and framed and hangs in the church's session room in what was the former Union Bank and later Bank of Scotland building beside the church. The two upper storeys of this building were acquired in the 1970s, after the merger of the banks made their Church Street branch redundant, and an interior connection from the church, directly into their new premises has helped to ensure that these are well used by the Sunday School, and indeed, by other church organisations. In 1969 Rev. Russell Walker preached his last sermon in the Old Parish, having retired after serving the congregation for 44 years, and in 1979 a beautiful stained glass window was dedicated to his memory in the church.

In 1968 a new vestry was opened and dedicated by the High Kirk congregation and at the same time, aware that their organisations were rapidly outgrowing their premises, they made plans for a suite of halls on the same site. In September 1969, Lord Stair laid the foundation stone. Exactly a year later the Very Reverend Dr. Nevile Davidson, a former Moderator of the General Assembly, dedicated and declared open the new premises. These were used for services in May 1990, when parts of the ceiling within the church fell away and the building was out of use for a few weeks until repairs eliminated the danger. Two years later a 150th anniversary service was held, coupled with a visit from the Right Reverend Hugh Wyllie, that year's Moderator. Since then, long-running negotiations with a mobile telephone company came to fruition and when their equipment was being installed on the church tower in 1998, the opportunity was taken to carry out intensive repairs to the tower and to remove the bell. The bell is now displayed on a plinth beside the entrance to the High Kirk.

St. Joseph's Church also celebrated a 150th anniversary, that of the establishment of their parish, when in 1996 a special Anniversary Mass and Reception had Bishop Maurice Taylor as celebrant and guest. A couple of years earlier the congregation had faced their biggest problem for some time when it was discovered that the roof of the church needed replacement. Surveys showed that parts of the flooring and underpinnings also needed renewal and after the Christmas services in 1995 the church was closed and Sunday services took place in St. Joseph's School. Other churches in town kindly offered use of their premises for weddings or funerals, an offer which was used on one occasion, before their own church could be used again for Easter, 1996. Much more work than had been first thought about, had taken place and the opportunity was used to rearrange the seating and install replacement pews. Faced with a heavy debt, the congregation went in for fund-raising in a big way and, with the aid of two bequests, cleared it off in four years. In 1997 the congregation had another cause for celebration when the sisters of St. Joseph's Convent marked the centenary of their coming to Stranraer.

Centenary celebrations had also been held at St. Ninian's Church in 1984, recalling the building of what had then been the West United Presbyterian Church, though the foundation of the congregation went much further back in time.Three years after the 1984 celebrations St. Ninian's became linked with Portpatrick Parish Church, with a special service in the village to mark the tie-up.

St. Andrew's Church was another of the town's places of worship which joined in a linkage plan with a country establishment, in this case Inch Parish Church. A special service was held at the latter in October, 1982 to mark the occasion and Rev. Tom O'Leary came in 1983 to be first minister of the linked charge. In 1998 the congregation of St. Andrew's marked the centenary of their church building, though here again the beginnings of the congregation went back much more than a century before the first stone of the present church had been laid.

We should go back in time too to look at the establishment of a Christian Brethren congregation in Stranraer, a group which, though affected like many of the churches by falling membership, still retains a good presence in the town. They were established in Stranraer in 1894 and their strong committment quickly led to congregations coming into being at Drummore, Portpatrick, Glenluce, Kirkcowan and Newton Stewart.

The early days saw the Stranraer folk meeting in the former Queen's Hall in South Strand Street for a short time and later in what was the original jury-room of the Sheriff Court in the New Town Hall. The main hall was also used for annual conference meetings which attracted large attendances. St John Street Hall, purchased in 1937, became their next home. This was the former mission hall built by the Ivy Place United Free Church in 1894, and it served the Brethren well in the many aspects of their work. Then in 1953 the congregation bought the former St. Mark's building in Lewis Street, their present place of worship.

The Reformed Presbyterian Church still occupies in Dalrymple Street the oldest building in town which has seen continuous use as a place of worship since it replaced an earlier church on that site in 1825. Over the last 33 years there has been no structural changes there though church and church hall were redecorated, had the heating system upgraded and a microphone and speakers installed to help members with hearing difficulties.

St. John's Episcopal Church, along with other buildings in London Road and Bellevilla Road, was demolished to make way for the new supermarket on the old Glenwell site and in March 1994, the congregation met in their new church in the upper storey of the new library in North Strand Street. With such a small but loyal congregation, the deal with Safeways came at a fortuitous time, giving them a brand new home just after their old church had passed the century mark.

The Salvation Army, which had operated until 1967 in the former premises of Sheuchan Free Church in Park Lane, had no headquarters locally from that date until January 1989, when they purchased The Kiosk building at Portrodie. Following extensive alterations and refurbishment they opened their new centre in October 1990.

Another notable chapter in the story of worship within Stranraer has been written by the Baptist Church. Following a non-denominational Christian gathering in St. Ninian's Church hall in the late 1970s, two men, anxious to see an evangelical church in town, made the initial approaches and found sufficient support at a subsequent meeting.

Initial services were held in the former High School, then in the Coronation Day Centre. When the Centre was being extended the High School premises had to be used again until a return to the Centre was possible. The Stranraer Baptist Church was formally constituted on 5th January 1985.

A fair amount of week-night activity with young people was undertaken and, when the Centre was not always available, use was made for a considerable period of the hall of the Reformed Presbyterian Church in Dalrymple Street which had been offered.

Meanwhile, an ongoing search for a permanent home had met with no success until the old Drill Hall and its attached house in Bellevilla Road came on the market. It was eminently suitable, having been built originally for a branch of the United Presbyterian Church in 1797. When that congregation moved in 1850 to Bridge Street the building was used for many years as a Templar's meeting place before being sold to the army in 1900.

A lot of hard work to restore it as a church and to form other halls and offices for the congregational work with children, young people and senior citizens was cheerfully shouldered and with the adjacent house transformed into a fine manse, the Baptist Church plays a full part in worship and work in Stranraer.

Perhaps the most remarkable story of all the churches in Stranraer belongs to the local congregation of Jehovah's Witnesses. As a very small group they met in the 1960s in a building in The Backrampart before acquiring a former war-time Nissen Hut at Clashmahew. From there their next move was to the old premises in Glen Street which had been built as a mission hall by the Ivy Place United Free Church. Then followed a short stay in Cairnryan village hall before the bold decision was made to build their own permanent home. The members acquired the corner site of Rose Street - St. John Street and in

1995, in the space of literally a few days, their Kingdom Hall was built, decorated, furnished and in use. With volunteer tradesmen and labourers from their own congregation, plus others from other congregations, it was an astonishing example of planning and teamwork in a pattern used by their members worldwide. The women and youngsters played their part too, catering as well as carrying to the builders, and not least impressive to onlookers was the sight of the workers, pausing momentarily for combined prayer breaks during the work.

DN

HEALTH and SOCIAL WORK

Stranraer, in the early days of Dumfries and Galloway Hospital Board, undoubtedly benefited from the provision of better health services. The opening of the Health Centre in 1955, on ground adjacent to the Garrick Hospital, and the extension of the Garrick itself in the late 1960s meant that the town, the Rhins, and a good part of the Machars were well catered for in so far as medical and surgical services were concerned.

In 1974 Dumfries and Galloway Health Board was formed to oversee and manage health provision in the region bringing together all health services. In April 1994 the Acute and Maternity Trust became the body responsible for the provision of acute medical, surgical and maternity services. In 1995 a second Trust was formed for community and mental health services. In 1999 these services were taken over by the Primary Care Trust.

The Health Centre has expanded in area to provide more accommodation for the doctors, nurses and ancillary staff. In order to achieve this, individual practice waiting rooms were dispensed with and replaced by a communal waiting area. Stranraer is home to 17 doctors, some part-time, in 4 practices. Staffed by practice nurses, clinics are held in the Health Centre for patients with ailments such as high blood pressure and diabetes. Qualified nurses see to inoculations and change dressings in the Treatment Room. Out-of-hours medical treatment is provided by local practices on a rota basis.

The services at the Garrick Hospital were improved with a new extension in 1982 to provide accident and emergency services. However, problems have occurred over the years. Major operations were banned in 1986 as resources were considered not to be up to standard. Local people then signed a petition to plead for major surgical services at the Garrick Hospital. The Health Board agreed in March 1987 that the resident surgeon Mr. J.W.Galloway would decide which operations would be carried out locally. It was decided in October 1988 that the surgical unit be upgraded at a cost of £100,000; however, in 1989 local doctors expressed concern for the future of such services in the town.

By October 1991 a replacement for the Garrick Hospital appeared in future spending plans of the Health Board, one year before the Garrick celebrated its centenary.

In the 1990s a helicopter Air Ambulance Service was provided for serious cases using London Road Playing Fields or Rephad or Stranraer Academy grounds as a landing place. In June 1993 the helicopter landed on Edinburgh Road to transport a seriously ill patient to Dumfries.

Yet another petition was signed by local people in April 1996 and a public meeting was held to express fears over down-grading the Garrick. The following October the Health Board indicated that work would start in two years to build a new £5 million replacement. In October 1997 a campaign was relaunched to fight for surgical services. More than 1000 people attended a protest meeting because claims were still being made that surgical services were being reduced in the new plans. By February 1999, the new Garrick Hospital was to be the Health Board's main project. In March 2000, the Primary Care Trust announced that a new integrated health complex would replace both the Garrick Hospital and the Health Centre on the site of Waverley House, building to start in the middle of year 2000.

The present Garrick Hospital has 42 beds and is served by three resident surgeons. Family doctors visit their own patients in surgical and medical wings although seriously ill patients continue to be treated in Dumfries, Ayr, Glasgow and Edinburgh. Consultants from Dumfries Infirmary visit the Garrick weekly to provide specialist services. Physiotherapy and X-Ray Departments are provided in the complex. Accident and Emergency cover is provided on a 24 hour basis by associate specialist surgeons and family doctors. The Treatment Room is staffed by qualified nurses.

The Clenoch Maternity Hospital closed in 1976 when Dalrymple Hospital opened to serve the elderly. The Clenoch Ward with 12 maternity beds is housed on the upper floor. Modern practice allows the mums and new babies to go home after a much shorter stay - two days or so, instead of the former 7 to 10 days.

Waverley House served the needs of the elderly, but latterly homeless families were housed in caravans at the old Home before it closed its door for the last time in 1976, having served the community for more than 100 years.

Dalrymple Hospital was built in 1976. It serves elderly and stroke patients who need a longer period of treatment and recovery with caring nursing and physiotherapy treatment. The Day Hospital was extended in 1991. The Palliative Care Unit, comprising two bedrooms and a sitting room, was built and furnished by the Order of St. John and staffed by Dalrymple nurses, and opened by Her Majesty The Queen in August 1996.

Attached to Dalrymple was Rhinsdale House, a home for the elderly opened as a joint venture by the Health Board and Social Work Department. Bellevilla House was established by the local authority in 1962. Two wings were added in 1986. These two comfortable modern homes were both well supported by the community.

With changes in requirements for such homes, e.g. en-suite bathrooms as an integral part of each resident's room, a new home, Thorney Croft, opened in 1999 at a cost of £2.3 million. It has six wings, can accommodate 60 residents, provides one wing for patients with dementia, and has a Day Care Centre for the elderly. Rhinsdale and Bellevilla Houses are now closed.

Thorney Croft is owned and run by a private, non-profit making trust. Belmont House, a privately owned home, is the other residence for the elderly in Stranraer town. There is also Corsewall House in Kirkcolm and Sycamore Lodge in New Luce.

Coronation Day Centre for the elderly was improved and extended in 1987. The upgraded building was opened by Princess Alexandra in July, 1987. Two Domus Units, Innistaigh and Darataigh, were built in the grounds of Dalrymple Hospital to serve the needs of elderly dementia sufferers. In July 1997 one unit was to be closed, but after local resistance there was a temporary reprieve. Since 1998 Darataigh is home for people with severe learning difficulties, replacing Cromarty House which was opened for their care in the early 1980s.

With the publication of the Beveridge Report in the sixties, the Social Work Department was established to bring various welfare services together. The Social Work (Scotland) Act of 1968 brought General Welfare, and aspects of Mental Illness, Child Welfare, Care of the Elderly, those with Severe Learning Difficulties and the Probation Service under one umbrella within the county, based in Stranraer.

Wigtown County, in the van of progress, formed a co-ordinating committee to advance the work of providing for the needs of the population. The Committee included representatives of Social Work, the Community Medical Officer, Housing Officer and Child Welfare. This liaison between departments was extremely successful in dealing with a variety of problems. The Health Service still shares responsibility for the mentally ill, child health, school health services, the mentally handicapped and care of the elderly. There were changes for Health and Social Services with Care in the Community legislation around 1990. Community nurses, health visitors and school nurses serve the town of Stranraer.

On the reorganisation of local government in 1975, the headquarters of the Social Work Department was based in Dumfries, with a branch office in Stranraer.

Amenity flats for the elderly, with warden supervision, won a Saltire Award when they were built in Sun Street. Kirk Care flats, built by the Church of Scotland in Dalrymple Street, and Millburn Court on the site of Hannay's Mill in Sheuchan Street both offer flatted, supervised accommodation.

Margaret Blackburn housing for the physically disabled, adapted to the needs of the individual, is available at the south end of the town.

The Social Work Department also converts and adapts bathrooms and provides aids to ease the day- to- day living for the elderly and handicapped.

Rowallan, in Bayview Road, has been converted by Cheshire Homes in order that a group of mentally handicapped adults can live independently, as have Key Housing Association flats in Dalrymple Terrace. These homes have supervision by carers.

A Home Help service is also provided for those living at home.

All these provisions are designed to enable "Care in the Community" to become a reality.

The community is served by three pharmacies in Stranraer, a reduction by half since the sixties.

Home nursing is available for terminally ill cancer patients through the Macmillan and Marie Curie Nurses, greatly funded by charities, and for other patients through the Order of St. John.

Dental services are provided at five surgeries in the town, as well as the school service with its mobile caravan surgery, and premises at the Garrick Hospital. In the 1990s four of the practices switched from National Health Service provision to private treatment for adults.

Residential care for adults with learning difficulties was provided at Cromarty House and the Activity and Resource Centre was set up for the stimulation, interest and education of adults with learning difficulties as a day centre.

The present Chairman of the Health Board is a local man, John Ross, Portpatrick. Another local man, James McIntyre, Stranraer, previously held the same position for many years.

CLW

VOLUNTARY GROUPS

It is gratifying to reflect on the interest, time, and financial help contributed by the folk of the town towards its well being. The voluntary sector is now recognised as the "Third Force" in the nation and Stranraer benefits greatly from the hard work and enthusiasm of so many volunteers in so many aspects of the town's activities.

Mention is made in the early part of this book of the Knights Hospitallers of St. John being active in Stranraer in the early days of the Royal Burgh. This group looked after the sick but was apparently disbanded in the early 19th Century. However, the Order of St. John, its modern equivalent with the same aims of committment to the sick, was re-established in Stranraer in the 1960s, to the benefit of the town and district.

One of the Order's first ambitious projects was the establishment of a day-care centre for the elderly, attached to Dalrymple Hospital, followed by the addition of the St. John's Palliative Care Unit, opened in August 1996 by Her Majesty The Queen. This is a two- bedroom unit with lounge and comfortable facilities for relatives and is constantly maintained and made homely by members of the Association. The Rotary Club made a generous donation to assist with the initial capital cost of the unit.

A transport service to and from Dumfries for patients travelling onward to

Edinburgh for radiotherapy is provided on a weekly basis, and a recent addition is a Hospice at Home scheme for the severely ill. The annual art exhibition in the North West Castle, charity concerts, suppers and sales support those ambitious projects locally. The Eye Hospital in Jerusalem and the Mountain Rescue Service in Great Britain are two projects further afield helped by donations from the Stranraer members.

In the town the Hospital League of Friends visit with a trolley of treats and toiletries for residents in hospitals and old folk's homes.

Inner Wheel members visit Thorney Croft and Kirk Care residents each month for a social get-together playing bingo. These ladies also spend their winter evenings knitting rugs, bed jackets and bed socks for the comfort of the elderly in the town.

The Women's Royal Voluntary Service delivers Meals on Wheels on three days per week for the elderly and frail living at home. They also operate, on a fortnightly basis, the housebound book service for the local library.

Charity shops in Stranraer are a fairly recent introduction, of benefit to those who donate, those who buy and the charity itself. The shops are manned by volunteers.

One of the oldest groups is of course The Red Cross, whose good work is known world-wide, and whose local first aiders staff fetes, fairs and cattle shows, as well as instructing in First Aid.

Dumfries and Galloway Citizens' Advice Service, Stranraer office, offers advice, information, assistance and advocacy.

Alzheimer Scotland has a branch in Stranraer to provide voluntary help for patients and their carers, and the Phoenix Club provides stimulation for handicapped adults. The Gophers, for the physically disabled, enjoy a busy active programme of social activities. Volunteer counsellors support those with problems involving alcohol and drugs.

A new venture, keenly supported in the community, is the Stranraer Cancer Care Drop-in Centre, which opened its doors on the 12th January, 2000.

Christian Aid raises astounding sums of money locally each year during a month of fund raising involving all age groups in the community.

The Talking Newspaper for the Blind is produced weekly on tapes by an enthusiastic group of local volunteers, who make the recordings and arrange for their delivery and collection through the Post Office.

Wigtown Council for Voluntary Service, formed in 1988, offers advice, secretarial and other services to voluntary groups.

The Royal National Lifeboat Institution inshore lifeboat, manned by volunteers has been based in Stranraer since June,1994, when a D-class lifeboat was presented by the Rotary Club. It was housed for one season in the Roads Department building, then in a concrete shed in Agnew Park. This was replaced in 1996 by a purpose-built boat shed which now houses their fourth boat, *Tom Broom.*

Branches of national charities such as the Arthritis and Rheumatism Society, Multiple Sclerosis Society, Action for the Crippled Child, Marie Curie, Macmillan Nurses, Cot Death Society and RSSPCA raise funds through sales and street collections. The funds are used locally and nationally.

Most societies, clubs and pubs in Stranraer show their support by donating to local charity needs and appeals - a generous town with folk prepared to give time and money for the benefit of others.

LAW and ORDER

The town's two most visible symbols of law and order, the police station and the courthouse, have both been greatly extended in recent years, reflecting substantial changes in policing and the administration of justice.

The police station extension, involving the addition of another storey in 1981, was partly the result of The Troubles in Northern Ireland from 1969. The need to prevent the movement of terrorists, weapons, and explosives between the mainland and Ireland led to the formation in Stranraer in 1972 of a special Ports Unit. The increase in its powers from the Prevention of Terrorism act of 1974 meant that the Dumfries and Galloway force, the smallest in Scotland, did not have the necessary manpower resources for the unit's new role and officers from the City of Glasgow Police, and later Strathclyde Police, were seconded to Stranraer to assist. This arrangement continued until 1978.

Since 1976 the Ports Unit has been responsible not only for the Loch Ryan ferry terminals at Stranraer and Cairnryan but also for all small ports and airstrips in Dumfries and Galloway. For this latter task a Small Ports Unit was formed in 1997.

The Ports Unit comprises police officers, now all drawn from the Dumfries and Galloway force, and civilian search officers. In addition to its primary task of implementing the Prevention of Terrorism legislation, the unit's jobs are the identification and arrest of wanted persons, the identification of persons involved in drug trafficking, and co-operation with customs and excise and immigration agencies. The results of its activities in those roles are frequently recorded in the national media.

During its early years the unit experimented with search and other equipment on behalf of the Home Office, including portable x-ray units, explosives' vapour detectors, and radar.

In addition to the police ports unit both ferry companies employ their own private security units.

After the Lockerbie air disaster of December, 1988, a considerable number of officers from Stranraer were seconded to that town for periods of weeks or in some cases months.

Police dogs, first introduced to Dumfries and Galloway in 1968, soon made their appearance in Stranraer and are today a familiar sight in a variety of roles.

The first firearms instructors for the Dumfries and Galloway Constabulary were introduced in 1974 and 1975 and one of those was based in Stranraer to train selected officers. Originally a handful of staff trained at West Freugh two or three times a year, using surrendered weapons and ammunition. However, in Stranraer as elsewhere in Dumfries and Galloway the firearms capability of the force has significantly improved and expanded over the years.

In the field of the administration of justice, the reason for the courthouse extension lay in the changes to the structure of local government in Scotland in 1975. These in turn led to alterations to the system of courts in the former county of Wigtownshire. Until 1975 sheriff courts were held in both Stranraer and Wigtown with sheriff clerk and procurator fiscal facilities in both towns. But in that year it was decided to have only one sheriff court in the area, at Stranraer. The accommodation at the courthouse in Lewis St had to be expanded in consequence and the building now houses two courts.

Alterations in the division of Scotland into sheriffdoms mean that Stranraer is now part of the Sheriffdom of South Strathclyde, Dumfries, and Galloway.

JH

HOUSING

Mention was made elsewhere of Stranraer being officially recognised as a growth point in 1966 and the fact that the council had made excellent use of the areas awarded to them by burghal extensions in 1955 and 1960

The spread of municipal and private housing was part of the reason for the boundary extensions, plus the necessity of having more of a land-bank to cater for future needs. Despite a good record of provision in the municipal sector, Stranraer councillors were facing the stark fact that their list of would-be tenants was growing faster than they could cope with.

In 1968 another boundary extension was proposed to take in private housing development at Leswalt Road and plans for 87 houses at the former Sheuchan Nursery site were approved. The town was slowly spreading towards the Gallowhill.

The older part of the town, however, was not forgotten, not that it could be, for there was a central swathe, stretching from Lewis Street right across to Dalrymple Street which was composed of a mixture of poor housing, derelict properties, and commercial concerns which were beginning to look out of place.

First talks with the planners regarding what would become known as the C.D.A. (Comprehensive Development Area) took place in 1970. Wigtown County Council, as planning authority, would eventually be responsible for acquiring – compulsorily or otherwise – all the ground and properties in this area, while Stranraer Town Council would be responsible for the eventual use of the ground and for house-building. It proved, initially, to be a somewhat uneasy situation, with committees of both authorities starting out with differing aims and it would be true to say that County Clerk David R. Wilson deserved most of the credit when, eventually, between 1974 and 1976, almost 150 houses, flats, parking areas and a large and necessary public car park came into being.

While these lengthy negotiations were proceeding, more houses and flats had been erected and brought into use on the last of the fields belonging to the former Sheuchan Farm at the West End. These also replaced the old houses and byre between the field and Sheuchan Mill and occupied the rest of the field to the Leswalt Road and Leswalt High Road junction and back along the latter to the Sheuchan Bridge, with the Lairey Burn forming the boundary between the new estate and the 1946 prefabs of Millbank Road.

In succeeding years the rest of the greenfield area between these prefabs and Seabank Road was filled with private housing and three new roads: Willowdene Crescent, Millfield Avenue and Dalriada Avenue. These occupied what had been the former Mill Dam Field, an area which in hard winters became a playground for skaters. Also to disappear with this development was The Golden Well, just off Seabank Road, a favourite spot with walkers for a long, cool drink on a hot summer's day.

Various smaller sites had been "filled in" between 1968 and 1970, utilising untidy gaps and older or derelict buildings at Sheuchan Street, Corsewall Crescent, and Arran and Kintyre Courts, and in the Dick's Hill area the gap between the pre-war and post-war buildings, running from Mount Vernon Road to John Simpson Drive, provided space for eight homes. Also in 1970 plans were laid for more flats, to replace the West End Garage on the old foundry site in Foundry Lane, and to replace the old buildings and yards on the southern side of Sun Street at its Lewis Street junction.

In 1971 attention turned to the lower ground to the south of Belmont Road and Belmont Crescent and 179 houses were constructed to form Old Port, St Ninian's, Glenwell, Antrim and Galloway Avenues. It was one of these houses which in March of that year was opened as the town's 2000th council house to be built.

Later that year, the plans for Phase One of Hanover Square got the final nod of approval from planners, after many changes and arguments, and the massive task of demolition, clearance of properties, and rerouting and culverting of the Town and Laundry Burns could at last get under way.

At the close of 1971 there was also a decision to demolish the old steel houses in Royal Avenue but within a couple of months agreement had been given for their replacement and in 1974 14 new homes were let. Further houses and flats were built in 1972 at Laurel Grove, Park Lane and Foundry Lane, more boundary extensions were sought and Stage Two of the C.D.A. was approved.

The councillors were also seeking approval for the modernisation of all pre-war houses and in June, 1973, work commenced on this programme in the Dick's Hill area, work which was estimated to cost just under £1 million.

1974 was a busy year for a town council which was coming to an end with the reorganisation of local government, but also a year which brought other bad news with a warning of lean times ahead.

The first of the Phase One Hanover Square houses were ready in February and Trade Street – the old Tradeston – was fast disappearing as the demolishers prepared the way for Phase Two. But early in the year plans for 50 houses on McMaster's Road were being held up with sewerage problems in Cairnryan Road and in October the first blow of what would be many in later years was delivered to further modernisation plans in the shape of government cuts.

There were further fears for the future before the big change-over in May, 1975. Dean of Guild Courts and the County Buildings Authority were both to disappear and with decisions in these functions to emanate from Dumfries there were gloomy mutterings from local councillors about "long-distance planning".

New sewage works at Portrodie were opened in April by Provost Mollie Murray, Stranraer's last civic chief and the only woman ever to hold that position.

While not having planning authority, the new Wigtown District Council was responsible for housing and quickly got down to business. They agreed to allow a garage on the site of the old tanyard within the Hanover Square complex and in their first year of office pushed forward plans for another 90 houses at the East End. In 1976 they continued the former policy of tidying up with houses built in Rephad Crescent and in the Hanover Square area.

Their plans for the East End matured in 1977 and 1978 with the building-up of the housing estates in Aird Avenue, Lochinch Place, School Road, Whinbank Terrace, Provost Road and Fairway, the last of these houses taking them into 1981.

The Eighties were to prove to be years of change so far as municipal housing was concerned. Government made it clear that rented housing would no longer be left largely with local authorities and there would be positive discrimination in favour of housing associations. Kirk Care, Loreburn, Margaret Blackwood and Key were such associations which locally were to play a part in the new housing strategy as laid down by central government and district councils had to learn to live with those as housing support grant was slashed year by year until it disappeared altogether in this part of the country.

These associations, regarded somewhat warily at the outset, largely because of their right to "choose" tenants, came to play a valuable part in housing as funding for local authorities dried up.

Kirk Care opened their first local development in December, 1981, when 38 sheltered housing units on the former Regal Picture House site in Dalrymple Street, came into use.

The District Council, still with a large demand to satisfy, had produced plans for 260 houses on land at Auchtralure in June, 1980, estimated to cost £4.5 millions and the largest-ever housing scheme in the county. In the same year, with government still pursuing their housing policy, the council accepted, perhaps with some trepidation, the tenants' right-to-buy scheme.

Key Housing Association opened their new unit on the edge of the Hanover Square area in May, 1983, and in July of that year the council brought forward plans to spend £870,000 on the modernisation of the 65 Stranraer prefabs. Later in the year the council, still keen on the long-held idea of a seafront promenade from East End to West, opposed plans for private housing on the former Sheuchan Creamery site. Their objections were upheld, despite a planning appeal.

Meanwhile, building at Ochtrelure (the name had somehow changed spelling in the planning and building process) was going ahead as, indeed, was a large private housing development by builders Robison and Davidson to the south and east of the council site and work on these areas continued throughout the Eighties.

The final tidy-up development of the Church Street - Sun Street corner got under way with the demolition of the former commercial premises and their replacement with flats in 1987. Two years later Loreburn Housing Association opened their first development in Stranraer at what was to become Princess Victoria Court in Sun Street, the site of the former market garden, bowling green and later tennis courts. And two years on, in 1991, Loreburn also opened Millburn Court, a £1.3 million development on the ground left when Sheuchan Mill had been cleared.

In Ashwood Drive the council replaced what had been the old Lewis Street Free Church School and later government offices with a small block of flats in 1990 and a few yards away from that Loreburn opened their Garlies Court development in 1996.

As mentioned earlier, private building was proceeding briskly in the Ochtrelure area and from the early 1980s Robison and Davidson, Loreburn and the Margaret Blackwood Association were all involved in building for sale, for rent, for shared ownership and for special needs. A substantial amount of the council's land-bank changed hands as it became generally accepted that meeting need and demand for new homes required a shared approach.

With the southern and eastern slopes of Ochtrelure filling steadily, the emphasis shifted to the northern limit, the Old Portpatrick Road end, and by the time the year 2000 came on the calendar Loreburn had built almost 250 homes and Robison and Davidson had erected just over 700.

DN

TRADE and INDUSTRY

As Stranraer moved on from its celebrations to mark the 350th anniversary of the granting of the burgh charter, the councillors were hopeful that the industrial site which had been established would attract much-needed industry to relieve the high unemployment situation.

They were to find that Stranraer's geographical situation, far from centres of large populations and large markets, made this no easy task.

In early 1968 Baby Deer were moving into a new factory on the estate and later that year the Sunchild establishment there was taken over by the nationally known Ladybird group.

Miss Sheena Drummond, the then Miss United Kingdom, was a popular visitor in July, 1970, when she officially opened large new premises for Stranraer Cash and Carry, a wholesale business which had been built from scratch by local businessman Andrew McMillan. Four months later his brother, Mr Hamilton McMillan, who in the short space of eight years had converted Sir John Ross's former house of North West Castle into the most modern and successful hotel in the South of Scotland, added an ice rink and extension to the hotel. The ice rink provided a massive boost for the already-popular sport of curling locally, attracted many more to the game and was to bring a fair measure of international fame and success to local curlers. Six years later the hotel had a swimming pool added.

In 1971 the British Linen Bank became the Bank of Scotland and the George Street branch of the former was extensively rebuilt and opened in March, 1975. In the following month the firm of James McHarrie (Stranraer) Ltd., celebrated its centenary and it was remarked on during the celebrations that what had started as an ironmonger's shop had at one time been part of a family concern that had owned five farms, three creameries, a dairy shop in Edinburgh, and the largest dairy utensils manufacturing plant in the county in addition to its motor and agricultural engineering concern.

Another old business, the gasworks in Harbour Street, had been 150 years in town when the site was taken over by the council in April, 1976, and cleared as part of the proposed promenade. Natural gas had been tankered into town since 1973 and local production had ceased then, with the business moving into a new storage-only complex on the industrial estate.

In May, 1976, the "Free Press" moved from Castle Street, where they had been since 1843, to a new plant in St. Andrew Street, marking the change-over with a new name and leaving hot-metal type-setting and letterpress printing in favour of more modern production methods.

Stockton Haulage, in October, 1976, opened a new freight terminal, dealing mainly with steel shipments, at former rail sidings near Culhorn Approach. A couple of months later the Scottish Development Department announced a 10-acre extension at the Blackpark industrial site.

An open-air market, something not seen in Stranraer for well over a century, was opened in September, 1978, on what had been a penned area for the Auction Mart at Glenwell Park. It was to prove very popular.

But if some old ideas were being resurrected, others were disappearing and the sky-line at the West End was altered in October, 1978, with the demolition of Sheuchan Mill tower, a dominant feature in that area since 1895.

Another unfamiliar sight was the Old Castle encased in scaffolding in the summer of 1979. Restoration work was being carried out by the Scottish Development Department's Ancient Monuments Division and the intention of the council was to open it again to the public with suitable displays in some of the apartments. At the same time the former "Free Press" building in Castle Street had been bought by the council and part of it was taken away to give greater prominence to the Castle.

That same year the former Regal cinema was being demolished and the same fate was earmarked for a line of properties on the south side of the lower end of George Street to allow redevelopment. Nine shops would form the new part of George Street and South Strand Street with a single unit on the Castle side of the latter street, which would also become pedestrianised but with vehicular rear access to the nine shops. Building was in full swing a year later and in early 1981 the first of the new shops was occupied.

A decision was taken in 1981 to close the town slaughterhouse. Alterations to meet new regulations proved to be too costly and, while the decision did not meet with universal approval, many were not sorry to see its disappearance from such a prominent site at Portrodie.

Some of the manufacturing concerns on the industrial estate were experiencing hard times in the early Eighties and redundancies and short-time working had to be accepted there and in the local building trades. Fears were also being expressed for jobs at West Freugh, where plans were revealed to replace Civil Service staff with private contractors. Coincident with the closure of the slaughterhouse was the demise of McHarrie's and the reopening of the refurbished courthouse with an additional courtroom at a cost of almost a quarter of a million pounds.

Brighter news in 1982 was of plans for new plant costing £300,000 at the Galloway Creamery and alterations which would mean an investment of £1.3 million over the following year.

The George Hotel came under new ownership in 1983 and plans were approved for the demolition of the Co-operative buildings in George Street and the erection of a new store. During the demolition an old well was discovered below the buildings of what had been Carse's Close, a street which had disappeared years earlier. The new Co-operative store was opened in November, 1984, but, after some years of dwindling trade, was closed in March, 1997, and two years later the local Chamber of Commerce took it over for community purposes and reopened it as Stranraer's Millennium Centre.

In the early 1980s there was a noticeable shift in shopping patterns and the top end of George Street lacked the activity which had marked it in earlier times. Wm. Low in April, 1983, announced plans for a new supermarket in Charlotte Street on the former McHarrie's site. With other competition moving into town the plans did not progress as swiftly as expected but eventually the firm did move from George Street to Charlotte Street in June, 1987.

Sunchild took over a new advance factory in 1983 and with new jobs and operations increased their output by a third. At the same time Stockton Haulage trebled their secure accommodation at the rail freight terminal with the opening of a £400,000 extension. Burgess Motor Services opened a new garage and car showroom in North Strand Street in June 1984, and extensive alterations by the McMillan family at North West Castle Hotel the same year led to the enlargement of the hotel's dining room and a new Alpine Restaurant and bar in the ice rink.

In November that year a new introduction to Stranraer was a small fish processing plant in the former Wheeler's Garage beside the Breastwork.

A favourite haunt for bus travellers and townspeople for many years, The Kiosk at Portrodie closed its doors in October, 1985, when Josie Adami retired. The café and shop had been extensively altered in 1950 but many older patrons still remember its unusual central and hexagonal island counter, which had been taken out then. After lying empty for some years, the premises were bought by The Salvation Army and reopened in 1990 as a goodwill centre.

Reid and Adams in March, 1987, refurbished part of their garage premises in Bellevilla Road and opened new workshops and ancillary departments behind their new frontage. A year later, Wigtown Rural Development Company revealed plans to spend £1.3 million on the vacated "Free Press" premises in Castle Street, a building which had been a private hotel until the printers had moved in there in 1843. In the same year an exciting new future was forecast for West Freugh with plans to develop part of it as a satellite-tracking centre. This was opened in April, 1991, and further units have since been added.

Planners gave the thumbs down in May, 1991, to a local businessman's idea for a £2 million hotel on the old woodyard and gasworks site at Portrodie but, undeterred, he continued to look for partners for an even larger scheme to have shops, a restaurant and other commercial undertakings on the same ground. In November that year another commercial concern disappeared from Market Street when demolition work started on the grain store which had been erected there in the 1930s.

Another national retailing combine came on the local scene when Safeway indicated an interest in 1992 in a site taking in part of Bellevilla Road, London Road and Royal Avenue. People in London Road were not happy with the proposal and in March, 1993, organised a petition against the development. Safeway won their case with the planners, swept away the old auction mart, Reid and Adams, stores and office premises in what had been the burgh yard, St. John's Church, an engineering workshop and the regional library. It was a massive undertaking, with Safeway helping in the relocation of some of those premises and their new superstore and a large car park were opened in 1994.

Because of this Stranraer's last cattle market was held in March, 1993, and a new library, incorporating premises for St. John's congregation, was opened a year later.

Boots the chemists returned to Stranraer in 1993, taking over premises in Castle Street. There was a fair amount of consternation that same year when the Post Office plans to move their counter business into Low's supermarket were revealed and even more indignation when, at a public meeting organised by the district council in protest, postal officials made it clear that a deal had been signed with the supermarket. The Hanover Street post office, built in 1964, was closed and the new department in Low's opened in March, 1994.

Another international retailer, Lidl, announced plans for a store on a site at Belmont in 1994, then looked at the possibility of building at Portrodie, but with amendments to their original plan finally went ahead at Belmont and started trading there in November 1998.

The Galloway Creamery had trading problems in 1994 and for a time the outlook seemed bleak with many staff members laid off. A consortium retrieved the situation and it went into production again as the Caledonian Cheese Company in February, 1995.

Complaints had been made from time to time that Scottish Gas services fell short in Stranraer because of the system of road delivery by tankers. That body's eagerness to export their commodity to Northern Ireland led to plans for a pipeline from the Stewartry, through Wigtown District, and thence across the North Channel. The completion of this late in 1994 gave Stranraer a vastly improved service.

An unusual contretemps flared briefly in 1997 when traders at the weekly Stranraer market on the old Waverley site at Dalrymple Street claimed the right to set up stalls at The Cross. The claim, of course, had no foundation as there had never been a market in that location, early markets and fairs in Stranraer operating on the foreshore, which later became Market Street.

In May, 1997, the old house at Burnfoot, opposite North Strand Street, largely rebuilt but retaining its central arched frontage, was opened as Stranraer's new tourist centre with other office accommodation upstairs. It was renamed Burns House. Later in the year Aitken the jewellers opened their new shop in the lower part of George Street, a few yards away from the premises the firm had occupied nearer The Cross since 1870.

Following the successful refurbishment of Burns House, the owner received planning permission early in 1998 to demolish the old joinery workshop and shellfish depot on the seaward side and build new office accommodation to be used by Stena Line. Then the project came under threat after access problems along the sea-front were raised by Dumfries and Galloway Council. These were finally resolved in the following year and in November, 1999, staff moved in to the new premises, with an official opening in February, 2000. Just prior to this the ferry company announced their intention of spending £2.6 millions on a new road, rail and ferry interchange at Stranraer harbour. At the same time, a group was formed of ferry companies' representatives, businessmen and politicians, committed to fight for much-needed improvements to the A75 and A77 routes on which the Irish link was so dependent.

At the opening ceremony of Stena Line's new offices, jointly performed by Bo Severed, president of Stena, and Tom Gillespie, chairman of Dumfries and Galloway Enterprise, both gentlemen made a strong plea for a commitment by government to the upgrading of those roads to Stranraer.

Towards the end of the millennium a strong fight was waged by local councillors to save textile manufacturing jobs in Stranraer when Unidoor, who had acquired the former Sunchild business, threatened closure. These were saved when negotiations led to a successful takeover by Grasshopper, who started recruiting in March, 1999, and only four months later opened a new factory on the industrial estate. Towards the end of the year there was more good news with the announcement of an extension to the Blackpark Estate at a cost of £875,000. At the same time, the traders who came weekly to Stranraer to hold their market found a settled site at last when they were accommodated in the town's Millennium Centre.

Over the period covered by this latest look at trade and industry in Stranraer, it is obvious that there has been a distinct change in shopping patterns. No less than eleven fairly large grocery establishments, most of them in George Street and Hanover Street, served Stranraer just after the Second World War and there was also a fair number of smaller outlets off the main streets, in the busier side-streets and scattered around the periphery of the town. These smaller establishments could be classed as general merchants but, again, with a dependency on foodstuffs.

By 2000 there was only one of the major concerns left and many of the smaller shops had withered away in the face of competition from the four supermarkets which had appeared.

In the 1960s Stranraer had approximately 165 shops (retail only) but by 2000 this number had dropped to 140, on reflection not as great a drop as might have been expected. What was clear was that this loss of numbers came entirely from George Street and Hanover Street (28 in total) and while others had gone to boost that total there had been new retail developments in other streets, notably St. John Street, which had more than doubled its 1967 figure.

So far as manufacturing industry was concerned, while firms moving into the industrial estate provided new jobs, in the older part of town not a few one-man outfits disappeared, mostly of the service variety. Traditional cobblers were perhaps the best example, with not one left in a town where sixty years previously there had been more than a dozen, around half of them one-man businesses.

And it was not only the one-man outfits which were disappearing. Within the last half-century an amazing number of drapers, ironmongers and confectioners were lost to the town.

DN

SHIPPING

The popularity and success of *Caledonian Princess* and the good back-up service provided by *Stena Nordica* in the early and middle Sixties led to the planning of the *Antrim Princess*. She was launched in April, 1967, and in December of that year became the fourteenth "Princess" on the Stranraer-Larne run.

But, despite the success of the first two vessels mentioned, it was still obvious that the Loch Ryan route was far from being the primary concern in the minds of the top planners and holiday peak demands from Holyhead led to the *"Caley"* being taken from Stranraer in September for a short spell. This, along with persistent newspaper rumours that control of the route would be taken from the Railways Board, did not help matters and questions were asked in the House of Commons by Mr John Brewis, the local member.

A White Paper on Transport in the last month of 1967, making a firm proposal to exclude the route from Scottish control and keeping it under London and the Railways Board, led to a firm promise in the House by the Board of Trade. The Board went further by stating that the route would have either a new road to feed the port or a restored rail line for Galloway.

Less than three months later it was announced that day-to-day control of the route would go to the Scottish Transport Group rather than London and hard on the heels of that news came a first intimation that the *Antrim Princess*, having proved herself in a matter of weeks, would possibly be joined by a sister ship.

British Rail did consider the idea of using hovercraft on the service and though one of these craft was seen on the former flying-boat launching ramp at Wig Bay nothing more was heard of that.

An announcement in October, 1968, that the route had broken all previous records, showing an all-round traffic increase, was followed three months later by confirmation that a sister ship would be built and while what would become the *Ailsa Princess* was still on the stocks at Venice a third vessel, *Baltic Ferry* was taken on charter to deal with the increasing freight traffic.

"Ailsa" was launched in December, 1970, and at the same time plans were revealed for a new ramp and an increase to four sailings each way on weekdays with two on Sundays. Improvements and changes seemed to be happening almost every month and in 1971 the new ramp, despite initial problems, was in operation; the *Stena Nordica* returned to Sweden; another new ship (the *Dalriada*) was ordered and the *Ailsa Princess* arrived.

In 1973 the *Neckertall* was a fourth ship on the route and the following year a new ferry terminal was opened and another fourth ship (the *Ulidia*) promised to replace the charter vessel (the *Preseli*) and take sailings up to 18 per day. Business was booming and figures for the previous year showed that just over half-a-million passengers had surpassed the previous total by ten per cent. By 1976 the yearly figures were over 200,000 vehicles and 680,000 passengers.

In December, 1976, plans by the Railways Board indicated an intention to reclaim land between the piers at Stranraer Harbour, an area approximately 250 yards by 90 yards, to build a new 400-foot jetty and install a new double-decked ramp and to carry out extensive dredging between the new jetty and the original pier and the approaches to both. Within a week of this announcement the Board publicised their intention to build another new vessel at a cost of £10 million which, combined with the harbour alterations, would bring the total outlay at Stranraer to £14.5 million.

In September of the following year the order for a new ferry was placed with Harland and Wolff, Belfast, and a month later work started on the harbour redevelopment. Dredging in the channel between Stranraer and Cairnryan commenced in May, 1978, and was halted briefly when the Colchester Oyster Company, which had seeded large areas of the bed of the loch with oyster spat, took the matter to court. (Five years later the legal question was finally settled when compensation of £108,000 was paid to Lochryan Oyster Fishing Ltd. for an estimated loss of almost half-a-million oysters).

In August, 1978, the *Darnia*, first of a new generation of double-decked ferries, took over from *Dalriada* and in the following January the *Stena Timer*, from Denmark, was used as relief ship. In May of that year the latest Princess, the *"Galloway"*, slid into the water at Belfast; at 7000 tons she would be the largest ferry to sail on the route.

Mr George Younger, Secretary of State for Scotland, came to Stranraer in June, 1979, to open what was easily the largest-ever single engineering project to be carried out at the town's harbour. Seven acres taken from the sea provided much-needed parking and marshalling facilities with a ramped approach road to feed the new double ramp and a jetty which had grown from its original 400-foot specification to 500 feet. New terminal buildings had covered walkways for passengers and some 800,000 cubic yards of material had been dredged from the berth in anticipation of the new *Galloway Princess*. Total cost, including the new vessel, had risen to £20 million.

Stranraer had a new pier and in a commendable gesture the planners asked the pupils of Stranraer Academy to suggest a name. The Ross Pier was the eventual choice, a historic link with the little jetty built more than a century before by Admiral Sir John Ross on a site now covered over by the latest development.

The 1980s started with the arrival of *Galloway Princess*, the first one-class vessel to serve the route. She came almost a year later than planned and her arrival brought into use the new security complex at Ross Pier. At the same time there were strong hints of a sister ship for the £14 million ferry, but the new decade was to bring problems. Cairnryan had provided growing competition following the establishment of a ferry service from there in July, 1973, and sailings from Stranraer were cut in August, 1980, from 22 to 20 per day, shifting down to 18 in the winter months. There was concern about jobs and suggestions in national media that "too many ships on Lochryan (were) chasing too few lorries".

Government was also dropping hints that Sealink, as it had become, could be ripe for sale to private enterprise, which in turn raised fears that the Stranraer-Ayr rail link could be in danger of closure if British Rail no longer had a ferry interest.

By 1981, with traffic still shading off, *Ulidia* was transferred to another port and at a conference in Stranraer's Old Town Hall to discuss the effects of a possible Sealink sale it was made clear that European Ferries, operators of the Cairnryan – Larne service, were interested in the port. Another blow came when it was revealed that later that year Stranraer would lose its direct day-time rail service to London, but, in December, the Monopolies Commission turned down a bid by European Ferries (owners of Townsend-Thoresen) for Sealink.

In December, 1983, an engine-room fire on *Antrim Princess* left her without power after she had sailed from Larne and passengers were issued with life-jackets and the life-boats made ready as the ship drifted towards the Irish coast. An 11 a.m. Mayday signal brought a fast response and within a quarter of an hour the first passengers were being winched off by helicopters. By one o'clock all 108 passengers and 23 non-essential crew members had been landed at Larne. *Galloway Princess, Darnia* and *Europic Ferry* had stood by during the emergency but with the fire put out and some power restored the *"Antrim"* was finally anchored safely some 800 yards offshore and towed into Belfast the following morning.

It was all change in March, 1984, with the disappearance of the B.R. motif from the Sealink ships. The familiar blue hulls, white superstructures and red funnels gave way to white hulls and superstructures with blue funnels and gold banding, incorporating SL, based on nautical uniform sleeves. The new colours were finally seen in Stranraer the following year when the *St. David* arrived as relief ship.

Strikes had marked the latter half of 1984 and indeed there were to be more towards the end of the decade.

In May, 1986, a weekly ferry service from Stranraer to Douglas was inaugurated by the Isle of Man Steam Packet Company using the *Lady of Man*.

Further changes in harbour facilities and terminal buildings were announced in 1989 and 1990 with an expenditure of £7.5 million in the latter year and in November, 1992, the company earmarked another £5 million to be spent over three years with £160,000 for upgrading their terminal building. Of equal significance was the announcement in October that year that they had carried their millionth passenger of the year.

Perhaps the investment figures were triggered to some extent by the competition which had arrived in 1992 in the shape of SeaCat. Sea Containers had started work in March to dredge a new berth at the West Pier for their Tasmanian-built, high-speed catamaran. They had also leased part of the Breastwork for a terminal building and parking and marshalling facilities and installed a linkspan and covered passenger walkways. Dredged material from the harbour bed was pumped into the former Marine Lake under an agreement with the council as the company planned to build a permanent terminal block on that side of the pier. By June they were in business and by October had carried 250,000 passengers.

In addition to the much faster crossing, they also offered another change in that their Irish terminal was Donegall Quay in the heart of Belfast. There had been a Stranraer (West Pier)-Belfast link more than a century-and-a-half earlier but this new service brought the offer of a link which had the prospect of business in Dublin and a return to Scotland in the same day.

Stena quickly answered the challenge. In July, 1993, they announced orders for two massive high-speed catamarans and a year later indicated a delay in the building of the new terminal they had planned, presumably to give flexibility in the deployment of these new vessels. Three months later their intentions became clear when they indicated that the second of these vessels would operate from Stranraer to Belfast and that investment in new ramps, berthing facilities and other harbour works would reach around £10 million.

In March, 1995, these figures were confirmed and six months later they indicated that they would shift their Irish operations to Belfast where a new £12 million terminal would be erected. Towards the end of the year they also changed the company name: "Sealink" would disappear and the ships would carry the designation "Stena Line".

European cash was offered the following year (1996), sums of £3 million to help build new terminals for both SeaCat and Stena, and in July the *Stena Voyager* arrived at Stranraer. This vessel, as different again from SeaCat as the latter had been from the older, conventional ferries, was enormous and a tremendous amount of work had gone into the creation of its berth and facilities.

Meanwhile, SeaCat were showing the plans for their new proposed terminal on the former Marine Lake site, formally submitting them to the planners in February, 1997, but by October of the following year they were no further forward and asked for an extension to the temporary planning consent for their use of The Breastwork. However the council, as planning authority, not happy with the way things were going, issued a three-month notice to quit in March, 1999, and three months later the company announced they were lodging an appeal against the council's refusal to renew the temporary planning consent. Matters had not been helped by an earlier announcement by SeaCat that they were withdrawing some sailings from Stranraer and operating these from Troon.

Following a public inquiry at Stranraer it was announced in February, 2000, that the SeaCat appeal against the council had been upheld and the Reporter extended the planning consent for the use of the Breastwork until November, 2002. A month later

SeaCat announced that in the previous year, despite the truncated service, their Stranraer berth had dealt with more vehicles, 53,000, than any of their other ports.

But matters were coming to a head. In April, 1999, Dumfries and Galloway Council, in their capacity as landlords, had given SeaCat notice to quit the Breastwork and The West Pier on the expiry of their lease at the end of April, 2000. This was in consequence of Seacat's decision to move most of their sailings to Troon and their delay in proceeding with the new Marine Lake Terminal. In the event SeaCat moved their entire operation out of Stranraer six weeks before they were due to be evicted and on Monday, 13th March, 2000, the SeaCat catamaran sailed from The West Pier for the last time. Within a week some pierside equipment and fitting s were being dismantled.

On the other side of the harbour things were very different: towards the end of 1999 Stena office staff had moved into a brand new headquarters in Burns House, on the site of a former woodyard and electricity board store. The new complex, built and leased to Stena by local businessman Mr William Burns, was widely accepted as a decided improvement at the harbour area and was opened officially by Stena president Bo Severed and Tom Gillespie, chairman of Dumfries and Galloway Enterprise, the company which had supported the much-needed development at Stranraer's sea-front.

Between the move into the new offices and the official opening, Stena had shown their further commitment to the Stranraer-Belfast route by sending their second high-speed catamaran to Stranraer to cover the annual refit of the *Stena Voyager* and had also announced plans to spend £2.6 million to create a new rail, road and ferry interchange at Stranraer harbour.

During the last quarter of the 20th Century Lochryan had seen another newcomer on the Irish ferry scene. Part of the former, war-time port of Cairnryan was opened by Townsend Thoresen in July, 1973, with the arrival of *Ionic Ferry. Free Enterprise III* and *Bardic Ferry* were there the following year when a new link-span came into use and the service quickly built up to offer five sailings per day.

Free Enterprise I followed and in February, 1976, the fourth vessel of that name became the largest to operate out of Cairnryan. She became a very popular ship on the route until 1985 when she was replaced by *Dragon.*

Other things had been happening at Cairnryan with shipbreaking at the former South Deep Wharf. The 43,000 ton *H.M.S. Eagle* came in September, 1978, and three months later almost caused havoc with the ferry services when she broke most of her moorings and swung out across the channel before she was brought back under control. On another occasion there was a massive fire aboard her and four fire engines were needed to deal with that problem.

Across the Cairn harbour a double-decked ramp had replaced the single in July, 1980, in anticipation of larger ferries and in the same year the possibility of a ship repair complex and a terminal for shipping out lumber or aggregates from the old Multilocular site at Innermessan, but using a new 600-foot jetty, was mooted by Roaleo Marine Ltd, but, following the first announcement, nothing more was heard of the idea.

Later that year, the remains of the *Eagle* were shifted to the inner side of the South Deep to make way for *H.M.S. Ark Royal*, the fourth ship of that name and at 50,000 tons the largest vessel in the Royal Navy.

After sheltering off Belfast Lough because of weather conditions the *"Ark"* was held at Corsewall Point to wait for the tide and she was hauled into Lochryan with only a few feet of clearance between her keel and the bed of the loch at various points. Thousands of people saw the last few miles of her last voyage before she was tied up at the South Deep, her massive bulk dwarfing the pier.

A couple of months later the *European Gateway* returned to the Cairnryan route after a refit which included a "stretch" job to add fifty feet to her length.

In 1982 the breakers at Cairnryan started work *on H.M.S. Blake*, a 12,000 ton cruiser, and this ship was quickly followed by *H.M.S. Mohawk*, a Tribal Class frigate. Two years later it was the aircraft carrier, the *Bulwark*, which was being scrapped but in 1988 this work ceased when Queenborough (Shipbreaking) Ltd. announced the closure of the yard.

In 1989, W. & J. Barr (Scotland) Ltd., purchased part of the port and in June the following year there was another brief spell of shipbreaking when some Russian submarines arrived at the Cairn.

1992 was a good year at the former military port. The first of what were described as superferries, the *Pride of Ailsa*, arrived in March, to be followed later by the *Pride of Rathlin*. And in September that year P&O, who had acquired the ferry service, announced the building of a new terminal at a cost of £600,000. While this work was going on the following year, parts of the decking of the South Deep collapsed and access to it was cut off.

In 1995, with business booming for all the ferry operators, P&O brought an extra ship into service and in June of the following year they joined the "fast ferry race" when their *Jetliner* arrived in the loch. With her 35-knot top speed she set new records for the trip to Larne and that summer there were calls made for speed limits to be set in shallower waters as the washes from the new, fast vessels were sending sudden and large waves ashore.

In 1999 P&O announced further developments, placing an order for a £33 million high-speed ferry and starting work on a multi-million pound berthing, marshalling and terminal project, which, with help from European funding, quickly got under way.

By April, 2000, new premises at this complex were completed and their new *SuperStar Express*, which came into service in April to replace the *Jetliner*, was heralded as the only ship which would cross the Irish Sea, from port to port, in one hour, carrying 800 passengers and 175 cars.

Earlier that month Stena announced that after negotiations with the owners of Larne harbour they would, later in the year, resume sailings to that port with their conventional ferries and, because of the shorter sailing time, increase the frequency of this service to twelve sailings per day. The H.S.S. would continue to sail Stranraer – Belfast.

DN

RAIL and ROAD TRAFFIC

Compared with the cataclysmic years immediately before the publication of the History in 1967, no upheavals in the local railway system have occurred in the intervening period. The privatisation of British Rail and break-up of the national network have not to date led to closures in our area. Fears for the continued existence of the Stranraer-Ayr line have so far proved unfounded. On the other hand, hopes for the reopening of the direct Stranraer-Dumfries line have not been fulfilled.

A recent proposal for a new station or halt closer to the town than the Harbour Station aroused interest as did the possibility of upgraded rolling stock, passed on from the Glasgow-Edinburgh service. The advantage of a no-change rail link with Gateshead's famous Metro Centre is offset by the timetable and length of the journey. However, Stranraer remains the only town in Galloway with a railway station.

With road traffic the situation is very different. The huge increase in commercial traffic on the short sea route since the 1960s has made articulated vehicles an omnipresent feature of the local scene. The main consequent road improvement has been the construction of a link road from the A75 on the eastern outskirts of the town to the industrial estate and the A77 in Stoneykirk Road. It was officially opened in 1994, its main engineering feature being the railway bridge across the Stranraer-Ayr railway. Plans to concentrate all ferry traffic on a widened Cairnryan Road with a new road linking to the A75 at Cairney's Corner have not made progress.

As regards local, town traffic Stranraer, unlike some other comparable towns, has not moved towards a vehicle-free town centre, South Strand Street being the only pedestrianised thoroughfare. Instead, in the late 1960s Wigtown County Council, the roads authority, continued their policy of demolishing town centre properties in order to widen junctions. Thus in early 1969 the 147-year-old Stair Arms was demolished to widen the road at the corner of Lewis Street and Bridge Street. Interestingly in 1985 the Director of Physical Planning for Dumfries and Galloway Regional Council described this policy of the earlier authority as "catastrophic".

In more recent years more than one scheme for removing cars from the central area of the town has foundered on opposition from local traders. Instead a variety of measures, including one-way streets, parking restrictions, and traffic-calming techniques, has been introduced and frequently amended. 1985 saw the installation of the town's first automatically controlled pedestrian crossing, in Hanover Street.

Outside the town centre proper, three houses were demolished in 1975 in London Road to widen the junction of that thoroughfare with Stair Drive.

JH

LEISURE

Clubs, Societies and Organisations

Cultural and leisure activities abound in Stranraer as the new millennium comes in. Participants can generally be split into two categories - those who organise and perform and those who become the audience and attend to enjoy.

For the children of the town, the Scout and Guide movements, Boys' Brigade, Sea and Army Cadets are still active, changing programmes with the times we live in.

Stranraer Drama Club, formed in 1891, still produces plays, a Christmas pantomime each year, and participates successfully in the SCDA One Act Play Festival, reaching the Scottish Final on several occasions, including the year 2000.

Stranraer and District Amateur Operatic Society, revived in 1967, continues to entertain local audiences each spring with a week's run of a musical or light operatic production.

Wigtownshire Music Association continues, renamed "Music for All", bringing professional ensembles to the town each year. They succeed in living up to their title, by including string groups, brass groups, jazz groups, woodwind and organ recitals in their programmes.

Music for All celebrated the Millennium by bringing a full symphony orchestra to Stranraer for the first time ever. The 120 players of the National Youth Orchestra of Scotland enthralled the audience of more than 500 in the Games Hall of the Ryan Leisure Centre - the most capacious accommodation in Stranraer. This was a huge undertaking, which proved to be a great success.

Creative Theatre for young people caters for those from nine to seventeen. Members of the Ryan Centre Youth Theatre write and perform their annual show for three nights in the spring, having rehearsed on Sunday afternoons throughout the winter. In addition to workshop sessions, they have also ventured further afield to entertain in other parts of the region.

Although the Choral Society is in abeyance, Stranraer Ladies' Choir, formed in the last decade, gives pleasure to large audiences and raises money for charitable causes.

Shows and performances by those organisations used to take place in the Masonic Hall in Sun Street, then from 1965 in Stranraer Academy Hall in the east of the town, until the Ryan Theatre opened as part of the Ryan Centre on the site of the old Stranraer High School in Lewis Street.

Audiences can now sit in comfort on tiered tip-up seats, and enjoy access to cafe teria and bar facilities.The casts have comfortable changing rooms, while stage crews have state-of-the-art lighting and sound systems, and generous storage space for scenery.

The Ryan Centre itself offers a busy and varied programme. Professonal theatre, ballet and entertainers as well as cinema are promoted throughout the year. It also provides most suitable accommodation for conferences. In all, it is a wonderful facility for the town and surrounding area.

The lively Speakers Club is well supported, as is the Bridge Club. The Burns Club, revived in 1985, celebrates the Bard's birthday in the North West Castle Hotel, provides an interesting programme for members throughout the winter months and holds a competition in Scots verse and song for local schoolchildren.

The Rotary Club was formed in Stranraer in 1953. Part of Rotary International, the enthusiastic club meets each Monday for lunch and usually has a speaker to give a short talk on a topic of interest. Rotary and its related organisation Inner Wheel both meet their aims of Friendship and Service, friendship for each other and service in practical help for others in the local community, and fund raising for charities locally, nationally and internationally.

Likewise, Round Table, Ladies Circle, Tangent and Lions cater for a younger age group and have similar aims. The local Lions Club hosted a very successful National Conference in the Ryan Centre in December. The Probus Club was started by Rotary for retired business people. There is also a B and P Club for business and professional women.

The local lodge of Freemasons meet in the Masonic Hall in Sun Street and are supported by the Order of the Eastern Star.

Churches in the town have their own groups and clubs which meet regularly - Old Folks, Young Mothers, Sunday School and Bible Class to name but a few.

The Scottish Women's Rural Institute, very strongly supported in the district, includes a Stranraer Branch.

The Gardening and Floral Art Clubs cater for those with green fingers and for the ornithologists a branch of the RSPB meets regularly. The Photographic Club holds competitions on various topics within its membership. The Model Engineering Society was very active in the mid-nineties when they ran the first model railway in Agnew Park before its redevelopment by the Council. The Stranraer Model Aeroplane Society meets at the former airfield at Cults. The Stranraer Branch of the Royal Scottish Dance Society has met in the winter months for many years. The enthusiastic members from a wide age group perform dances old and new.

In the last twenty years, pubs and hotels have changed beyond recognition. Food - bar lunches and evening meals - are served in most and live entertainment, including karaoke is provided, particularly at weekends. No longer is alcohol the only beverage served, but soft drinks, coffee and even milk can be requested by the patrons. Perhaps the legal limits of the consumption of alcohol for drivers, and the introduction of breath tests have assisted this enormous change. Licensing laws have eased and children are allowed to be served with food and soft drinks in pubs, and licensing hours too have become much more flexible. Several nightclubs thrive in Stranraer where the young folk over eighteen can dance the night away.

The ability to borrow books at no charge was established in Stranraer in 1921 by the County Library Service. In 1994 Stranraer Library was relocated to North Strand Street, where a custom - built facility was provided to maintain the lending service of books, including tapes, video cassettes and CD Roms. The library houses a historical collection of local reference books and micro-fiche records for study in situ. It also has a spacious exhibition area, and two sizeable lecture rooms on the upstairs floor, one accessible by lift, which provide welcome accommodation for clubs and societies.

Stranraer's historic Old Town Hall, built in 1776, is the home of the Stranraer Museum. The ground floor houses a permanent exhibition of archaeology, local history and farming while the one time council chamber hosts changing exhibitions. Following on the redevelopment of the centre of the town, the imposing Castle of St. John is open to the public during the summer months. In addition to hosting displays of the town's history, it offers stunning views of the surrounding area from the battlements.

The Antiquarian and Natural History Society, which takes a great interest in the heritage of the area, has met continuously since 1955, holding a monthly lecture during the winter followed by outdoor summer outings.

A new group was formed in 1998. Stranraer and District Local History Trust is a charitable trust which was formed to research, record on tape, and publish books on the local history of the area. In 1999 four books were published. The History of Stranraer, the Trust's millennium production, is a facsimile of that produced in 1967, with an appendix researched and written by members to bring the story of Stranraer to the year 2000.

The citizens and young people of Stranraer really cannot say there is nothing to do in a town which offers such a choice of leisure activities for life-long learning, interest and fun.

Sport and Recreation

The Ryan Theatre is only one part of the ambitious enterprise undertaken by Wigtown District Council in the latter years of its existence. It is a part of the Ryan Leisure Centre, which was built on the site of the former High School in Lewis Street, most convenient for the town centre. It has parking space for cars although this proves to be limited when the theatre is busy. The town at last has a complex of swimming pools with fun activities in a leisure pool and training lanes in a larger pool for the serious swimmer. Trained staff instruct all stages from beginners' classes to lifesaving. There is a spacious games hall, which has hosted national sporting events, and fitness rooms with state of the art equipment.

Agnew Park, another council owned facility, was redesigned in 1996, with help from the European Fund. The Marine Lake was filled in to become a car park, while the grassy area to the west is an attractive activity area. A walkway has been laid along the shore of Loch Ryan, with seats provided to admire the view and spectate on the busy ferries sailing on the loch. The boating lake with play island, crazy golf, miniature railway, adventure playground and cafeteria make Agnew Park a busy attraction for visitors and local folk in the summer months. The monument to the Princess Victoria has been re-sited within the gardens of the park.

Stranraer Football Club continue to play professional league football at Stair Park, with two new stands and much improved facilites provided during the last two decades. The club's success in winning the Second Division Championship in seasons 1993-94 and 1997-98 gained it promotion to the First Division. However the fact that they were the only part -time outfit in the league contributed to their being relegated at the end of the following seasons. In 1996 Stranraer beat St. Johnstone to win the Challenge Cup. In February 1989 about 3500 fans supported Stranraer's visit to Ibrox for a fourth round Scottish Cup tie. Although Stranraer lost 8 - 0, the Rangers team was packed with Scottish and English internationalists.

Junior and amateur youth football for lads of all ages remains a popular sport. Weekend and evening games use council pitches in the Academy grounds (floodlit during the winter) and at McMaster's Road and the Coronation Park.

Wigtownshire Rugby Football Club operates at London Road playing fields. A handsome clubhouse provides comfortable changing rooms, a squash court, bar and activity area for members. The club plays in the National League.

The curling rink at the North West Castle Hotel is now famed country-wide, indeed world wide. Competitions and inter-club games are played from September to

April. Hamilton McMillan of the Stranraer Club was unique in holding the Scottish, European and World Championship titles in 1999. Although winters have not been cold enough for outdoor curling for many years, Stranraer is a popular mecca for enthusiasts of the "roaring game".

Stranraer Golf Club continues to prosper at Creachmore. A very superior two-storey clubhouse was opened in 1994 and gives superb panoramic views of the course and Loch Ryan from the upstairs clubroom.

Stranraer Bowling Club opened 150 years ago, followed by the West End Club some twenty years later. This popular pastime has many adherents during the summer months.

Tennis and cricket are still played, and although all-weather tennis courts exist at Stair Park, neither game has many participants at present.

Badminton, a popular game in church and school halls in the 60s and 70s, does not enjoy great popularity at the turn of the century.

The Angling Club continues as a sport on Soulseat and Loch Magillie, while Loch Ryan offers a challenge to those after bigger fish. Angling is still the most popular sport in the district.

All the local schools hold their Sports Days in the summer term. Those inspired by success continue to train throughout the year. A superb facility was provided by the Sports Council in the grounds of Stranraer Academy and has an all-weather four-lane running track, jumping pits and a safety cage for field events.

As we look forward to the new century, we can confidently say that the sports facilities in Stranraer are first class and are available to all who wish to take part.

CLW

LOCAL MEDIA COVERAGE

Newspapers

Little change has taken place in the local newspaper field since the original History was written. Local government reorganisation in 1975 led the then Wigtownshire Free Press to change its name to The Wigtown Free Press. At the next change in local government, in 1995, the disappearance of Wigtown District led the newspaper to another name change, this time becoming The Stranraer and Wigtownshire Free Press. In 1976 the Free Press editorial offices and printing works moved from Castle Street to a purpose-built complex in St Andrew Street. While the Free Press has changed to tabloid format, The Galloway Gazette has remained in broadsheet. In spite of widespread changes in newspaper ownership elsewhere both local papers are still owned by descendants of the original proprietors, the Free Press by the Earl of Stair and The Galloway Gazette by a limited company with strong local representation.

At various times a number of free news sheets have been published locally in keeping with national trends but in the past all of those have had a limited life span.

Television

The main difference in local TV coverage from 1967 is in the source of the programmes received. In 1967 Stranraer fell into two areas as far as reception was concerned. People living on the east side of town, out of the shadow of the Gallowhill, received both their BBC and ITV programmes from Ulster by means of a roof-mounted aerial. However on the west side of Stranraer the bulk of the Gallowhill prevented any direct TV reception by most homes. The majority of residents here received their programmes by way of a cable relay system from a mast on the Gallowhill. This had been established in 1960 by local firm A. McKenzie and Sons and offered, as they came available, Ulster and Border TV, BBC1, and BBC2.

The opening of a transmitter on Balker Moor in 1977 means that today only a small aerial, not always externally mounted, is required to receive programmes anywhere in Stranraer from BBC Scotland and Border TV, the two companies officially designated as serving Stranraer. The inauguration of the Balker Moor transmitter, a satellite of the larger version on Cambret Hill behind Creetown, led to the demise of the cable relay in 1983. At present the town lies just outside the official reception area for Channel 5.

With rare exceptions TV programme coverage of the local area consists mainly of items on news and sports bulletins, the former often relating to the ferry services.

Radio

Major innovations in local radio provision have taken place in the last 20 years. In 1983 the Dumfries and Galloway region received its first local radio station when the BBC established Radio Solway in Dumfries with a reception area covering the whole region. The new station had two opt-out slots on the Radio Scotland frequency, in the early morning and at lunchtime. The total broadcasting time varied between 60 and 90 minutes daily giving the opportunity for not only news and weather bulletins but also feature programmes of local interest. In Stranraer an unmanned studio was set up in a building in Castle St for local contributors.

However in 1993, just before the station's tenth anniversary, BBC Scotland fundamentally altered its local radio provision and Radio Solway was one of the stations discontinued as a separate entity. The BBC retained a presence in Dumfries and now provides specifically local coverage in the form of four news and weather bulletins on week days, these totalling approximately 25 minutes daily.

Independent local radio came to the region in 1990, when Ayr-based West Sound Radio, which already broadcast to West Ayrshire, Arran, and Cumbrae, was awarded the Independent Radio Authority franchise for Dumfries and Galloway. However the west of the area, including Stranraer, lay outside the range of the West Sound transmitters until 1998. In that year, as a result of West Sound's takeover by Scottish Radio Holdings, coverage was extended to include almost all of Dumfries and Galloway, including Stranraer. West Sound broadcasts for 24 hours daily, concentrating on music programmes, and claims to be the most listened to radio station in its franchise area.

JH